MW00977952

A CHRISTIAN DOCTOR
VS.
HOMELESSNESS:
FROM TENTHOUSE TO PENTHOUSE

Sara Harris-Bowditch

authorHOUSE®

AuthorHouse™
1663 Liberty Drive
Bloomington, IN 47403
www.authorhouse.com
Phone: 1 (800) 839-8640

© 2016 Sara Harris-Bowditch. All rights reserved.
Edited by author

No part of this book may be reproduced, stored in a retrieval system, or
transmitted by any means without the written permission of the author.

Published by AuthorHouse   03/22/2016

ISBN: 978-1-5049-8666-3 (sc)
ISBN: 978-1-5049-8664-9 (hc)
ISBN: 978-1-5049-8665-6 (e)

Library of Congress Control Number: 2016904767

Print information available on the last page.

Any people depicted in stock imagery provided by Thinkstock are models,
and such images are being used for illustrative purposes only.
Certain stock imagery © Thinkstock.

This book is printed on acid-free paper.

Because of the dynamic nature of the Internet, any web addresses or links contained in
this book may have changed since publication and may no longer be valid. The views
expressed in this work are solely those of the author and do not necessarily reflect the
views of the publisher, and the publisher hereby disclaims any responsibility for them.

KJV - King James Version
Scripture taken from the King James Version of the Bible.

CONTENTS

DEDICATIONS

1. First of all, this book is lifted up to the Creator of heaven and earth. First Corinthians 8: 5, 6 states, "For though there be that are called gods, whether in heaven or in earth (as there are gods many, and lords many) but to us there is but one God the Father, of whom all things, and we in him, and one Lord Jesus Christ by whom are all things and we by him."

My testimony is that, had it not been for the Lord, where would my hope be. When I lost a vital part of my vision, the center vision, as a young woman, I would have been committed to a nut house, no disrespect for mental institutions. But it was the capable hand of God who stabilized my sanity and soul until this very day! And for that I shall be eternally thankful!

2. To my daughter Angela, the first of her family peers to earn a college degree. My Little Girl has been an armed warrior in the Lord's church for many years. God have blessed her with the wisdom to keep others encouraged even through her own infirmities.
3. To my grandson (G-son) Brandon Jackson, AKA Brickz, his DJ name, who earned his Bachelor's degree from Georgia State University! May God keep him safe and healthy in these uncertain times! I pray that his faith gets strengthened day by day. From your G-ma!

4. To: my husband, David Bowditch, as of May 8, 2012. David is also the Christian man I needed in my life. If his loving support had not been there, both spiritually and financially, it would have been near to impossible for me to re-write this novel. May we continue to hold on to each other and especially hold on to God's strong hands!

5. To my sisters and their husbands: James and Frankie Elliott. I will always be grateful to them for bringing me the good news about Christ and his church many years ago! May God forever bless them!!

6. To Barbara Wilson, who, one can set a clock by her routine ways. And also meticulousness becomes her in every way! May God be longsuffering with her as He is with all!

7. To: Kirkland and Charlene Hart. My baby sister, Char. Is an angel in disguise? For sure, without their unselfishness my journey on the first novel would have been very bumpy. They are always in my heart and prayers!

8. To: Isolene Jewell, my deceased older sister. She always had a strong desire to finish her education, but she became a victim of her surroundings at an early age. She became an alcoholic and had to drop out of school. So, to honor her, I named my first book after her. Her nickname was Tulu and the book is, Tulu and The Yetti: Help America. I love and miss my dearest sister!

Below are a few more shout-outs.

a. My preachers at the Church of Christ: Brother Wesley R. Brown and Brother Orpheus J. Heyward.

b. My deepest thanks, to the staff at North Georgia Blind and Low Vision Services! Hello Nancy Parkin/Breshezi. Nancy, I am really sorry the publisher who did, Blite, did not put my dedications in the book as I had hoped. They did me a dis-service!

c. I would like to thank all the staff at Center for the Visually Impaired. Hello Angela, Desmond, Rasheda and Paris. You guys rock!

d. Thank you Doctor Rebecca Weiman, with Buckhead DDS, PC. Doctor Becky, you gave me back the smile I had years ago! God bless!

AUTHOR TESTIMONIAL

©2008–2016

As a poor girl, in what was called, The Fourth Ward of Atlanta, I must say that I encountered many homeless and low-income families. And even in the 1950s and 60s, a little before the Civil Rights Movement, decent families had to live in dilapidated houses with cracks in the floors. Families rented those houses. I recall one house we lived in had a toilet on the back porch. And in the Deep South, in those days, winters seemed more ridged than nowadays. If we would use a toilet inside, it was a metal slop-jar, or so it was called. The slop-jar was used at night for 5 girls and our mother. Thank God there were no males in the house to contend for the slop-jar. We 5 girls shared duties emptying the slop-jar. And God forbid that anyone had diarrhea during the night and you were the one who had duty the following morning.

However, the blessing was that the run down house kept a leaky roof over our head. But the demon was that the rent was so steep, until our mom could not always pay the rent off of our father's Social Security. And if a family could not pay, they were evicted the very next month without hesitation. And to have your furniture sat out on the streets was a scary scene for too many families. And sometimes my family would fall, victim. And there had been no shelters for us in those days. Or if there were temporary housing, we had no entry rights. So what families did was to pile up with a family who was in a better financial standing. Then the following month when check time rolled around, that family could rent another house and even that same house, if it was still available. There had never been a credit check, just as long as you paid rent on time every month. The people that rented those ragged houses did not care if you had a job or not. So many families did what they could to make money. Even down to selling moonshine liquor to neighbors. White folks would bring in the moonshine for families to sell in order to make a living. Thus my mother and oldest sister sold and became alcoholics. Both of them died at very early ages as the result. However, some families had working parents or one working parent in the house. Sadly, the only job that was available to them was in White folks houses or washing dishes and mopping floors in restaurants. Those downtown Atlanta, Georgia, restaurants that they had not even been allowed to, sit down and eat. The Fourth Ward was within walking distance to downtown Atlanta where most families had worked.

Nevertheless, I thank God that He brought us through. Not that my family was so religious, we were not. But now that I am a member of the Church of Christ, I realize that God's provisions were upon me and my sisters, who are also now Christians. God knows who will obey the gospel call, and who will disobey. But being such a loving Father, He gives all people a fair choice to come to Him. He is omnipotent (all powerful). The Lord God omnipotent, reigns. Rev. 19:6. He is also omnipresent (everywhere at all times). In the book of Jonah,!: 3, Jonah was sure he had evaded the presence of God, but God's Spirit was also there on the ship. So God sent a great wind into the sea. God is also omniscience (sees and knows all, even the evil and the good, Proverbs 15:3). So in light of this, I know He knew us as poor children before we came to Him.

One of my testimonials is about my sisters and I, some of us preteens. There had been a mysterious man that suddenly came into our neighborhood. This one-armed, up to the shoulder, middle-aged man always wore overalls. He befriended my mother. The unlit-cigar-chewing man was called Mr. Sy-Sy. Whether that had been his real name remains a mystery until this day. The kind faced Mr. Sy-Sy would come through our neighborhood pushing a wooden-hand-made push cart. The cart contained all kinds of used clothing. We would watch him and think he was the strongest man in the world to wheel that cart with only one arm. He would always come down the back where there were dirt roads only. Why the front of those houses had paved roads and the back was unpaved, I guess I'll never know.

Well, Mr. Sy-Sy would come through about once a week. Later we came to know him as the community rag-man. Then he informed my mother that he picked up and sold used clothing to the rag-house down the streets. He did all of his work on foot. And the summertime could be just as melting as the winters were ridged. So Mr. Sy-Sy never failed to save out the more wearable clothing for my family. And the clothing we would exchange with him was only good for scrubbing floors. Of course he would only sell them by the pound, as the rags they really were.

As I can recall, we would strain to hear his bell once a week. And when he would finally come and dump those clothes on our back porch, we would go through them like we were at a department store sale. The rest of the clothes, we would just pitch into a closet in our house. And whenever we would need something to wear, we would go shopping in that closet. And believe it or not, God kept us clothed through that closet. We would pull out a dress or skirt and blouse. With washing and homemade starch, made with flour and boiling water, and then using an iron heated on the wood stove, we were ready for school. As far back as I can recall, we got ourselves up for school, and did our own preparing clothes for school.

So now, as a follower of Christ, I pray diligently that God gives me the wisdom to share and teach the spiritually and physically un-endowed to seek and depend on Him. My praises and glory goes to God for helping me to rewrite this story in order to pull others up from Satan's pits and snares! I pray for both the homeless and the well-off. We all need Him to fight Satan and to get us into heaven!

PART ONE

CHAPTER 1

Around 8:30 that morning on the snowy streets of Neal, New York, there on the ground wrestled two ragged clothed men. And with clear determination in his dingy enraged eyes they bared yellow teeth. The men tried relentlessly to be the first to hold high in victory the eyeball of his foe. There in front of the busy liquor store the men, one Black and one White, mid-thirties pounded through layers of clothing . . . neither being affected by the whacking. The multi-raced crowd some warmly dressed and others just as tattered as the determined grapplers, cheered for them to gouge just a bit harder not really having a favorite. All they wanted was to see the snow turn red with human blood. Absurdly the demon behind this quarrel was a bottle of artificial colored grape wine that had not been opened and was on a slow roll away from the dueling duo, "It's my turn to take the first swig!" one huffed through a puff of steam. "You took the first drink from the last bottle!!" reaching desperately for the rolling bottle.

"No, I didn't, you went first the last time!!" yanking his foe's arm back into the melee. One would think the frenzied crowd would be use to that kind of scene among the city's homeless alcoholics. This day was no different from any day of the week, even on Sundays. These men had pitched in to buy the three-dollar bottle. He knew that if he was allowed the first drink, he would guzzle more than his fair share, in almost one desperate toss-down.

In that extremely indigent neighborhood even against the more sober resident's rebuttal to shut down liquor stores, the stores opened early mornings for the sake of homeless alcoholics. Every day the men and occasionally women, already hung-over would rush in for booze rather than food. Plus the addicts had long since discovered that when alcohol was poured into an empty stomach the high was sure and quicker. And once he was drunk he would be propelled into a wonderland blotting out his woes and fast fading hope. Also the other world would shield him from the brutal winter of New York. And once intoxicated and asleep just anywhere, once again he would experience temporary peace. Then he would only awaken to the disappointment of still being alive in this world. So with his weary face buried in dirty hands, "Dog-gone-it, another day of eternity in this hell!" he would literally cry. "It's impossible for a body not to depend of booze down here!"

So, the crowd cheered as the two men busied vying for mastery on the snow. Little did they suspect that a younger Black homeless man had swooped up, the free bottle. He held the prize high and away he scurried towards the alley, skillfully keeping his balance on the ice. The crowd roared, "Run, run!" And as he ran he twisted off the cap. Finally all the cheering for the younger man alerted the fighters that they were no longer the focus of attention. The two men on the ground also began to look after the running man. The younger man now had the bottle open and was taking a greedy gulp where some grape liquid tinted the snow. And from within the crowd, "Do you need a figure skating manager for the Olympics?" one man yelled, cracking up the crowd. The two on the ground at last realized their hard begged for three dollars was about to go down the gut of someone who had not even chipped in.

So now on the same page the two fumbled and helped each other up. The older men began a more slippery pursuit of the younger thief. Eventually they did catch him, but much too late. Thus the hefty beating they laid on him was futile. He was too drunk and still trying to squeeze another drop out of the empty bottle.

Meanwhile in a warm auditorium in Manhattan just about 30 miles from that scene a podium sat high upon a political-set stage. The stage had been painstakingly constructed by some unemployed or homeless men who had jumped at the chance to at last have work. The down-spiral of America's economy had tested everyone's faith.

There among the packed audience only anticipated breathing could be heard as hundreds stared at the astute looking White man as he stood up beckoning a very beautiful young Black woman along with him. Both stepped behind the sturdy wooden stand. And in a tastefully fashioned suit the man holding a custom-crafted plaque heartedly extends his hand to the just as affluently dressed woman, who takes a proud breath accepting his hand. "Doctor Hadassah Desoto. . ." he bears pearly whites behind thin lips, "On behalf of the state of New York we're more than delighted to present you with this prestigious Humanitarian Award. You've not only rehabilitated, but also made entrepreneurs of so many homeless veterans, ex-minor-offense convicts and those citizens who've recovered from substance abuse!"

Hadassah, which name was given to her by her grandmother is Esther from, Esther 2: 7. "Thank you Mr. Senator!" the Psychiatrist also bares pearly whites behind full glossy lips, "It's my duty to please God through serving others!" Then snickering out over the audience, she added, "I'm also delighted God has allowed me to have taken many of these people from a tenthouse situation to a penthouse status!" Her comical air drew laughter among some in the audience… the ones who knew the hidden joke. Those that now lived comfortably in upscale apartments and no longer in cardboard boxes. She was most proud of the homeless ones who had been members of the Church of Christ but had fallen down and did not have the strength to get up. Some felt as if God had let them down until the doctor discovered them and convinced them that God never leaves His obedient saints. But rather their faith had faltered and let them down.

As a Christian, Doctor Hadassah Desoto felt a deep responsibility to show them first how to repent in order to strengthen their feebleness.

Especially since herself was once impoverished and was bought up from a flimsy lifestyle to a literal mansion. Though she never slept on the streets she still had her grievous testimony. Had she run away the way she had contemplated many times over, she would have wound up on the streets or even worse. After all she had been a breathtakingly beautiful girl with a body to match. But now as a doctor she has been afforded great success in counseling others on how she had learned to walk with God rather than piggy-back on others. Also she wholeheartedly feels that her Christian compassion has been greatly rewarded. God has blessed her with wealth through the makeover program and with a flourishing private psyche practice. Thus she feels the least she can do is to recycle some of that income for benevolence. Not only is the doctor wealthy but profoundly believes the Holy Bible to be the mind of God. Thus she zealously counsels the poor downtrodden to lean on the word of God for their daily survival. In the scriptures she read where God provides for His own as Psalm 37:25-28, which King David affirmed in the long ago, "I have been young, and now am old: yet have I not seen the righteous forsaken, nor his seed begging bread . . . verse 26, "He is ever merciful, and leads; and his seed is blessed . . . verses 27, "Depart from evil, and do good, and dwell forevermore. . . verse 28, "For the Lord loves judgment, and forsakes not his saints; they are preserved forever; but the seed of the wicked shall be cut off." And in that same passage in regards to saints is preserved forever she believes the statement that saints will be preserved forever and inherits the earth means that the obedient is promised food, clothing and sheltered. God would provide for saints from the good fruit of the land forever. Forever meaning for as long as saints are alive on the earth they will inherit the fat thereof. Unlike some false religions who believe that this is one of the scriptures that refer to God allowing the *earth* to stand forever and the saved would inherit the planet Earth. Not so! But rather this entire passage points to God feeding and caring for not only the spiritual needs of His servants, but also for their physical needs, while they are presently living on the earth and before they would succumb to a fleshly death. Another scripture which some man established churches use to twist this meaning is Matthew 5: 5, when Jesus said in his Sermon on the mountain, *"Blessed are the meek for they shall inherit the earth.*" This particular scripture relates to Psalms 37, in that all of the fat of the earth belongs to God's obedient anointed people for as long as they would live on the earth. It is absolutely necessary for these scriptures to be rightly divided in order to be spiritually digested. And then on the last day God will destroy this present earth as we know it. According, to 2 Peter 3:10, this present earth will be burned up in the end. "But the day of the Lord will come as a thief in the night, in which the heavens shall pass away with a great noise, and the elements shall melt with fervent heat, the earth also and the works that are therein shall be burned up." Doctor Desoto testifies to those who believe that God will not destroy His own creation, "God can and will indeed destroy the earth as He promised because after all He created it for His saints while they are yet in the flesh and have needs!" she says, "And when He takes his saints to heaven, He'll no longer need this earth!" And on another note, this particular passage in 2 Peter proves that the earth did not begin with a big bang (the big bang theory) as the Darwinism doctrine suggests, but rather the planet Earth will *pass away* with a great noise (big bang) just the opposite of what that man-made doctrine teaches. She was amazed at how those, so called Bible Scholars delight in deliberately rearranging God's already totally composed Word just to make it fit their ideas and practices. Also she discovered further proof that this present earth would be destroyed. In Revelations 21:1, which the Apostle John spoke by the inspiration of the Holy Ghost, wrote, "And I saw a new heaven and a new earth: for the first heaven and the first earth was passed away; and there was no more sea." The Jehovah's Witnesses and some other religions totally ignore this particular scripture and believe that they will have the privilege of remaining on this earth in peace throughout eternity. However, in their error they failed to rightly divide this scripture also. This passage exhorts saints that God has prepared a new heaven and a new earth for souls and not for physical bodies to dwell throughout eternity—on the new spiritual earth. This new dwelling place will not be physical as some claim, but will be a spiritual place with streets of spiritual gold and walls of spiritual Jasper for the spiritual souls to enjoy. The saints will also be spiritual in that they will have shed this physical body at Christ's appearing (1 Corinthians 15rh chapter). Also, to prove this point the book of Revelation speaks of spiritual food (seas) as oppose to physical food. "And there was no more sea," that passage reads. Whereas, on this present earth, which is physical, humans depend on the seas for fish (food) and water (seas). But on the new spiritual earth there will be no more dependence on the seas to provide daily provisions—spirits have no need of fish nor water (food). This passage determinedly refutes the doctrine that saints will physically live on this present planet Earth. If the Jehovah's Witness were to remain on the planet, then where will they get their water and food from? Even if there are herbs, they would eventually need water to grow more herbs. Doctor Desoto recalled having said to one of those false teachers who had once walked into her office and offered to teach their doctrine, "I think you're the ones who need to re-analyze the theory of you all forever inhabiting this earth, Ma-am and Sir!" she had invited the man and three women to enroll in a free Bible study with the Church of Christ. They, of course, adamantly refused and rushed out of the office never to return. They had come to the office because solicitors were unable to gain access to her undisclosed home. Also in her studies she had read a passage as an answer to a question a client had asked her one day. The woman had asked why did God create Satan if, God knew that Satan would rebel. Then Dassah recalled her preacher had answered that same question one day. He had said that God gave Satan a choice to serve Him as He gave any other angel. God also gives man the choice to obey or disobey. God never arrests man's will to make a choice. So Satan, God's angel made a choice not to following His commands. In essence, God created angels and man to make conscious choices.

Thus the doctor also has to deal with the homeless skeptic. These are the ones who firmly claim the Holy Bible to be merely men's words. She would testify that it was indeed God and not man, who allowed King David to proclaim God's goodness. The words that David spoke held a double promise—one, the disobedient is admonished, and two, the saint is given peace of mind. In spite of the stiff disdain from the unbelievers among the homeless, the doctor yet refers them to the scripture in 2 Peter 1:21, concerning those doubts, "For the prophecy came not in old times by the will of *man* but holy men of God spoke as they were moved by the *Holy Ghost*." Furthermore, she would logically reason, "The Bible could've never been written by mere men because a carnal mind would never condemn itself by commanding that himself shouldn't steal, lie or commit fornication. . . and we know it's not the nature of man to sentence himself to hell the way God's word frowns on sin!" she would attempt to convince the cynical ones that the Bible was only written with the pen of men, but was worded by the Holy Ghost, "Just take time to study the scriptures and take note of the longsuffering and mercy of the Almighty, which is far from what man would ever do for another man." Then, being careful not to boast on herself she would humbly tell of the many times she had read the Bible never once to find inconsistencies when rightly divided. She attributes that to God enabling her to justly divide His word and shows the homeless skeptic 2 Timothy 2:15 proving how with prayer, study and meditation she was able to understand most any scripture which God revealed to her. One has to study the entire Bible in order to be able to rightly divide any particular scripture. 2 Timothy, 2:15 reads, "Study to show yourself approved unto God, a worker who needs not to be ashamed, rightly dividing the word of truth." Then she would counsel the homeless, "You too can obtain wisdom in order to understand the Bible, but you first must be saved … get into Christ's body his church!" She would confidently defend by showing James 1:5, which reads, "If any of you (Christians) lack wisdom, let him ask of God who gives to all liberally and upbraids not, and it shall be given to him." The doctor warns how futile it was to ask for enlightenment if faith was amiss and doubt that there is one true God. She would say, "It amazes me why Christians even waste their breath talking to a deity they don't even believe can deliver!" **She believes that if the brothers who conduct the Bible classes could only convince the homeless to accept God's single plan that God has already laid out for all to obey, then man's obedience would provoke God likewise to keep His promise to provide their daily necessities. As a female doctor Hadassah performs her psyche duties, but in the church of Christ only the** men saints are allowed to lead group Bible classes where there is a male/female audience according to 1 Timothy 2: 12, where the Holy Ghost instructed Apostle Paul to instruct Timothy to set the church in order, "But I suffer not a woman to teach nor to usurp (seize unlawfully) authority over the man but to be in silence (not to over-ride the men)." At first the doctor thought that command seemed a bit chauvinistic on the brothers' behalf. But then she had a fast change of heart when she realized who was in charge of all living. So she had recalled another scripture in 1 Corinthians 14:36, 37, "What? Came the word of God out from you? Or, came it unto you only? 37 if any man think himself to be a prophet, or spiritual, let him acknowledge that the things that I write unto you are the commandments of the Lord. Then she had said, "After all, the brothers did not command this, God did! He is the Supreme One who lays down the rules!" So she repented and was glad to relinquish all the church leadership to faithful men, "We as humans run our own houses the way we wish and He as the Creator rules in His own house His church as well!" she says. Too many secular preachers do not understand how the Bible teaches against women preachers. They do not understand why women have a specific place in the Lord's house, the assembly gatherings. Rightly divided this male-female law was a comparison of Christ and his church-his bride, Christ (man) being the head of his wife (woman). The doctor was so proud to have been added to the church of Christ where she learned the true doctrine in its purest form. However, in a non-church setting like her mental and professional counseling sessions she is allowed to counsel men and women about spiritual things and about God's promise to supply food shelter and clothing to the obedient as well as invite them to secure their soul for the judgment. Many did get baptized after hearing the gospel call. In the past several years she has been responsible for about 195 men and women being added to the church of Christ after having been taught the truth. More importantly, among that number were some fallen Christians who are now happily back in the worship services.

And she emphatically stresses that daily bread did not necessarily come by way of handouts. There were Bible instances where God even commanded the Israelites *not* to petition benevolent favors from other nations. Even today under the New Testament God endows followers of Christ with the ability to be independent working citizens. In 3 John God, through John commended the church for supporting each other and how they were forbidden to ask assistance from non-Christians who were called Gentiles (those who were not yet baptized for the remission of their past sins). Third John 1:7 reads, "Because that for his name's sake they (Apostles) went forth, taking nothing of the Gentiles." Still, as a rational psychiatrist she realizes that nowadays there are times when a tax-paying Christian the same as a non-Christian may suffer from mental or physical disorder and are in a dire spot and may seek decent assistance wherever they can obtain that help. And those Christians as unemployed tax payers deserve governmental assistance according to the laws of America.

But mainly Christians should first petition their own for benevolence. In an attempt to encourage the poor she advises that working, dignifies a person. In Deuteronomy 24:19-22, the able bodied poor was commanded to work by 'gathering' their own food like Ruth did in Boaz's field (Ruth 2:15). And God in laying out the Old Testament law to the Israelites through Moses had forbade the wealthy from gleaning (Harvesting) their entire field. So that whenever food fell on the ground the reapers could not gather over it a second time in order for the strangers, fatherless and widows to collect the leftovers. In light of the poor also having to gather daily food was proof that God never tolerates laziness. "Working for one's daily provisions are designed to bestow honor. Slothfulness denotes that one is even too lazy to run from approaching danger to save their life!" she would recall the passage in Proverb 26: 13, where a lazy person would rather just sit there and simply cry out, "There is a lion in the way; a lion is in the street." This Proverb shows that he was too lazy to even get out of the way and would rather allow the lion the opportunity to devour him and others. Thus, during the recruitment of the homeless her first proposal usually is, "Would you like some work?"

Another important lesson she learned from that scripture of the harvester was that the rich or whoever is able is commanded by God to share with their *truly* helpless neighbor. And thinking of the magnitude of land on God's earth she is often reminded of how God created this earth for all humans and not just for the rich to monopolize. And if the truly poor have no roof over their head, then the rich should make a roof affordable for their income or lack of income. However in reading the Holy Bible she also learned that the poor should give back to God as well as the rich gives back. The following is not a direct command for the New Testament church but the principles still applies: In the book of Exodus, Moses required all of the Israelites from the age of 20 and up, to bring a certain amount to sacrifice for the work. "Everyone that passes among them that are numbered, from twenty years old and above, shall give an offering unto the Lord." The poor were not instructed to give less than the rich at the time. However under the New Testament everyone is required to give as God has prospered them. I Corinthians 16: 2. "Upon the first day of the week let every one of you lay by him in store as God has prospered him." There were also poor saints in the church who this command included. Dassah knew that meant that God gives the poor saint a certain amount of income and God expects him to make a sacrifice just like everyone else. If the poor made only five dollars that week then he should purpose in his heart how much of that he would give back to God.

Back to her thoughts, "Sadly, since I've been in this practice, I've seen the efforts of affordable housing come and then funding gets cut before it is given a fair chance to work!" she had accessed one day in a jam packed homeless recruitment meeting. Then one day in front the television she dabbed at tears while watching the news. There was this housing authority office that had so many poor people mainly Blacks waiting out in the cold just to, get a Section 8 housing voucher. Then the tears really turned on as most of those nearly homeless souls had children outside with them. Later that night she heard that 300, 000 people had been there fighting for only 30,000 vouchers. She felt that if the tears she had already shed could get all 300,000 families into a home then every last one would have a place to tuck their children into bed. She recalled a thought she'd been relishing lately. The idea was that since Blacks are the majority in crisis here in America even when it comes to simple renting, why is it that those Blacks who could not make it in America would not try their hand at living in Africa. But when she had suggested that to a fellow doctor he had astonished, "There are people breaking the door down just to come into America!" he had replied, "And you are saying the poor should beat the door down to get out of America? I don't get it Dassah!"

"Well, you know that I am not a racist," the very fair skinned doctor had said, "But look at it this way a group of immigrants with white skin stand a far better chance of being granted immunity into America than a whole group of black skinned people, so the government might let poor Blacks go! Wouldn't you agree?"

The dark skinned man paused and looked long at her a fellow doctor of the mind. "I guess you're right… again." He had snickered. "Darker skinned people have been unduly stereo typed here in America."

She continued her thought about the land in Africa being plenteous, though mostly undeveloped. She figured every homeless and hopeless Black person should band together and petition the government to fund that forty-acres-and-a-mule promised and fund a Back to Africa Exodus. The government could allot relocation fees as slave reparation atonement payment. That way the still pending law suit would be officially over in the Supreme Court. But she did realize why the suit was not yet settled. The report is that the government is struggling with deciding which age group of Blacks are eligible for the slave reparation payments. She had long since figured that any poor Black person, who are willing to leave America should be eligible to leave. And America should set them up in Africa and protect them the same way America protect White America who are in Africa. Additionally, Blacks in America over the age of 80 should never die from heat exhaustion or freeze due to an inability to pay utilities. Furthermore, as slave reparation no elderly African-American should ever have to worry about nursing care for the rest of their short life. But she was very grateful for the private energy programs for the disabled and elderly. And also for Medicare and Social Security which she assisted so many to apply for.

However, in today's politics the Republican Party seems to hover in Congress like vultures trying to gobble up and do away with every assistive program that would help poor American citizens! And when it comes to the poverty polls in America Blacks make up the majority. It has been like pulling teeth without pliers for President Obama to even get the jobs bill for minimum wage to pass in Congress at a meager 10.10 per hour. Yet most of America, in the President's first term was asking why hasn't things gotten any better since he has been in office. Dassah simply answers, "Blame Congress!" As slave reparation those who work should at least get paid that amount for their hard labor. The doctor vows to begin a support group for a Black Exodus to Africa. Although she is well aware that she would never be allowed to get a Black support group inducted into the Web Internet line-up. She had learned that the hard way one day when she scanned the net fervently trying to find a stable Black support group and was not able to locate a single one. Then she asked herself had Black support groups stopped trying to make a difference as a forgotten nation? Or did all the Black Webs get blocked for some unfair reason?

The doctor as of late is amazed how when the families of the victims in the 911 Trade Center attack in 2001, was overjoyed when President Barrack Obama was responsible for finally tracking down Osama Bin Laden and had him killed. Those families and other Americans were appeased now that Bin Laden had received a just reward. But, on the other hand, some of those same people when it comes to Blacks getting what is rightfully due to them through the Slave Reparation Act they will boldly butt against that fairness for Blacks. "How down right hypercritical!" she had huffed. "So, in their opinion, what's good for the goose is not also good for the gander! Should Blacks simply go on and forget what the government allowed to happen to their ancestors, and is still denying Black rights today?" she says. "Well, in the same sphere, why wouldn't the families of the victims of 911 go on and forget about what Bin Laden was accused of having done to their American families!?"

There in the auditorium during the award for the famed doctor. The room was just as packed as those voucher lines. At last the ex-homeless now white-collar multi-race, largely African American audience gets the chance to go wild with applause. Most of them was ex-homeless men. Some of them were there with re-united families and was looking so polished and polite.

The doctor sat poised on the panel with several governmental officials. And as usual she was teary-eyed and this time with pride just to know that a large number of those men had become small business owners. He was now able to uphold the title of Head of Household. She was even proud that the rest simply had good livable jobs. The Christian in her knew that God had appointed a special day in which he would reward their hard work by giving them a place to prop up their feet in comfort. And she felt that God had allowed her to resurrect those poor people men in particular from their graves of destitution.

As she sat there among the elite her beautiful light brown eyes scanned the audience. Her beautiful eyes met with a set of dark healthy looking handsome eyes. The buffed mid-20s younger than herself man winked at her. And immediately she returned the gesture and mimed through glossy lips, "Hi Step" along with an inconspicuous wave of well-manicured fingers.

Stephanas Carter was her bodyguard and had just this morning fought through the snowy traffic in her limo just to get his boss to the meeting on time. Even with the packed busses and subways, New York traffic still remained bumper to bumper most of the time. It appeared as if everyone who visited New York was convinced that relocation should be their next move. Stephanas Carter was born in New Jersey, but had been in New York for the past 6 years since he went to work for Dr. Desoto. When Step was just an 18-year-old the doctor had plucked him from the deadly vices of the streets along with some other wayward boys. He had been so strong and sure of his goals that the doctor saw his potential and chose him to be her extra set of eyes and ears. With great determination to achieve he had completed the makeover program within 12 months as opposed to the required 24. Now she and he were the special pair that was able almost to read each other's mind. Step was single with many admirers longing to put an end to that. But he felt that at 25 he would have to spend a lifetime with one woman. "I'm just not ready to turn into an old man like some of my friends have done!" he often used as an excuse to have his cake and eat it too. He was just not ready to part with the 3 honeys he always kept around. Step was not a Christian, though Hadassah had unsuccessfully lowered the evangelistic hammer on him. "Your soul should be the first thing you should clean up!" she constantly says.

"Oh, I believe in God and plan to get saved some day!" he would only promise and leave it at that.

Then on another day soon after the Award ceremony and back in Neal, New York, it was 7:00 am. Once again the meteorologists had mutually predicted the weather. That Saturday in January was wintry with moderate accumulating snow. Only a few folk were out driving and some carefully moving even slower just to gape at the black limousine strangely gracing their shoddy neighborhood. A few people squinted curiously trying to peer through the tinted windows which the driver had pushed the remote for more darkness. Thus they surrendered to ever seeing in, and simply watched whether the vehicle would master the only snug vacant parking space. Finally the limo was nestled between two regular vehicles. And again the driver sighed of gratitude for the snow chains—special plastic designed so as not to damage the tires or the road. But they were designed for her cars mainly to give added traction on ice.

Inside the spaciously designed for maneuverability, plush was Doctor Hadassah Desoto the only passenger. The good-looking man who had winked at her in the auditorium sat behind the wheel. Stephanas Carter's legs stretched far under the wheel. The two peered through snow pelted windows into different races of observers still trying to see inside. "I'm glad the law allows limos such privacy," the stunning, 38-year-old doctor breathed cross-legged and as composed as the surround-sound music. The half Black half Puerto Rican casually dressed woman glanced at her handsome 25-year-old bodyguard only to receive a baritone grunt.

"Is it too early for you, Step?" humor sounded through sophistication.

"You'd better believe it Doctor Dassah!" he yawned still relishing in the mentally-tantalizing late night date with a not only striking but intelligent woman. Step dated several times a week—a different women each time. He had yet to run across the woman that made his heart as well as his loins jump for joy. Many of his peers his age were deep into exclusive relationships or married. He also would not mind having one girl. But that just never happened. Not that every woman he dated had not attempted to pull him into the cage with her. Only to have him rebut, "I don't think you'd like me as much as a husband!"

"Why, would you suddenly grow fangs and a rattle on the end of your tail!?" one had inquired.

"No, I'm sure you wouldn't approve of me bringing home other kittens to cuddle!" he would truthfully admit. "I just haven't found that special kitten yet!" The gentleman in him would certainly not be trying to hurt her feelings. He knew that leading girls on could cause serious repercussions. He would not give anyone a reason to torch his penthouse.

Even though Step was not a Christian he had certain morals. He had gone to the church of Christ during his rehab in the homeless program and was moved by things he'd heard.

There in the limo the doctor glanced over at her drossy ex-homeless employee, "Now, you knew we were going scouting this morning", subtle authority filled the air as she uncrossed her legs snapping off the seatbelt and then added, "For the price of these wheels this car should read minds and unbuckle seatbelts too!" humor.

A lazy snicker, "Want me to start unbuckling your seatbelt?"

"No!" she glanced over irritated, "In the six years you've known me you should know when I'm only kidding!" She popped open the dash, reached in and pulled out a pair of leather fur-lined gloves that matched the hooded coat draped over the back of her seat. And beginning to wiggle slim fingers into the softness, she paused. Then like a bored child deciding not to play with that toy suddenly she yanked the glove back off, "We'll just sit here and have another coffee break. . . It's still pretty early," she glanced over full lips glossy, "Of course we could've waited and come out this afternoon, but as we know by then the homeless men would be gone in all directions in search of booze or food. . . We'll have better success while they're bedded down you know?" only a reminder of what Step already knew.

"Yeah Doc, I know," the apology was as sincere as it sounded. He sadly recalled also being among the homeless prior to getting rescued by her six years earlier. So the morning routine in search of the homeless was no stranger to Step.

Dassah was out that morning scouting for homeless people, men especially for her makeover cotton growing and all types of food farm in South Georgia. Some of that food would be shipped up to Manhattan to her three, all-organic restaurants. She also encourages her church members to buy her organic foods both meat vegetables and fruits. "This chemically grown food is the culprit behind all these illnesses from cancer!" she always warns.

She had extended her once mediocre psychiatric practice into a legitimate profitable empire—a program to rehabilitate homeless veterans and ex-minor-offense convicts—some living on the streets as a result of past substance-abuse or mental disorders. Though the doctor still performs regular psychotherapy her unusual and profitable passion now is to offer the homeless a jump start at life again. "It also gives me a rush to see just one man get baptized and complete the program with a renewed positive attitude!" she had once said to a fellow doctor. "Plus, not *all* of it is about the Benjamins, you know!" And at the thought of money she recalled never forgetting her childhood fantasy where she had lived impoverished and was angry about it! So she had vowed to make plenty of money when she grew up. And at that point in her life she promised to get rich at any cost. But that was before she got saved and began to pray about those selfish ways. Yet she was still young and angry while in med school. Thus she would dream about being wealthy simply to erase any memory of a penniless past. "In a dream one can have whatever one can dream up!" mostly she would walk around in her make-believe-world. Whenever she would be on the way home from school on the bus she would block out the numerous conversations going on around her. As a young girl who wore outdated clothes she would sit staring at her image in the big window of the bus. She would will herself to be clothed in the latest design and the cutest hair style.

Then soon after med school and laden with student loans she was added to the Church of Christ which put an iron handle on her cup of goals. She could only wish President Obamas' Educational Reform Plan was in force when she had been in school. At that time she had to pay back 150.000 dollars. And that loan was did not include the free grants she got. Nowadays she would be required to pay back only about 10 to 50.000 dollars if even that much! "So many people haven't an inkling of an idea all the good this President has done in such a short time!!!" she had huffed to a fellow doctor who also had a load of school debt. "And, as for the health care reform soon many poor people will be able to get mental health and not have tax-payers foot the bill. . . And God bless the President for signing the unemployment benefits and then the many extensions he has ordered! Just think of all the unemployed people who would've become homeless had it not been for unemployment benefits," the wise doctor had pointed out. "And I'd bet a dollar to a dime some of those 25 million people who chose not to vote for him is benefiting from that extended unemployment insurance!" she had wagged her pretty head that day.

It was after she was saved that she discovered how having the right heart herself was the true key to helping others. "Sincerely serving the poor rather than mere lip service makes all the difference in their hopeless lives," she had said to her fellow doctor. Yet in the mist of assisting others she held on to her vow to someday be very well-to-do. "Though in my wildest dreams I never dreamed I'd be as rich as I've become," she had smiled at the financial statement she had spent the entire morning re-checking her accounts. She only trusted her accountant and broker to a certain yardage of her money. One day while looking deeply into the accounts she had snickered, "In God I trust, but in all others, I investigate!"

There in the parked limo, recalling how that prosperity had blossomed in only a matter of a few years also made her naturally full moist lips smile big.

In the limo snow misting Step under the wheel Dassah recalled how she finally was able to finish med school at the age of 32. Subsequently along with the addition of the makeover program to her practice by the age of 35 her first ten-million was in the bank. Two of those millions the government had funded her program. So by the age of 37 her worth had excelled to twenty million. "Not many psychiatrists can sport around a small carrier plane and two limousines off of a mere psyche stipend," she thought, picturing her two freight planes sitting on the rented field at the airport. She used the planes to ship food from Georgia to New York for the restaurants and also to other states. She envisioned her two limos, Mercedes Benz and SUV at her 29-acre mansion where all her house employees were ex-homeless people.

While in the parked regular limo Dassah smiled about her present worth of 95 million dollars not to mention all the successful investments. While the downward spatial of the economy had affected the others she had her farm and many stores and 2 plush hotels. "God has put me in a good position because people need always to eat wear clothes and have somewhere to sleep overnight!" she smiled about her blessings of which she always gave God the glory. However her real estate firm was a bit sluggish but with those minimal losses she made up in the restaurants. There was 2 restaurants in Upper Manhattan and the other restaurant was In Lower Manhattan. She made the lower one affordable to the poor. All of her stores were assured to serve organic meals, even to the poor. And the apartment complex was rented to section 8 seniors had not done too badly. "Senior citizens have always proven to be dependable!" she had said. "Plus the government doesn't fool around when it comes to reinforcing Section 8 rental payment policies! Section 8 tenants in order to keep their vouchers must keep up their rent and utilities!" she smiled at the fact that she do not have to pressure senior tenants to pay each month like she does the able bodied young folk.

Outside in the cold new observers squinted to peer in, fine snow before their eyes. But hard-bodied Stephanas had simply reclined eyes closed to the soft music. And as usual Dassah took her thoughts to her booming makeover program. The homeless veterans and ex-cons she recruited were once tax-paying citizens some who had fought for America and deserved a helping hand. Even though many of them may now be battling substance abuse. "Stumbling into a life of habitual sin can happen to the best of us!" she would defend those now repentant substance-abusers. "I often meditate on the scripture that warns us, 'Wherefore, let him that thinks he stand take heed lest he fall!'" she would sternly warn the cold critics who feels they are above having compassion on the weak. "Apparently any homeless person would succumb to some kind of mental disorder!" she had said to a fellow doctor one day in their discussion about a young female ex-homeless patient. That young woman had yielded to homelessness because she could not find a job and her Supplemental Income had been terminated. In the past she depended on her husband ever since they came out of high school and got married. They never had children and were now divorced… leaving her with no special shills. Many of the other governmental assistant programs had rejected her simply because she had no children. Thus the young American citizen was in a different state than her family. When the government cut her off she was finally stripped of all self-esteem. Eventually the exhausted woman wound up on a hospital wing after she alerted people she was contemplating suicide. Dassah had treated the woman at that hospital where the doctor volunteered quite often. "Some American polices apparently needs modifying regarding helpless people who have no children!" she had huffed to the weeping woman that day.

There in the parked limo that Saturday morning the doctor recalled how gravely in her recruit efforts she would approach men and women either on the streets in shelters or dejectedly exiting the doors of a jail house. Some of them had been released without a clue as to what their next move would be before the doctor and Step had approached them. The doctor side of her was grateful that coming fresh out of jail some alcoholics and drug-abusers had already been detoxified. But that depended on the amount of time spent in prison. Fortunately that purging helped Dassah not to have to waste precious time and expense cleansing them out. Some disabled men that was released from prison with an IQ below 69. He may have been incarcerated for a long period and had no hope nor intelligence to fend for themselves. So alleys and loitering on corners would become a hellish haven for them. For those retarded Black men she knew of no foreseeable future goals. Even mental facilities would quickly reject them. And it was a fact that too many Black mental men got sent straight to prison instead of to a humane rehabilitation facility. As a doctor of the mind she avoided playing the race card. But she knew that White men and women were in the majority in mental hospitals. "Why is it that Blacks are deemed criminals while Whites who commit the same crime are declared mentally deranged?" she often huffs at the sin of showing favoritism.

But as for the other homeless people her job-offer and hopefully business-ownership was the miracle those men had hoped for. So with a ladder extended she had assisted many to start a careful rung by rung climb to a fruitful future. But it saddened and then angered the stern psychiatrist over the conscience decisions some of those homeless men had made. Many of them chose to continue to wallow in a life of vagrancy. Her own strict pre-requisites made her sad whenever a man would not qualify for entrance. Working on her demanding farm was a far cry from just sitting and driving machinery all day. Thus the damaged alcoholics and mentally ill beyond repair would be back on the streets in no time flat.

She recalled one of her heavily guarded recruit meetings. It was the day she had counseled a mentally disabled Black man whom she had patiently sat down with him face to face. That man in his early twenties had sat there so stiff still and quiet. The beautiful doctor had softly and motherly asked, "Seeing I can't allow you to enter this program and you have no place else to go would you like me to take you to a mental care facility?" her knowing full well he did not even know what a mental health facility was. And even if she had broken the statement down to the lowest denomination he still could not figure it out. "How in God's would does anyone have the heart to put someone like him in a prison with hardened men?" she had cried. So there with the man all clean as much as possible. He was seated across from her with a confound gaze. He had simply nodded "Yes" just like the little child he was. Even with all the patients she had seen like him she could not control the tears swelling in her. Then her eyes met with a much smarter security guard standing by. He was also an ex-homeless man and could only shake his 30-something head in hopelessness. "Now its back to being just another statistic once he gets out of the hospital!" she had said. "That is if he's let into the hospital at all!" she had thought that day walking the frightened young man to the exit. "This young Black man will only wound up back in prison making furniture for fifty cents a day and getting sodomized by his fellow inmates!" she had said to the guard. Then the uniformed guard had said, "Doc, as much as I dread saying this but in prison he'll at least have a roof and three squares a day!"

Dassah only shrugged slim shoulders hating to even admit that was sadly a valid point he had made. Anyway, she personally took him to the mental facility where she volunteered knowing that after a few weeks perhaps days would be discharged. And unfortunately back on the streets the mentally disable man would be last in line to receive help. She also knew that retarded people had no knowledge of how to panhandle. Just like a child he and like a hungry animal he would eat anything right out of the garbage. And in reality too many people fail to realize that when a truly mentally disabled person approaches them he is only hungry and rarely poses a threat. As much as possible she appeals to the public on how to respond to the homeless mental people, "Some people don't even take time to figure out who's really mental and who faking homelessness!" she would argue. "Just suppress your fear and ask him if he need something to eat. . . Then if he's retarded he'll immediately nod. . . Then you can take that hungry person and buy him some bread and bologna! Even if you hand him a dollar he'll go and buy some kind of junk-food. . . Most mental people know that money can be exchanged for food. Even though he may get taken advantage of at the counter concerning any change owed back. And some nice store owner might just give him more for his dollar." she would say to people. . . "I thank God for the few benevolent people in the world!"

Concerning turning men away from the program the doctor tried all she could to allow everyone rehabilitation. Having to institutionalize anyone made her feel her quest to save everyone from homelessness had fallen flat on its face. "Nowadays even most governmental institutions are so badly in need of funding!" she thought there in the limo. "But there are also institutions that unfairly take in patients of their own biased choosing!" First-handed she had witnessed inequality in institutional preference just like anywhere else. As much as she hated to admit there were racists in every facet of life. "That serpent called Satan is all over the place!" she huffed. "Satan also influences the rich not to donate to mental causes!"

There in the comfort of the limo she recalled the beginning of the program. She had designed it for re-making the eager to be rescued homeless man. And women were welcome in the beginning. Then the farm phase of it for females took a flawed nose-dive. Afterwards women regrettably got banned. But she still allowed women to utilize certain aspects of the services in order for women to also become fruitfully mainstreamed. As a psychiatrist Dassah felt that men should be given priority in order to provide for his abandoned children. Thus she flat out mandates that he takes care of his children even while on the paid program. Also at the end of his training the man could not simply skip on his merry way and not be responsible for any children he had fathered. It was policy that before he could even begin the two-year work pursuit he must find and then own up to his abandoned off-springs. Even though he earned a minimal income from the program, the government would temporarily assist him in providing for those children while he worked for Dassah. Then when he finished and began his business with the money he was required to save in an investment fund, along with the governmental grant, he was on home base. With a smile there in the limo with her lovely eyes fixed on the snow and through soft music, she recalled how soon she and the government were blown away with the success of the program. "Nevertheless, every twenty-four months really tells the success stories!" she thought. Every two years was when the men received his cap, gown and grant money. He would be all polished and ready to crank up his small business. But before graduation he would have been financially productive for her and proudly for himself. He would have worked on the farm and in her numerous lucrative stores.

The doctor and her large staff had thrown themselves tirelessly into restoring the men both mentally as well as physically. However, it was not a surprise to her that it would be like pulling teeth with just her fingers to get the Black men to submit to couch therapy. "The Black man's reluctance to admit something is wrong with his psyche is something even med school had no answer for!" she had said to a fellow doctor one day. "Maybe since the government is so liberally handing out grants for unnecessary research, they will do some on why Black men think they are exempt from mental illness!"

Dassah thought about her finances. The quarterly status reports to the government tell how many men came through had exceeded her expectations. So, there on the streets of Neal, New York, in the parked limo with Step behind the wheel, a warm feeling engulfed her. She visualized the men who had already left the program as small business owners. Visions of those business meetings prior to the graduate purchasing his business came to mind. She sat there painting a vivid picture of the business suppliers and government staff around an oval table. They sat awaiting the ex-homeless men's anxious rehearsed entrance—rehearsed to impress. And in the meeting each supplier would be in plain view of the men who was about to enter. The suppliers would sit jaw-dropped over the ex-paupers marching in, heads high. Down the spacious aisle they would prance. The aisle became their catwalk to freedom. The men would move confidently with their briefcases containing well written business plans. They now sported leather instead of plastic grocery bags. The leather monogrammed case would be awarded to the man who produced his completed business plan. She recalled how impressed the suppliers would nod at them. They were in awe that those men had once slept in a tenthouse, in alleys and begged on every available corner. Dassah found herself having to prove these were indeed the same men she had taken off the streets. She found it necessary to take before and after snap shots, "Are you sure these people were ever slept on these streets of New York? Are you sure you ain't just pulling a fast one?!" One female official had challenged wide-eyed.

"Here you go!" Dassah would proudly fling the pictures it on the table. They showed the portfolios of a two-year time progression of the men, "Surely my foolproof program speaks for itself!" she had smiled proudly one day.

Then while checking out the before and after fingerprints they would apologize for having doubted her honesty. But deep down Dassah was impressed that she and her capable staff had done such a fantastic, unbelievable job. She was also proud that the men had been so willing to hang through the duration of the rigorous program.

Dassah recalled that one of her exacting rules was that each man partner in business with four other ex-homeless partners. Each graduate would have been taught and passed a strict business ethics for entrepreneurship before completing the work program. Since Black people had such a reputation for not being able to get along in business situations she would prove them before they would partner together. They had many classes on respect and how to talk it out, rather than duking, it out. However, coming from the streets of prison life, fist spoke louder than words. And concerning the business plan, the strict matriarch would emphatically remind them, "Now if you can't put together a fourteen-page business plan, then you couldn't very well run a small business, could you?!"

She recalled one beginner's recruitment meeting. It was in a huge security guarded conference hall. It was prior to putting that crew to work on the farm and also to begin his transformation. She had informed them, "Recruits, its basic math," the smooth, feminine woman sitting in a room full of rough necks, had bravely huffed, "Five business partners might. . . " Then suddenly she hesitated, keenly eyeing the confused gaping men, "I stand to be corrected, she continued, "Five business partners *will* be more successful than a single owner!" seeing fit to remind grown men of the obvious, "You must never say, I *might*, or *if* . . . You must always say and think, I *will*, if the Lord is willing that I should live! Because success begins only with that assured attitude and trust in God!" She had stood up and questioningly, briefly paused again, and then continued, "Recruits, I'm sure you've heard the phrase, 'No ifs, ands, or buts about it?'" again pausing, giving them time to soak that in.

Confused, heads slowly begin to nod in the affirmative they had heard that phase before.

"Well, beginning this day I want you to drop the, ifs and the ands, and get up off your butts!"

Now enlightened, immediate laughter erupted from the new ex-homeless recruits.

Dassah knew the more mature men among them should already know those basic business concepts, but absurdly even they had no prior teaching about finances. Also many had come right out of high school and straight to jail without ever learning common business sense in the least. She was well aware how young Black boys in very poor neighborhoods were conditioned to fail and to turn over their lives to the prison system. While, White kids came out of school, and was taken into the armed forces for a better future, Blacks kids came out of school, and were taken to prison. "But little did the government realize that a war in the east would happen and take those White kids lives before they could even get fully grown!" she sadly thought. The doctor thanked God that some kids managed to escape the judicial system by having gone off to college. Even then some of those poor boys were unable to ride out the storms of family financial problems. As a result they were driven to the streets. And, while they were in that cruel arena mental degradation got grinded too deep for them to ever envision any hope.

Many street people were there as the result of being forced out of their dwelling place. In many cases an apartment may have burned down around them with no renter's insurance. Some of those homeless had simply been poor managers of money thus their debts had chewed them up bones and all and spit him out on the streets. Others had lost jobs with no other skills to get another one.

In this present dangerous economy so many unemployed people find a dire need for extended unemployment benefits. That's why the compassionate Democratic President has presented a bill for that imperative extension. Were it not for those extended employment checks there would certainly be more homeless people out there. But then for some those benefits did run out and those ex-tax payers found themselves faced with an eviction warrant that put some on the streets. The doctor had heard so many true stories from so many homeless citizens. "Though America tries to feed clothe and shelter the homeless the rate is growing too rapidly to keep up with them all!" she says. "Especially since so many people from other countries are also depending on America to feed them. . . Foreign families enter America with loads of children and the government has to take from Americans in order to feed them!" Dassah had sighed to a fellow doctor one day.

She recalled the new recruit class that day she had seriously continued to say, "But when poor people grasp the importance of unity then managing money and business will come much easier! Also remember that in your business don't be afraid to take on reliable partners." She continued to say, "Preferably from within this program. . . And that any prospective business partner who may be fresh out of jail for a misdemeanor may not have the money you require as his investment. Nevertheless that person male or female very well may be the diligent worker you need . . . And his wages, which you would normally fork out to any hired help could be used as their investment . . . of course it would be humane if you would allow that poor worker some kind of extra money to live on. Try not to take all his wages for the investment installments," she had gone on to counsel that day, "And in no time with a payment plan that prospective partner would have paid off his investment fee and be a most trustworthy partner. . . anyone who would hang in until the end surely has proven his reliability," she finished that day. Then she had solicited questions from the recruits of which there were always many questions from new ex-homeless group. She recalled one of those questions that has stuck with her. One young White recruit had seriously asked, "How can I be sure I won't take the business money and do Meth again?" He had been a senior year college drop-out whose family lived in another state. In the beginning of his drug journey some friends had dared him to try Meth . . . or had they been his friends at all? He admitted how he really liked the way that first hit of Meth made him feel . . . feathery-headed without a care in the world. Watching him had saddened her. Too many young White kids were getting nailed into the ground by Methamphetamines—their drug of choice. Also she saw too many Black kids get strung out on cocaine in the form of crack. Thus the Blacks wound up in jail or prison. "Meth users usually get referred to rehab and crack users get long jail sentences!" she had hotly told the truth in a mixed raced meeting one day about the obvious inequality in the judicial system. "Or is it a rich verses poor thing?!" she had a quick change of heart. "More White parents have money or property to bail their kids out of jail than do Black parents." She thought.

Then she had replied to the White man that day, "Well, all you can possibly do is allow the Lord to add you to His church. . . That way you'll have the privilege to approach the Father in prayer . . . you'll stand a better chance of remaining drug-free. . . It's a blessing to have a relationship with the Lord and have access to ask things of Him. . . Christ can give you a new mind the Holy Ghost. . . " Then she picked up a Bible from the stack she kept handy. "Here read Philippians, chapter two, verse five." Reluctantly he took the book from her. And flipping haphazardly through the pages, he admitted, "I don't know where that book is!" he jutted the book back at her. Then one man had snickered at the downtrodden White man. Dassah stepped abruptly over to the snickering man and handed him the Bible, "Here, you think you can find it? She nodded knowingly. The snickering man with dirty fingernails took the book and skillfully flipped to Philippians, 2 verse 5 in no time flat. He also began to quote the passage without even looking at it but rather he was looking at her, "Let this mind be in you which was also in Christ Jesus," he said and proudly jutted the book back to her.

"Impressive!" she smiled at him. "It seems you know your way around the Bible!"

"I have a Master's degree in Theology, Ma'am. The brown shinned, 30-something man exposed. "But now I don't have a common place to lay my head!" he huffed as the other recruits gazed on.

"But what happened? She slid into the chair beside him.

"Just five and a half years ago I had my own congregation among the Churches of Christ" he took off the grungy overcoat.

"You were a member of the Lord's church too!?" She smiled. "So am I! Well, hello there. . ." She looked at the name tag that she required all the men to wear to meetings Then, she tended her right hand. "Brother Cedric Baldwin!"

"Yes, that's my given name! He shook her hand.

"Brother, I really didn't mean to interrupt you . . . go on." She was so happy to be bringing a fallen saint back to the Lord . . . her number one goal.

Cedric went on, "I grew that church from just thirty people to one hundred within a little over a year," he sighed. "Then, suddenly some money came up missing, a large amount . . . we few members gave very liberally . . . then fingers started to point from one brother to the other, and guess who the fingers fell on?" he sadly sighed. Then the White man at whom he had snickered said, "All fingers pointed to you but did you really take it?"

"Look Man, I didn't spend all those years learning what God expected of me just to sell my soul for a measly ten-thousand dollars! No, I did not take that money! The church even told me that if I promised to pay back the money, then I would not have to spend time in prison." wagging his head. "But if I tried that then I would be saying I took it! I did not and the one who did knows I did not steal it!"

Then Dassah said, "There's another who also knows you're innocent." she assured him. "The Good Lord is Omniscience and knows and sees all things. . . It'll all come to light one day!" she had comforted him.

Then she had gone on to counsel the man with the Meth issue. She told him that past substance-abuse was a day-by day process just the same as a Christian trying to abstain from committing any given sin on a daily basis. "I'll pray that you reach your goals Troy," she had promised and had been mindful to keep that promise of prayer for all the recruits to come to the Lord. Then she had turned to her newly discovered brother in Christ. "Cedric, surely we'll talk later to try and get to the bottom of who really took that money!" And later she went to the brothers of that congregation. They were familiar with her work and were able to settle everything. When the deacons of that congregation, began to do a diligent search, they all looked into the safe that the money so suddenly disappeared. Dassah was there when they conducted the search. "The police has already simply eyeballed the safe!" one deacon had said as they were re-examining the safe.

"And how old is this safe, anyway?" she looked at the rusting of it inside and outside.

"It was here when moved in about seven years ago!" Cedric informed.

"This safe appears to be an antique." She said as she got down on her knees to get a closer look inside. "Cedric, can you recall that long ago, where you placed the money in question?"

"I put the collection trays, two of them, one tray on top of the other, on this top rack, right here." He touched the very spot. There was another rusty rack under that one. Dassah felt around on the top rack and to her surprise, something at the top of the rack tore across her gloved hand. "What was that?!" She yelped and looked to see what it was. A wire had broken through the cloth lining of the decrepit safe. Thus she became very suspicious, "Cedric, how high was the stacks of money you put in that top tray?" Then Cedric though hard about that, "It had about three or four stacks of paper money. . . I would wrap the money in stacks and put it in this spot always!" he promised.

Then while still was on her knees, Dassah took out her phone and shined the flashlight into the old safe. The cloth was literally rotting away in back. That was where the top stacks of bills had been accidentally raked by that metal piece and had fallen behind the cloth. The torn cloth had served as a pocket. So she ripped away as much of the cloth as possible. And to everyone's surprise, out tumbled two stacks of rubber-banded dusty bills, rubber bands nearly rotted. She picked up the money and handed all of it to the minister. "You will probably want to count this, Brother."

"Yes, I will personally do that, Sister, thanks!" He went to a table and right there counted out ten stacks of 100 dollar bills and some more loose bills. There had been no checks in those stacks. The checks were always given right away to the secretary for bookkeeping. Then Cedric could do nothing but plop down on a chair, put his hands to his face and weep sorely. "Almost six years of my life flushed down the drain!"

The minister, who had not known Cedric, went to Cedric and tried to console him, but Cedric shoved him away. "You just don't know how hard it's been trying to forgive the church!" tears on a roll. "I even found myself blaming God!" Then he slid from the chair to his knees. He bowed his head, seeming not to care who prayed with him. However, everyone present bowed the head. Some even kneeled with Cedric. He said, "Please forgive me, Father for forsaking you all those years!!" he pleaded with intense sobs. "And thank you for allowing this error to come to light! I am so glad that people now believe that I was innocent. And, thank you that none of your children stole that money!! In the name of Jesus Christ, Your dear Son, amen!!"

Then everyone in the room gladly said Amen! Then Cedric hugged and kissed his She-ro, Dassah.

Needless to say, the church had a meeting and decided to give the money to Cedric as pay for his lost time from society. And, Cedric's wife took him back, and now his ten year old son stands a chance of mot becoming another statistic. Cedric decided to remain in the makeover program. He will use that money to go along with the wages he will make. He is also back faithfully in church where the old members simply cannot do enough to prove how sorry they are. Instead of a small business, he wants another congregation. "And this time I'll let the real deacons handle the money!" she laughs about it now. And as for getting his name wiped out of the justice system, Dassah put Callie, her person attorney on the case. But Callie warned Cedric that he had to be patient in that effort. He said to Dassah, "Patience has become my middle name, wouldn't you agree, Sister Doc?"

Dassah recalled that in those meetings as she answered questions sadness would engulf her to see more African Americans than any other race. Though, women of any race in attendance were very few. "Such a pity there're so many homeless middle aged Black men in these United States of America too!" she would think of the lack of unity among that age group as she had looked out over the packed audience that day. Most of those older men were 45 and over sat there not even talking to each other. Then she brought her mind back to the present in the comfort of the limo and suddenly glanced over at her bodyguard reclined

"There certainly wouldn't be as many homeless Black men if they would only take a lesson from the locus!"

With a head-jerk in the direction of his once silent boss, the unsuspecting man startled, "Huh!!?" that frown yet unable to diminish his coffee-skinned good looks.

The pretty brown-skinned doctor with hand gestures of frustration flatly huffed, "What I mean is in the book of Proverbs chapter thirty, verse twenty-seven, says that the locus have no king, yet go they forth all of them by bands!" she informed Step, "And you know what that swam of locus did in the land of Egypt, don't you?!"

"Break that down in laymen terms, Doc," a snicker from masculine lips "You're talking to a Bible novice, you know!"

"Well, when Pharaoh refused to let God's people go so that they could worship Him, God sent locus into Pharaoh's fields as one of the deadly plagues . . . then the locus without having any leader were unified enough to destroy all the food substance in that land. . . King Solomon in Proverbs makes a comparison that even without a fleshly king unity can still work wonders. . . And in my opinion it appears that ever since the Civil Rights Movement Blacks feel they needed a major leader to move forth in the struggle . . . and without a leader they would rather abandon the cause. . . But God is showing that the locus has no king, but still being unified they manages to achieve what they set out to do! God was their King!" She popped open the dash and pulled out a very worn Bible. "The moral of the story is, with God at the forefront Blacks could become dignified people once again!"

"Now I see what you mean," now smiling about Black victory. "If Black men were to quit rubbing against the grain of the struggle and flow in the same direction they could virtually wipe out homelessness . . . And not necessarily with physical violence but with mental strategy love for God and unity!"

Questioningly the beautiful biracial woman leaned over, "Now you know I'm no racist don't you, Step?" She ignored the new faces out in the snow trying to peer inside the limo.

"Yeah, I know that, Doc."

"Though this may sound pretty prejudice it's not intended for hate. . . But in my opinion if Blacks were to stop trying to be like other races for a while and just concentrate on working on their own plight, some positive changes might manifest. . . They need to work on reinventing their own identity. But instead they are trying to look like other races and be just like them!"

"You're right! In the eyes of other races a Black man will never be anything but losers. So we should act like the proud Black men we know we once were!" The young man began to get ticked-off. Step, just as most young African American males felt that Black men were only lost and confused in America. And also in any country except in Africa, "Here in America we're like spiders without their natural webbing abilities!" he turned to Dassah and continued, "Blacks would be better off in Africa though I've never been there!" he huffed. "Contrary to popular belief I heard there's some good land in Africa! I would like to urge Blacks to consider moving there to help revitalize that good soil. But, at this point it would be near to impossible to get many Black men to part with their White women to migrate to Africa!" Then, behind the wheel he paused briefly to think about that. "On the other hand," he continued, "I've heard that there are just as many White women in Africa as there are here in America. . . I've heard that some White women have even moved to Africa because they have that jungle fever!" he snickered knowingly. Step had encountered all races of women in his life of bachelorhood.

Dassah, an arched brow shot up, "What do you mean about young Black Americans relocating to Africa?" though she had already thought about that idea but was now on the curious side. She wanted to know his take on the possible exodus from America plan.

He sat straight up, "Well, since America still owes Black slave reparation, one way of repayment could be to fund a Black Exodus to Africa for the poor and homeless. Those who have no hope of achievement in America. . . Personally I think the homeless would rather work the land in Africa than to die under bridges and in alleys here in America!"

She glanced over, "M-m-m that sounds like a feasible idea. . . But how would they live in Africa?" she pried, but really knowing.

Suddenly being sleepy was at the bottom of his list as he hastily turned down the music, "As of late this idea has been my constant partner!" holding up one finger, he began, "First, the government should find out who's eligible to leave in the Exodus. . . Two, they should willing to fund it. . . Three, they should cultivate some good African land. And also give those people seeds, animals and machinery to dig for clean water. . . Fourth, they should provide protection for those Americans the way they protect White Americans there in Africa! Those Blacks should have weapons to protect themselves from terrorists also!" he excitedly laid it out.

"That's a splendid idea, Step!" her light brown eyes full of excitement. His expectations were better than hers for a possible Exodus Movement. So she innocently added, "Yes, and the government could issue stern warnings to terrorists to steer clear of those peaceful Black Americans," she was now pumped up. "And I agree that very capable weapons should be trusted to Black American families the same way they are put in the hands of White families!"

Glancing over at her, "And by now the government should trust Black Americans with weapons there in Africa seeing how in spite of all the abuse Blacks have endured here. Blacks never have tried to overthrow America as a whole using violent tactics. . . . Blacks aren't the race American government has to worry about. The government allows every country that hate America to come here! Other races have proven to be the enemies to beware of!" Then with a firm stare at Step, "We should talk about this issue a bit further but in the meantime I'll be pondering hard on it!" there in the parked limo that Saturday morning. "But right now we must jump to rescuing some homeless people for my desperate need!"

"Yep!" turning the music back up flipping through stations still playing Christmas music in January.

Plus she was aware that statistics reported more homeless families in shelters mostly mothers with children. Thus she felt an urgency to get men back to being leaders in the home to lift burdens off of women. Even those poor women in their own homes were whipped to a total frazzle having to act as both parents. But especially when it comes to the rearing of those confused rebellious boys! The astute psychiatrist would see that as many as possible of those women received free mental counseling as well as financial assistance. This assistance would continue until the children's father would be rehabilitated in her program. And she was equally as proud to report to the government that the men who went back to their families his children began to excel in school and has adopted positive attitudes overall. Most of those children's negative behavior had been the result of an incomplete home life anyway. And for that very fact during family counseling she refuses to counsel any child one on one. The parents was required to be present. She needed to access interactions of the family as a group. From that she was able to ascertain for sure whether the child was loved or not. "Given numerous sessions instead of just one it would be most difficult for a parent to front that long a period!" she had said to a colleague one day in their observations. "I can pick up on whether a child is being abused and I've exposed many abusers that way!"

"How could you tell?"

"Easy! If a child sits petrified for most of the session then that's not normal for children. . . Children are usually active to some degree. . . And if a child flinches every time the parent raises his hand then that's not normal. . . As a doctor you may secretly test the child. Hand the child a toy and see if he'll readily take it while his parent is watching . . . If the child meekly eases his hand to take the toy while moving his eyes back and forth from the toy to his parent that shows he's petrified. That's a sure sign that he may feel he'll get hit if he even touches that toy."

"But we can't really say a child is being abused just because he's afraid of his parents!"

"Of course we can. . . That's why we're called shrinks Girlfriend!!" Dassah had teased that day. "We can shrink those brains until we've rung the truth out of them'!" she pretended to wring out a cloth or something.

There on the streets of Neal as Dassah and Step sat in the parked limo fine snowflakes stuck to the windshield proving that not only was it wet but it was also cold outside. They stared out at the different races of passersby. It also seemed that every new person became curious and took his or her turn peeping in. Step was under the wheel sipping coffee now to soft music again. And in reflection about last might. Dassah as always was in deep thought about her ever increasing makeover program. She thought of how the conscientious ex-homeless men as part of the program would work. They would work either on her demanding farm in South Georgia or in her mall. Many worked in her two mega restaurants or in her security firm or famous hotel for two years. This paid work was only after three months of non-paid successful rehabilitation and farm work. This work was also only with free food and board. One of her requirements was that none of the recruits should have a physical disability to the point that it would hinder his work production. Also only the successful fulfillment of that three-month segment would qualify him to begin to apply for the small-business government grant while he worked. The doctor was especially excited to require each man to fulfill the mentoring of a juvenile male as part of the training. Though in her expertise she knew it was best that the man never be alone with any of those boys. She had already faced a law suit because of women living on the farm among men. So the cautious doctor unquestionably would avoid any more unwise unwarranted inconveniences. "Plus, my first concern is for the welfare of those boys! she said, "It appears too many men nowadays have abandoned the nature desire for women and gone a lusting after little boys!" angrily, she huffed.

She recalled that before the men would complete the program they would agree to hire if needed willing veterans and ex-minor-offense cons that had not gone through the program but still desperately needed jobs. But she knew that there were only so many jobs a business owner could offer in that he already had four business partners. So it was up to every ex-homeless person to try out for the program for themselves. There was one exceptional business that had many extra positions available for the homeless. And it had eight ex-homeless partners. That busy business was a nails spa in a very lucrative area in Manhattan where only celebrities were allowed a membership. The rich women in particular would frequent that pampering spa. Those wealthy women were usual customers at the male-manicurist-pedicurist spa. On any given day a woman occupied all of the fifty-chair spa surrounded in total plushness.

However, in order to prevent another sexual harassment law suit only services from ankle-to-feet, and hands-to-wrist, were executed. The women simply lavished in being pampered and massaged by a man's strong fingers instead of the soft hands of another woman. These women complained that their husbands never gave them a foot massage or even a spontaneous hand-rub outside of wanting to sex them. Also the ex-homeless business owners of the Spa would hire ex-homeless women to take care of the men who came in for manicures and pedicures. These earnest business men had worked very hard to become certified manicurists and foot masseuses. And hiring ex-minor-offense cons as opposed to other people would be part of the business owner's clause before he could qualify for any business grant. And to those ex-homeless men who were reluctant to hire other ex-homeless people Dassah would firmly remind those selfish men, "If someone hadn't given you a second chance we wouldn't even be having this conversation. . ." she would shake a well-French manicured finger done by his Spa, "No doubt you'd be still in that alley wearing ice sickles for pajamas!"

The beautiful doctor's heart began to sing right there in the comfort of the parked limo when she visualized the physical transformation the men underwent, both physically and mentally. She viewed that change as a miracle in itself. "You can't beat God-therapy, a wholesome diet, adequate work and plenty of clean water!" she contentedly had said in a meeting one day. She recalled that in conjunction with new leases on life in their businesses some men had even attracted independent professional women. But even if he did strike up a relationship with a woman other than his children's mother, still did not cancel his requirement to provide for the children. Dassah naturally full lips smiled big, thinking about some of the men who had diligently searched the shelters and housing projects to find his family. He would gladly go through the process of withdrawing them from those welfare programs. Thus those mothers with small children were totally shocked and more than ready to be reunited with him. Especially since he now looked so fresh and polished. Still other men were merely grateful just to be re-programmed, so to speak. "Now that's what profitable rehabilitation is all about!" she had beamed at the men coming out ready to crank up small businesses.

She smiled especially big about the reformed young Black residents in the program. They had been released from prison for misdemeanors of merely being locked up for a marijuana butt or residue from cocaine. Then after way too many unjustifiable years in a hard prison where they gave free labor. And now with no job or family the streets would became his permanent hat rack. Which some were even too young to fend for themselves—most having been incarcerated as merely, teens. Again she recalled how statistics report that young Black males are more likely to return to prison than any other race. "Society are placing the blame on the young Black boys but the adults and society are the real culprits!" she had said to a fellow doctor. "If our judicial system rehabilitated Black kids the way they do White kids then Blacks would also get a second wind! At a very young age the Black kid's record is purposely set up to condemn him to prison or to the streets for life!" Then with solemn sadness she thought of all the books and news about such undemocratic statistics concerning Black youths. So much so that society has become desensitized to the Black plight here in America. People are sick of seeing all those Black-abuse documentaries where people simply talk about it and do nothing about the situations. So society now turns deaf ears on all the negativity in the Black hoods. And yes there still exists Black neighborhoods where poor Blacks are forced to live. And all the police brutality against Black teenage boys sickened her to think about. The judicial system seems to be the enemy of those babies. The system would rather uphold those unrighteous cops than to tell the truth about what really happened as to why he was shot down in cold blood. So that makes the jury who gets the cops off unrighteous also. They will also get God's disapproval. The Bible condemns people who purposely perverts righteous judgment. She recalled a scripture in Proverbs 31: 5, where the wise King Solomon gave advice to another regarding his inability to make sound and just decisions if he had too much wine. However Solomon used wine to show his meaning. But a king or any person in power can be drunk off anything even drunk off to much pride. Can judges and jurors be too prideful to make just decisions without partiality? And that passage reads, "Lest they drink, this case pride and forget the law? Can they pervert the judgment of any of the afflicted (poor)? When anyone has been warned of their evil ways and refuse to repent his sins will be rewarded! And, he will not like the reward the creator is capable of laying on him!

And those judges, jurors and crooked lawyers will get their just reward for all the innocent Black kids they've shoot down. Some of those kids were shot in the back or as he already lay there helpless! Then Dassah said a silent prayer, "May God, comfort the families and especially the parents of those kids!"

But as a doctor she realizes that society haven't a clue as to what to do about the stagnated race-mess it has wound up in. "And that's what gives my makeover program the success to rescue these lost men who are not in their children's life to help rear them. . ." However, she knew that many of those Black boys had fathers in the home when the child was shot down in the streets. In fact many of those kids were from decent homes. She thought, "It really sad when cops are jealous of young kids!" Envy on the cop's behalf was the only excuse she could think of. "And it was not that the cop feared for his life either. Because those killer cops were the only ones in possession of a weapon at the time! So they can just come off that bold-faced lie!" she huffed.

Concerning the program the problem rested in the fact that there were not enough African American businesses around. There were no jobs to offer their own race. Only if Blacks would offer another Black a second chance! Again sadly she had discovered that Blacks tend to be their own worst enemy in too many cases. Black business owners rain fiery snobbish-ness down on Black wayward teens just as much as any other race will kick Black teens to the curb. Some Black adults will even indulge in negative dialog with other races about their own Black wayward teens. Whereas other races will flat out refuse to degrade their wayward teens to any Black person. Whites simply refuse to put their teens in the same category with Black teens. Do they feel theirs are better than Black teens? It has been proven that Whites will protect and uphold their children's bad behavior. "Just like that song about pants hanging down," Dassah had said to the doctor. "Black adults should never give any Black songwriter props for coming up with a degrading skit like that!" Any Black adult should lovingly pull such faddish teens to the side and explain the inappropriateness of the way he dresses. . . because overall children will listen to love. But kids will hotly rebel against rudeness!" she said. "Adults should try a tactic like this, "Son, I don't mean any harm but where is your belt? If you don't have one, can I buy you one? Look, Son, I care about how you look?" That will certainly catch his attention in a more positive manner than, "You ought to pull up those pants! Nobody wants to see your nasty underwear!" Then give him a few dollars to buy a belt. In all probability he will think that you are a weirdo. And he probably will not buy a belt with the money but he'll never forget how nice that grown up was to him.

"I like that song!" the fellow doctor had said, "It just might provoke the boys to pull up their pants, don't you think?" the fellow doctor had asked Dassah that day.

"Well, what I'm talking about are principles. . . Little White girls have been showing navels and cracks for the longest her race ever made an insulting song about that! Plus, you can catch more bees with honey than you can with salt!" she quickly replied.

"I guess you got a point there. . . What's good for the goose is good for the gander, huh? If you reprimand one race do the same for the another race.

"Yeah, and as a Christian I'd be the first to outlaw any public nudity, but for everyone and not just for Blacks!" she had defended that day.

As for the equal rights she thought about how the National Association for the Advancement of Colored People (NAACP), the Southern Christian Leadership Conference (SCLC) and the Equal Employment Opportunity Commission (EEOC) seems to have given up the fight for people of color. Even she was young enough to recall when these protection organizations were once reliable resources in the Black plight. She had once said to that same fellow doctor as they had walked down the corridors of a mental hospital checking charts, "The NAACP have simply gotten too big for their own breeches nowadays wouldn't you agree?" she glance up at the lanky doctor in his white lab coat. That day was just another typical one of their many discussions about politics.

"Yeah" the handsome doctor had calculatingly replied, "The whole problem is that those organizations are behind the scenes having that Black-on-Black gang-banging among themselves . . ." he shook an accusing finger. "Jealousy is the real problem there. . . You don't have to live in the hood to be part of Black-on-Black competition you know! And, on the other hand, when Black leaders get paid enough in governmental funding for their organizations, most will take a bribe not to rock the boat!" he had accused that day.

"I'm sure you're right!" she had breathed that day walking beside him doing their rounds. "And who feels the backlash of their little secret wars? It's the poor Blacks who depend on them to help. Those grey-headed leaders aren't doing anything but stagnating progress. Any of their stale ideas could just be thrown back into the ice age. Anyway, why haven't they been replaced by more innovative leaders who'll bring fresher tools to the workbench? I don't mean to disrespect Black civil rights leaders because they did a good job in their day!" she had sighed.

"True, and the last Black intercession I can recall the NAACP standing up for was the Jena Six issue at that college!" anger. "Too bad our poor Black citizens have no dependable representation. Not even as much assistance as the Latino race has here in America. . . . The Mexican protection groups are always on top of their game for justice!" he definitely nodded. . . And I think the NAACP does have a new president but very few people have even heard of him seeing the NAACP is kept so much from the media these days! And another negative factor in the NAACP is that they have a difficult time getting financial assistance from the Black community. . . Too many poor citizens are so busy working two jobs and sometimes three for a measly seven dollars an hour until where's the time to march or attend meetings? It's Just another ploy to keep the poor that way. The plot is the government refuses to pay more than seven dollars for hard labor. So the poor has no money to fight with. He has to use that puny wage to feed his family!" he had accessed that day.

Then Dassah quickly jumped back on the NAACP, "Black citizens as a people should be given the power to vote every one of those old NAACP leaders out like all the other politicians are polled nearly to death!" she had said that day.

Then, there in the parked limo her thoughts came back to the makeover program. Her mind was on those homeless men who had jail records. The famous Christian doctor was in the business of assisting any needy person. But her main aim was especially to save their souls. So to prevent being partial she was constantly reminded of the scripture in Acts 10:28. Peter claimed that God had hotly reprimanded him for calling another race common or unclean referring to the Jews as more superior over the Gentiles. Of course God was preparing to allow Gentiles entrance into the church the way He had opened the church door to the Jews on the day of Pentecost. She knew that meant that God embraces any nation who will obey Him. Then she was reminded of another scripture that proved God's love for all of mankind. In Acts 17: 26, the Holy Ghost, through Paul had said, "And have made of one blood all nations of men for to dwell on the face of the earth." All men were created equally by the Maker. So who was she to feel any differently towards any of the, homeless people. No matter what the race or gender may be? "And 'one blood' you racist means we are all brothers and sisters whether you like it or not!" she always says. Then she would say, "And if you are not a racist then my last statement should roll right off you like water does a duck. You should not get soaked!"

There in Neal, New York, snow sprinkled the burnish vehicle sliding down yet warm slick early that Saturday morning. The car had only been parked for about 15 or 20 minutes. Step, under the wheel was clad in slightly loose-fitting jeans and a tan fleece sweater. He stepped from under the wheel and into the roomy aisle bending heading to the back, "Want coffee Boss?" through a yawn mouth as wide as an alligator. The young man did not drink anything stronger than a virgin Bloody Mary, but felt like the hang-over of the century. When he lived on the streets he had seen so many of his homeless peers rot their guts with cheap alcohol until himself had developed an utter disgust for the stuff. "Cheap or not all of it'll eventually cripple you!" one of his older buddies had warned the young Stephanas while warming around a can of fire. That dirty faced White man was one who always fought to get the first drink from a bottle. "Lord knows I wish I'd been as wise as you, Son. . . Then my wife wouldn't have kicked my drunken butt out of my own house!" he had anyway turned up a cheaper can of beer there in the alley that summer day six years ago as Step could recall. That alcoholic veteran like many others had earnestly vowed to break the bottle. However he had a stomach that was so dependent on the stuff. And his stomach sent a message to the brain telling him that mountain was just a little too steep of a climb. And the ones strung out on other drugs had a fiercer type of demon to try to sever. Those with more costly addictions were unable to substitute for a cheaper brand—all drugs proved to be unaffordable for the homeless. There was no second choice of crack cocaine or Methamphetamines.

There in the limo at Stephanas' offer of coffee immediately Dassah chuckled, "You must've read my mind . . . once again!" Her mysterious, very light brown eyes moved to the clock. "It's only seven-twenty. . . Why don't we just allow those poor men another moment's sleep this dreary Saturday," she waved. "Most helping places aren't even open this early on weekdays!" It sounded like a complaint, but was far from that because her program was in desperate need of able bodied men. Then she stared slightly perturbed at the window which she could control to darken even more and pushed the remote, "These people act as if this is the first time they've seen this vehicle!" she huffed, "We come to this hood at least once every two months maybe not in the same area though." She said to Step. She did realize that people had moved in who had never before seen her limo there.

Then gazing out through the snow pelted window into new curious faces, Dassah very deep thoughts went back to the initiation of the makeover program several years earlier. And with a Black Farmer's grant through the National Black Framer's Association and a Psychiatrist grant through the government, she and her hefty crew got busy cleaning up the streets of New York. From city to city they had covered much ground. Those homeless workers would go through her farm with pay as part of training. Though she felt it was a shame before the Almighty

God how some Black farmers' grants were held up by the court when some White bloggers decided to cry "Governmental fraud an accusation against Black farmers." She had become so angry one day while reading that true article by Cynthia Gordy, on February 17, 2011 posted at www.BlackFarmers.org. "Most Black farmers are given such a difficult way to go here in America!" she had huffed after reading that accusation against many Black farmers. She was not one to play the 'race card' seeing herself was interracial but this incident called for a spade to be called just what it was. And she was also upset when White farmers now being so in need of workers had the gall to ask a city official to let them hire people who had been paroled. They would hire those paroled people to work on their farm really meaning parole them just so farmers could abuse them with no future incentive and below minimum wage. The smart doctor knew the problem with that program was that a great percentage of people getting paroled were young Black males who should not even be in prison in the first place. Also a great percentage of the ones being paroled were older Black males, "Will this bring back slavery with only minimum wages or less?" She knew the real reason farmers were now in need of farm hands was: The illegal immigrants they first had hired had either gotten wise that it was impossible to live off 3 dollars per hour, especially for this out-of-control for consumer economy. Other immigrants have left private farms to start their own farms here in America. Still others got deported back to Mexico. Now Black parolees are the farmers' last rope of hope. "Just when is it that Black folks will stop allowing themselves to be herded like, dumb cattle?!" Dassah wondered. "If Blacks were to agree to work on any farm, those Black workers should demand a stable future the way my program offers," she says, "What kind of future can you provide for my family instead of the same old bondage?!" they should demand. "If this kind of forced labor were permitted it would seem Blacks never came out of slavery!" she insists, "They get falsely thrown into prison and work for nothing and now parts of the government is attempting to prostitute them on farms. They will have no hope of livable wages and no future!"

Then she recalled how typically just as most other assistive programs do. She had also only applied for a governmental grant for housing, food and medical attention for the poor in general. Then she inadvertently discovered how she could also honestly monopolize financially off that needed effort. So one day in her then basic but still very nice psyche office she had asked herself, "Dassah now is your opportunity to live on the finer side of the track for a change!" Though as a prominent psychiatrist she had long since ceased to struggle just to make ends meet. But her vow years ago to be wealthy had now been passionately aroused. It was at that point that she decided to makeover the willing homeless which included women at that time. She would put them to work for her, let them make some money for themselves and lots of money for her. The honest scheme to use the homeless in a positive fashion has also earned her psychiatric practice a good reputation.

Many other homeless agencies had broken the law by working illegal immigrants. But her God-given wisdom had moved her to work only needy Americans. That way it would all be kept it in the family. "Then I won't have to answer to God for breaking his command to first show charity at home," she thought. "I do believe in the Judgment Day, so whenever illegal immigrants become legal citizens then I'll also put them to work and not a day before!" She also realized that the unemployment rate would be lower if more American employers would be fair and do the right thing. But instead they worship the almighty dollar and the government allows them to break the law. She recalled what one homeless man who was on the streets because he had been jailed for becoming delinquent in tax payments. That day in the new recruit meeting his dirty Caucasian face had grimaced, "Now if the law would crack down on illegal hiring the way they jacked me, a business man, then those crooked employers would be fearful! It seems the law cares more about illegal people making it big in America than they care about Americans becoming too successful!" he had flat out accused. I know we all should be law abiding too!" he had knowingly posed that day.

While in the parked limo the lovely doctor glanced up at the crucifix dangling from the mirror. She attributes the Holy Ghost as giving her total daily inspiration. She always feels that just to get through med school in spite of a penniless childhood had been a wonder. Then she angrily thought, "What childhood! If you ask me not having a prom or any school function to scrapbook about is prison-hood instead of childhood! Remember you had no play time, Hadassah!" sadly she thought, movement coming from the back where Step was. "You spent the most impressionable years raising your brother for a careless call-girl of a mother, remember?" And recalling her name, Hadassah as a child she had totally loathed that name, until her grandmother explained why she personally named her that. Her devout grandmother had read of Hadassah, who was Esther, in the book of Esther. Hadassah was Esther's Jewish God-given name. Though the Bible does not specify but 'Esther' could very well had been her bondage name. There were also many cases in the Old Testament where whenever God allowed the Israelites (Jews)to be taken into bondage because of their sins against Him, their captors would rename the impressive Jews.

Then suddenly the mental battle about her childhood which she had been battling for so long tried to resurface. But, once again with determination she willed triumph. Then she stubbornly exchanged those memories for happier ones about the initiation of the makeover program. "It's very clear that the generous grant never would have been awarded had I not been a board certified doctor," she thought now with a smile. But, because of her own hundreds of thousands she had already rehabilitated a few. The government now trusted that she could execute the plans she had so eloquently written on paper in the form of yearly proposals.

There in the parked limo with Step that Saturday morning they were preparing to go in search of the homeless men in particular. Dassah shrugged feminine shoulders beneath a long smooth neck. "The men and I are only using each other!" she thought out loud this time, Step still in the back making fresh coffee, "Everyone uses someone for one thing or another, but too many use others without giving back in return!" she reasoned.

"Are you thinking out loud . . . again?" the very handsome bodyguard, now sliding back under the wheel glared knowingly at his beautiful boss. In the elegance he pulled down a little metal table between them and placed the coffee tray on it.

"Oh, I guess I was thinking out loud!" Her comical tone drew laughter drowning out soft music. "Well, I ain't crazy, at least not yet!" she laughed revealing white even teeth. She knew that most people thought of psychiatrists as somewhat fanatical, them self. She found many of her new patients even trying to get into her head instead of her into theirs. Whenever she counseled a new patient she could hardly wait until the first session was over. Then a rapport would be established as to who were counseling whom. Then she would immediately think, "But at two-hundred-fifty-dollars an hour no Medicare accepted should I be complaining?!"

As Step poured coffee from the little four-cup pot Dassah recalled her plan aside from the regular practice. That goal was to get the homeless and the homeless Christians comfortably re-mainstreamed. She had already taken into consideration that they may not become filthy rich in a small businesses but a decent living and self-respect was a mountain of wealth to any ex-homeless person. He would go from a tenthouse to a penthouse likeness. "Anyway, not many people can expect to get rich in a basic business nowadays," she had said one day. "With this runaway economy you have to be self-employed just to keep a normal meal on the table. . . People use to get rich being basic business owners!" Even when she was in school business owners would yield high profits even after the first five years. Nowadays having a business was compared to having an 8 hour per day job.

Dassah recalled the beginning of the program how she as a doctor already had a pretty penny to invest with the governmental grant as most all grants would require. Then upon submitting the proposal the government had replied how her strong pitch had taken them by storm. "All the government needed was to be assured of a workable plan and a qualified citizen to implement that plan," she had smiled very proud about being a psychiatrist. "Thank you heavenly Father for leading me through those hard-punching days of med school!" she thought there in the limo that early Saturday morning with Step back under the wheel now listening to music and sipping coffee.

As she sat sipping coffee she thought of how she had been accused of being bias in that she no longer allowed the homeless and ex-con females into the makeover phase of the program. Though, in the beginning she had seriously offered women the same services. Consequently a lengthy and costly law suit had been her reward. One woman had claimed rape, robbery and brutal battery where two of the prospective ex-con men were the accused. The cunning homeless woman had an Associate of Science degree upon being referred to Dassah for assistance. She had been fresh out of college. Then drugs, prostitution and fraud had branded her soon after graduation. Dassah recalled how after the trial the nearly suckered in male judge had apologized for having been so naïve as to believe the woman's sob story. That day after he had issued a judgment he had said to the just as beautiful doctor "That woman could've totally smashed Hollywood's acting arena!" He shamefully shook his totally grey head. The woman's complete beauty had also kept the court mesmerized for the entire month hearing until finally she began to trip over her own lies. Then Dassah' not so slim but astute lawyer, Callie Greenhill, got so upset that it had been the woman's phony drama and perfect articulation that had prolonged the just verdict. Then after the woman received a four-year sentence and everything was back to normal Dassah had sighed to Callie, "Too bad that woman made the bed hard for other honest homeless women!"

"It's pathetic how people are so easily taken by a curvy body and perfect face!" the chubby attorney had huffed over lunch that day while woofing down a deep fried drumstick skin and all.

While in the limo fine snow flurries Dassah smiled recalling the outcome of the trial. The ex-homeless cons were innocent and Dassah was given the green light to re-boot the makeover program. The court had allowed her to continue working the out on bail men. And also the others who were already being rehabilitated but all recruitment had been banned until the accused were cleared. "Oh the war would've really been on had my psyche practice been restricted!" she had angrily wagged her beautiful head to Callie that day. Dassah recalled how she had been just as anxious as the ex-homeless men to get to the bottom of that accusation. Sadly Dassah shuttered at the mere thought of anyone getting raped. As a teen she had also been around that truly painful corner. But that woman actually had been abused and beaten but by the pimp that had forced her to scam the doctor in the first place. That was the incident that put a ban on females living on the farm. "No more co-existence farm living for this doctor!" she had promised herself. Instead other effective assistance were instituted for women. Only they could no longer physically reside on the mime-hundred-acre farm. The farm in South Georgia was always running even outside of harvest time. "There seems to be more homeless men than women needing assistance anyway," Dassah had said to Callie. And as a doctor she had found homeless women to be more pliable in survival tactics. "Put a woman in a tent and with ten dollars she'll turn it into a palace and feast off ground beef, beans and rice!" she had added. But she would never withhold general assistance from any homeless female. She made sure those women received temporary transitional homes, And then she would financially help them to move on as happily as many had done.

The doctor recalled how she also found it necessary to consider the men's mental stability before he could go to work in one of her stores. And after one man completed the program he had to move on for another one to have the same opportunity. Dassah discovered that the salary phase of the program was the most difficult pill for the men to swallow. In the process of convincing them to accept the small pay it took some fast talking. "When you start talking to poor folks about meager salaries a wall automatically raises!" she had once said to Callie.

"Yeah, I guess the poor souls had been in the dumps for so long until they want overnight success," Callie had replied. ". . . but one would think that after being broke for so long the smallest denomination of sturdy pay should seem like a million bucks!"

"Apparently not!" The doctor had to convince many of them that small salary was only temporary. However the less than minimum wages even without them paying rent or food was unappealing to some of the complaining men. Nevertheless Dassah decided to stick to her plans and most of the serious ones had thanked her for not giving up on them. After he had saved two years of the largest part of his paycheck and moved on with his small business and partners he was glad he had ridden out the high tides. "Not to mention the, from rags to riches look he'd leave here with!" she thought, glancing over at her picture perfect bodyguard under the wheel. She looked forward to the next Mr. Dig Me Now, fashion show for which she always solicited volunteers from among the men. Out of much respect for the men and for herself she would never force them to parade around like meat. At the beginning of the year most of the men usually would turn the pressure on her to let them model for the upcoming June show. Again, with a smile Dassah shot a quick glance over at the unbelievably new man at her side in the limo.

"What?" questioningly, Stephanas returned the glance.

"Oh, nothing . . . Just thinking out loud . . . once again." Her beautiful eyes moved to the windshield where snow had accumulated and new faces appeared into the side windows. Her eyes moved to the clock. It was 7:35. "We'll move out around seven-fifty or so, okay?"

"You're the boss," snatching his mind from the music. He had popped in a CD of decent hip-hop. Since Step was 25 he was heavy into the rap scene and was well capable of competing in dancing with the pros. The limber man had rhythm that could be marketed. Had he not become a bodyguard he would have opened a dance school with his grant. However, he and his four partners chose to co-op a security firm. Dassah also listened to rap, until the artist would start using profanity, which so many did. Then she would say, "You know I was really digging that song, until he messed it up with that unnecessary use of awful language!" she would angrily switch it off—she found herself switching it off quite a bit. But she knew there were some decent rappers out there and she did not condemn rap altogether. At times she found herself complimenting the poetry of some of the more talented hip-hop artists.

Then Dassah thoughts strayed to how she assisted the men with their savings by allowing them only a few dollars, mutually agreed upon, from their bi-weekly wages. The largest amount would go solely for his mandatory investment with the government grant. If the case was that he would decide to no longer save then he would be terminated with whatever savings he had thus far.

The Christian doctor sympathized with the few men who had and would fail to ride out the turbulent rehabilitation. Some men would decide he wanted to just up and leave with his little money. But rarely would he find a job before he became broke again. So too little too late he would realize what a blessing he had cowardly bailed out on. And it was times like that when she detested her own rule of not re-instating those men. She had deeper pity on the fallen Christians and the veterans that would quit. "However, she would remind herself, "Though my business, just like any successful business has to have guidelines!" She recalled how it took more than just a normal amount of will-power for her to say no to those who wanted to return. "I'm really sorry!" she would say to the sorrowful men. "But you should have listened when I stressed over and over again that frugality and honesty was one of the this program's mottos!"

While in the limo preparing to go out in the snow to scout for homeless men, Dassah visualized the ex-homeless men down in South Georgia on her very fertile farm. A very trusting staff of overseers and therapists always were down there with the workers. On Saturdays the men are off and most still in bed. There is no weekend work there but up in New York it is necessary for the restaurants to open seven days a week. Nevertheless, on Sundays she made it mandatory for the ex-homeless both men and women to attend one of the three church services and Bible classes. The church of Christ held their services on the farm. In New York she had store managers scheduled so that everyone would get to attend one service if not all services. The strict doctor had warned, "This is my house and while you're in it for the two years you're expected to abide by all rules!" The men came into the program under a non-binding verbal agreement. By that he could quit anytime he wished with only a small portion of the money he had saved. So some had agreed to remain and attend at least one church service and Bible study on Sundays. Some had refused and left the program, "I'm an Atheist!" a handful had earnestly alleged. Still Dassah stuck to her rules and those who did not heed were out. How anyone could pass up the opportunity to live on a health farm free of charge puzzled even the doctor of the mind. "Most people would pay for a membership to a health farm!" she had once complained to Callie. Nevertheless, she realized the farm was more work than play. But they would get free room and board and a paycheck to boot. She also had to respect that some people were just as firm about their religious beliefs as she was about hers. "Every soul is given a choice by the Maker as to where we wish to spend eternity because we all will someday leave the earth!" she would fairly affirm. Then she would think of Joshua who had declared in the long ago, "As for me and my house, we will serve the Lord!" God had allowed Joshua to make a choice. God never restrains us bet assures us what will happen to us if we chooses from the wrong menu.

Then her thoughts went to the humongous farm in Georgia in an unidentified area way down south. She also has a top-of-the-art rehabilitation facility in Manhattan for the workers there. The rooms on the farm and in Manhattan are spacious with sturdy furniture to accommodate rugged men. The gyms, the recreation rooms and every comfort are at their disposal. The men are allowed to make over time on the farm and in the stores within the two-year makeover period. They can also eat from her three restaurants where he may have been assigned to work. Dassah assured that the men working strictly on the farm had cooks who used only those healthy foods. Nevertheless, the strict no-cooking for the men, are firmly enforced. She realized that ex-homeless people were so adapted to living hazardously in alleys and cooking over open fire. And that habit was yet in their blood. "I've put too much time money and effort into this program to have it go up in flames," she had warned. "Now where would you ex-homeless men go if you didn't have this farm?" She knew the biggest challenge of all was getting the men not to smoke cigarettes on the premises which the farm grounds were sometimes too dry for that. But the stiff monetary fines were enough to convince them to do their cigarettes before being bussed back to the farm. Even her sternness extended to the non-homeless over-seers about smoking on the direct premises. However she was careful not to tick anyone off and cause them to vengefully commit arson. Even though the overseers would gripe but their usual pack-a-day, habit did gradually decrease. "Oh quit complaining!" she would teasingly fling back at them. "Quitting smoking will only save your lives anyway!" Plus she knew the overseers and therapists would be crazy to walk out on the liberal wages she paid. Thus, before long she had a completely smokeless environment. Consequently in their proud quitting-smoking testimonies they gave Dassah credit for her persistent persuasion. And they were not allowed to bring alcohol on the farm or even drink during a work week. Finally, contraband began to be a hundred per cent negative. For the most part the ex-homeless men were seriously striving to become law abiding citizens once again. "We'll have plenty of time to do what we want after twenty-four months and that's worth the sacrifice, man!" one handsome White ex-con had smiled during a guidelines meeting. "I prefer looking at it in months rather than years. . . It's like serving a two-year jail term, only getting set up in business for it!" he had laughed exposing now spotless teeth.

In a day's work the ex-homeless workers raised livestock, grew cotton and fruit. The lamb, goat, beef, poultry, fish and bison were organically produced with care and patience. The animals were kept happy and stress-free. The tomatoes, corn, oranges, apples, strawberries, cane lopes, watermelons and vegetables of all kind were the biggest and best in the south. "God surely have blessed this land and the program!" Dassah would boast. "It reminds me of the Canaan land of the Bible! When you're obedient, God blesses and gives good, fertile land!" She thought about those ex-homeless men that moved to Africa and begun their small business there. That was why she had been so taken with Stephanas' idea about the poor Blacks moving to Africa. Those ex-homeless men who had opened stores and farm land in West Africa had been totally blessed with the best vegetation and livestock from America. The water irrigation systems were always set up over wells of water. Many of the ex-Americans carried with them the mechanical and technical abilities they had learned in America. "We finally feel like we belong!" said some of the ex-homeless, small business owners there in several parts of Africa. Plus South Africa had some very good land and schools for the men to utilize. She knew that ever since America over threw Nelson Mandela, in South Africa and took the over that country, America is also now South Africa and have plenty of resources.

There in the limo that Saturday morning Dassah thought about the endless task of keeping the store positions filled with ex-homeless people. That in itself called for a master-plan from the prudent doctor along with her large staff of doctors and therapists. On top of being short on homeless employees with sorrow she had to give a few men the boot. They had failed to abide by sanitary techniques in the restaurant. She had to finally, after several warnings and his dishonorable discharge let him go. One day in a full to capacity meeting of nearly graduated men, Dassah had seriously admitted, "It never makes me happy to terminate anyone, but as you know that does occasionally happen!" As she talked that day the well-nourished, muscular faces of different races, mostly Black men and women, stared attentively at her. And with regret she continued, "But I refuse to allow anyone to tear down what it took so many sleepless nights and prayers to build!" She glared meanly out at them from her chair, armed guards all around the room. "Now if anyone does not have the guts to do what's right for a measly two years, let's hear it now!" Dead silence, and then she said, "And, if not for yourselves, at least think of your abandoned children!" She paused, firm but feminine body standing up in modest jeans yet revealing a voluptuous figure. As a Christian, Dassah tried to conceal as much as possible of her pleasingly endowed body. Plus with five-feet-ten-inches and amazon body, she really turned heads. So there in the meeting that day, she had said, "Come on!" beckoning challengingly. "Tell me if I recruited any more cowards who get a kick out of begging on the streets and looking and smelling like of heard of Billy Goats!!" Then suddenly, well buffed bodies began to shift timidly, exchanging 'not me' glances.

"Good! Now let's snap to the business of getting you back on your feet and keeping it sanitary in my restaurants. If I catch as much as a long fingernail, the whole lot of you, are through . . . So you had best start encouraging each other to keep the very short!" she wagged, "Furthermore, who do you think would want to eat the filth from dirty nails?!" She went through the crowd checking nervous outstretched hands. "Am I right and are we still friends?" she had purposely reverted to a curtly smile.

Heads nodded, knowing she was justified to lash out with reprimand. They also knew she had proven to be a friend as well as an employer.

Dassah considered herself blessed to have the majority of the workers tolerate her strict set-up. She was equally impressed to report to the government that over the years the program had about seventy percent rate in graduates. She looked forward to the tear-jerking speeches that followed those happy exits. Those public officials that were always invited to the graduation held twice a year also would beam just to see the positive returns on their grant dollars and the workers' paying taxes again. "It seems state revenue *has* increased since this work begun!" a prominent official had boasted to another. No longer having to dish out so much money to shelters and funding for housing and food stamps, had really pleased them. They were now able to concentrate on healthcare even for the middle-classed Americans who now needed healthcare. The government was overjoyed that the ex-homeless citizens now owned businesses and was also filing tax returns.

There in the parked limo as snow pelted the windshield, Dassah and Step were still sipping coffee. And as they began to bundle up to go in search of homeless men she recalled another meeting of new recruits. "I know that these meager salaries aren't anything to brag about," she had warned the anxious men. "But when you stick your heads into your money, no matter how small the amount, it'll come out smelling like green-backs instead of green rotten-lettuce!" she had laughed. They laughed in that the unpopular dumpster-diving flashed before their eyes. She recalled how some of the men were now proud owners of grocery stores, clothing shops, shoe stores, laundry centers, convenient stores, nails spa and other small businesses there in New York. Or they could relocate wherever they chose to live. And relocation altogether was the choice of many. They would take their reunited family along with them. Though, the juvenile system, and the Department of Family and Children Services had to be assured that they were serious about their teenage boys. It was a glorious day when so many children would be released into their father's custody. Some families were even able to adopt children that their child had known while in DFACS or juvenile.

"Doc, I never want to lay eyes on New York again!" one handsome young, Black man had firmly declared. "If Manhattan, were to even show up on television, I'm pitching' the darn tube out the nearest window!" in the meeting that day they all laughed happily with him.

Dassah was exceptionally happy to learn that same man and his partners had also relocated to Africa and was doing well in their home-builders business. These men had no children here in America, but had adopted four 16 year old boys from the juvenile system. The last she heard those boys were in school in Africa and two about to graduate high school. The new business owners had excitedly said to Dassah, "The demand for building services moves as swiftly as the gazelles over here! The boys work for us after school, and are making plenty of money!"

"Very good, and if more people moved to Africa and build then maybe some of those huts could be transformed into houses!" she had said.

Then Dassah recalled feeling sorry for the homeless who could not possibly hold a job let alone run a business.

There in the limo the beautiful doctor of the mind recalled doing her internship at a facility for the mentally challenged. One childish adult resident there had at first overwhelmed her. She was a student doctor at that time. And during any given day having to always scold a full grown person like she would a child, took some getting used to. An adult clients' age and body may have been thirty but chronologically he may have been only six years old. She recalled how that, many childish-adults would run to her literally bawling that his peer had pushed him, or took some item from him. During the day that type of occurrence were never ending. In that facility she had discovered that some patients should not have been placed with the more abusive category of mentally ill patients. Then one day trying her best to pry an abusive patient off of a mild-mannered one she recalled yelling, "These docile people shouldn't even be in with those combative patients!" She knew that the combative patient only had mental issues and was not brain damaged as were the legitimate retarded patients. Also, she found that even today there is yet an overflow of mixed patients in too many mental facilities. And with insufficient funding for care or staff willing to work with the mentally challenged, appropriate placement is virtually impossible—unless the family has plenty of money. The astute doctor had considered training more health professional people. Dassah thanked God for her huge staff—but was in the process of hiring more free-lance psychology therapists. She knew that would free her from having to pay out so much in health insurance and other required company insurance coverages. And she was also required to make sure all of her workers were insured. So she rejoiced when the President got the Affordable Health Care Act, passed. Most of her employees were now able to apply for coverage. However, the men coming into the program she had to get a package option which was more affordable. And then when they could afford to take out their own coverage, they would.

There in the limo with snow slightly pelting the windshield she sadly recalled an incident where a certain childish-adult patient who was about thirty-five when his fatigued late seventies father had checked him into the mental facility. His adult-child had suffered a head injury but had only physically recuperated from the injury. Even though the patient was mobile he had a mental age of about four or five. And his communication skills were also on that level. Dassah had cried reading the intake report about how the man had been normal and had finished high school. He had worked as a garbage truck driver with the city. Then he had been viscously attacked by a gang the reason for the attack had been robbery. Dassah recalled viewing his particular case as one of the saddest. Then the patient after being there for several years with an apparent vague prognosis his elderly father passed away. Thus, without any further funding the patient had to be terminated from the facility. Dassah recalled the last she heard of him he was wandering the streets begging until he finally was found dead. "Well, any adult-child of such low mental status would not know how to properly care for himself, wouldn't you agree?" Dassah had angrily asked the fellow doctor who had informed her of the man's death. "I wonder why people would take in an animal," she had huffed through grief. "And refuse to help a homeless human being?!"

"Probably, people just plain are afraid of the way mentally disabled people look and act, especially a Black man?" quickly replied the fellow doctor.

Dassah prayed that people would become just as eager to invest energy into mental facilities. They could volunteer time with those ill people and get somewhat used to being around them. Though, herself knew that some mentally unstable people could be very unpredictable and very dangerous. So she understood why non-medical people would shy away from the few they would encounter.

CHAPTER 2

T hat Saturday morning, Doctor Dassah Desoto and Stephanas
Carter her bodyguard sat in the parked limousine taking their last
coffee break and bundling up for the snow. The coffee would help
ward off the chill of having to trek deep into alleys in search of homeless
men and women if there were any women there. Very rarely were there
women living in alleys unless she was with her husband or boyfriend.
She knew that at that early hour the men would be bedded down in
cardboard boxed or homemade tents. As they prepared Dassah' light
brown eyes glinted against light tan skin. She glanced at the clock—it
was 7:45. "We'll just give them a few more minutes," she said, turning
up the last of the now warm coffee.

"I work for *you*, remember?" The handsome bodyguard was happy
just to recline under the comfort of the wheel, indulging in soft music.
As a 25-year-old, Step still loved modest rap but had tuned to some
music more calming for the early morning.

On the sidewalk as people strained to peer in, again Dassah fell
into contemplating about her booming makeover dynasty. The haring
struggle just to make it through collage and med school flooded her

thoughts. "I'm talking kick-backs of all buck-a-roos!" she thought with a big sigh. The four years of high school, which she attended along with a four-hour after school job had her young back bent. At the age of fifteen she had worked at a neighborhood restaurant surrounded by grown-up co-workers. That experience had taught the teenager grown-up ways much too soon. Now she feels that maturity was the blessing that got her through. As a teen she had been embarrassed by having to wear those vintage uniforms. But being mature had helped her shun the scoffing of her peers. But she recalled how grateful she was to have that furnished attire. And in those days there were no neighborhood thrift stores. Only plenty of liquor stores! "Plus, those uniforms enabled me to keep nice the only two school outfits I owned," she thought there in the limo. She was thankful when her feet finally stopped growing. Then her Shoes began to last a bit longer with a little cutting and gluing leather from one worn pair into the bottom of another pair. Then layers of leather painstakingly Super-Glued would become *doable* not *necessarily durable* soles. Lastly, an entire weekend the shoes would sit to dry. Now that she is wealthy she recalls how even though she had to work every day still having lunch money had been just a daydream. She had to use every penny in the house which she, her three years younger brother and healthy mother had shared. And neither did Jarvis, her younger brother have pockets that jangled. The four dollars an hour she made went for clothes and shoes for his ever growing body. "If baggy pants would've been back there keeping my brother in clothing would not have been an arduous task!" in the limo, she snickered under her breath picturing the handsome, lanky Jarvis. She always says that God gave vision to the designer of baggy clothes just to accommodate poor kids. "Nowadays a boy need only own a couple pair of jeans from middle school thru junior high!" she had laughed to a now grown Jarvis one day as they reminisced about those hard times.

She glanced over at Step and sleepily he glanced back. "What now, Boss?" he raised an attractively bushy brow atop of perfect dark eyes.

"Oh, it's nothing." She would refrain from revealing her past to the employees—only a few minor details they may have known about her. As a psychiatrist she was very elusive about her past life, and about her clients' problems. "As far as I'm concerned, I'm also my own client!" she would say, yet dealing with the revolting ramifications of a rape. The ordeal had happened to her at the age of only fifteen while still a virgin. Before psyche school she had no idea that holding such an embedded grudge could rot the mind while that one you hate goes on and live in peace.

With snow misting outside and amidst tasteful surround music she pushed her thoughts to Jarvis. The way she would tease him of having fertilizer under his feet put a smile of sheer love on her face. Jarvis finally finished college and heads her demanding real estate firm and security firm. Though, Jarvis is more than able to buy his own shoes now. The smile suddenly disappeared when she recalled at the age of fifteen and the only bread-winner in the household. She recalled having a promiscuous glamour-girl for a mother, now deceased. Her mother had given Jarvis and Dassah different fathers in those unbelievably grueling days. Dassah recalled that her mother was a stunning voluptuous African American with curves in all the right places. Jarvis's father was Black, whom Jarvis had seen only once—too young to even remember. And Dassah' father was Puerto Rican whom she never saw, or thought she never had seen him. All she recalls was this fair-skinned foreigner with a liquor store next to their house. The man would always peep out the window as she was outside in her yard. And so many people would go in and out of the liquor store. Yet others would hang around the store until closing. Then, surprisingly right after the death of her mother she discovered the man who had secretly spied on her. He had been her father. He and his wife, who was the same race as he, had been the owners of the liquor store. Obviously zoning laws in the forsaken neighborhood of Victory, Georgia had been broken or never fixed in the first place. She recalled how foreigners came there mainly to rip off poor people down to their very last penny. That was one reason she strongly advocated ex-homeless people to start businesses in their own hoods. The main goal is to force those illegal foreigners out of business. Blacks in particular should market and support their own the way other races wholeheartedly stick together. Blacks should stop buying a quart of outdated milk for unreasonable prices. "It's a crying shame how the poor are the very ones making the rich richer!" she had huffed to a fellow doctor. Dassah recalled there had been an American owned grocery store miles away from her house in Victory. "But then who could afford to go that far to market!" she sadly thought there in the limo. And very few people owned cars in those days. The public transportation was always so packed with grocery bag riders. "Even the public transit system made a killing off the poor by the constant fare hikes!" she thought. "Whoever said, 'the poor get poorer and the rich get richer' must've come from Victory, Georgia!'" she thought with a sigh there in the snow pelted limo.

An admirable smile turned up her luscious full lips over the fantastic job Jarvis was doing as heard of the real estate and security firms. Even in the mist of having lived in the most indigent part of Victory, the strict rearing of her brother had returned them both great dividends. During her immature mothering of him she had not allowed him to play outside of the tiny yard of the run down rented house. She would maybe allow one of his friends to visit Jarvis in the yard. He got most of his peer interaction at school and so did she. Whenever the immature girl would hear of statistics about the mortality rate of Black males, she would be appalled and petrified. On the other hand their mother was unmoved by that stacked chance. Having such an uncaring mother as theirs Dassah was the only one her brother could turn to. And she was grateful he took her advice for the most part. Nonetheless Jarvis never held back being the typical teenage boy about his sloppy housekeeping. At times Dassah felt she was born an old woman destined to be a mind-healer. She was molded to solve analytical issues. Nevertheless, she had the most difficulty understanding how any mother could ostracize herself so from her own children. "Some human mothers are worse than animal mothers!" she often says in her moments of longing to have a real mother. And, for the most part in their small house her and her mother had been like two unfamiliar boats passing in the night—her mother rarely touched Jarvis and her. Absurdly Jarvis literally only knew his mother's name as Mama. And he only called her 'Mama" because he heard Dassah refer to her as that all the time. Up until he turned 4 he had no idea she was even his mother. He thought of Dassah as his mom.

Watching snow fall onto the windshield of the parked limo Dassah recalled as a child wearing the last name of Foster. It was only when she became a doctor that she took on her father's name. "Though Foster is fine, Desoto just sounds more refined! But maybe it's more psychological in that my old name haunts me!" she had said, signing the papers the lawyer had handed to her.

Dassah recalled discovering how her father was married but had been a Sugar Daddy; to Dassah' teenage mother before Dassah was conceived. Then when Dassah was 8 Dassah' mother moved to Victory with two small children the youngest belonging to a young Black man. Later on the 'Sugar Daddy' Dassah' father had moved his liquor store adjacent to Dassah' mother house. She recalled her absolutely beautiful brown skinned mother who later died from AIDS had only gone as far as the tenth grade. The expensive clothing while her children wore rags was bought by the boyfriends she kept on the side. "What kind of mind convinces a mother to turn deaf ears on the cries of her own hungry children?" Dassah thought in the passenger seat, light brown eyes fixed on the snowy windshield where she envisioned her past playing out.

Now as a doctor she realizes her mother had a severe mental disorder. "And the main disorder was a case of outright selfishness!" she hissed within.

With music soothing, Step shot her another glance but kept from prying. In the six years he had been with her he had adapted to her 'moments'. "Of course what more is to be expected of a psyche than to hang around in a pool of quiet deliberation?" he thought. "After all she's literally got thousands of people and things marching through her head!" He knew her life was tied up completely in God and the makeover program. "You're going to wound up marrying one of your ex-homeless recruits!" he had teased one day just to get a stir out of her.

"The money you'd bet on that would be better off left in your pocket!" she had fired back that day. "It's not that I think I'm too good but you know my take on dating employees, and on becoming unequally yoked in marriage to an unbeliever!"

She had learned that from Second Corinthians 6: 14, "Be ye not unequally yoked together with unbelievers." She also knew that some preachers interpret this as idol worship only. But in her study of the scripture she knew how some preachers could mistake this scripture as against idol worship only. Because in First Corinthians 7: 13, it reads "And the woman which hath a husband that believeth not, and if he is pleased to dwell with her, let her not leave him." Dassah knew that in this case both she and her husband had heard this new gospel of Jesus Christ together. The woman had obeyed by being baptized into Christ but her husband had not obeyed. Well the now Christian thought it would be a just thing to leave her unbelieving husband. However, she would be restricted from wedding him if they had not already been married. God's command does not contradict itself. Why would God tell a Christian in one passage not to marry an infidel? Then in another scripture command one to stay with one? Apparently these New Testament saints had read how in the book of Ezra in the Old Testament where those priests who had married strange women were commanded to put them away, children and all! Dassah had heard her preacher refer to scriptures such as this, as Inferences" Though the passage does not directly say a thing, if you read between the lines, you would rightly get the meaning.

Snow flurried on the windshield as new faces appeared with no success of seeing in. Then in the passenger seat bundling up, and as much as she attempted not to, she began to reflect on her playgirl of a mother. The then 30thirty-year-old mother of a 15-year-old and a 12-year-old had not cared what skin-color her men were as long as his money was green foldable and not counterfeit. One thing Dassah as a teen and the only one working was not having to pay rent on their two-bedroom house. But later she discovered her married father had been paying the rent all along—he had bought the house for them but never to be a known father to Dassah. Growing up she had a father missing in action. She recalled many men coming in and out of their house. But the man next door never once set foot in the house. Not that she knew of anyway. And even now she blushes at the thought of her mother peddling her body to the highest bidder. Dassah thought, "Mothers sometimes do many unethical things just to feed her kids, but that certainly hadn't been my mother's excuse! My mother's addiction to a lavish lifestyle in an impoverished surrounding had ultimately become her children's suffering for food and clothing!" But Dassah did thank God that her mother was not addicted to drug abuse. Then she thought, "So she had been in a sober frame of mind when she was abusing us all those years!" It hurt Dassah even more that her mother had no valid crutch as a reason for hating her children.

Then another big sigh from her caused Stephanas simply to shoot a nonchalant glance over at her. They usually had general conversation about the program or about the first Black President, but today both she and Step saw that Saturday morning as a profound thought day for the psychiatrist.

In the comfort finally slipping on her jacket, Dassah recalled when the family first moved into the house away from her late grandmother, who had lived in another city. The 6-year-old Dassah had sulked long over having to leave the only home she ever knew. Dassah' mother had dropped out of high school when she was pregnant with Dassah. There in the limo she pictured her bright little room at 'Me-Ma and Me-Pa's house. Her grandfather was now living in a personal care facility at his own will. He wanted to interact with others his age after having lived so caringly at Dassah' house for several years after his wife passed. Her grandparents had been devout hard working Christians who'd had two children later in life—Dassah' mother being the youngest and the most rebellious one. As a little girl at her grandmother's house, her grandmother and mother would relentlessly butt heads about her daughter's laziness and dating too many men. "It's time you went back to school so you can take care of your children!" the big boned woman stood boldly eyeing down on her daughter one day. "You've already had two children out of wedlock," she had firmly scolded for the hundredth time. "And you won't have another baby—not in this house anyway!"

Dassah recalled the day finally she her mother and Jarvis, bawling, had waved goodbye to Kentucky and their loving Me-Ma and Me-Pa. That sad day was in the dead of summer. She was 6 and Jarvis was 3. Her mother was only 21 at that time. And as the three had walked into the dingy house in Victory, Georgia, lugging very worn suitcases, her mother too lavishly dressed for that surrounding, had agitatedly said,

"Dassah, you and that boy will just have to share a room!" Dassah recalled the repulse on her mother's face whenever it came down to having to mention her own son's name and she rarely called him Jarvis. At the house that day her mother as was her way became annoyed for no apparent reason. She sashayed off to a window and harshly switched on a rusty air conditioner that was leaning unsteadily inward. And with unnatural fear Dassah watched her mother's firm mini-skirt-backside strut off into another room. The girl knowing that before long her mother would be slapping her silly for no reason. She recalled how the healthy looking for the time being Jarvis had with his dark little face stood amused at the blast of air waving out strands of yellow ribbons. The ribbons were there to alert when the air had gone down. He'd known only central air at their grandparents' house. "Dassah!" her mother had screeched, jolting the girl out of her skin that day. "Shut that door so I can get some air up in here!" As Dassah recall her mother spoke cooingly only to boyfriends. During those entertaining visits Dassah barely recognized the soft purring of her mother. Her mother's Dr. Jekyll, Miss. Hyde attitude could have won her an Academy Award. Then her mother and the man would step out until early morning or locked up in her mother's room all night. And whenever Dassah and Jarvis would hear some man in the hallway or bathroom they dared not come out of their room. Only they sometimes would hear him when he came in or was leaving or standing on the porch. Her mother had never worked—not on a real job on her feet that is. That day the sheer trepidation overshadowing her 6-year-old light tan face as she stood in the doorway gapping at the griminess, Dassah could never forget. Then Jarvis in shorts exposing dark boney knees had run to Dassah and wrapped himself around her like a pretzel. "I want Me-Pa!" he had pitifully squealed.

"Shut him up! I don't feel like all that drama today!" her mother had echoed through the sparsely used furnished 3 rooms.

As usual Dassah had to be the one to play mommy again. So Dassah finally persuaded Jarvis with a half a bag of chips—setting him on the floor and put Teddy beside him. Afterwards on tip-toes daring not to disturb her mother, Dassah moved to the wobbly air conditioner. A sudden gag was choked back when a blast of mildew hit her clammy little face. But then the air soon cooled her thick curls. And with eyes closed she simply bore the stench. She pretended it was the aroma of apple pie at her grandmother's. Dassah recalled that when her mother had turned her back that day Dassah scowled, "A girl should not have to share a bedroom with a boy!" she only thought, realizing her grandmother could not come to her defense now. Standing at the air conditioner the girl softly touched her swollen lip from the embarrassing ordeal with her mother on the train just hours earlier.

Dassah and Step were in the parked limo that Saturday morning getting ready to go in search of homeless men for the makeover program. She also looked forward to the men she would pick up from the overcrowded jail and from the mission on Monday. The snow in Neal, New York had thickened. The few people out squinted through the dark windows. Dassah was thankful the police were not around. "If I have to repeat my reason for being here once more time I'll just barf in his face!" she verbalized to Step this time.

Her handsome bodyguard could relate to her frustration about the cops, and snickered. Many times he had witnessed her explain to the curious new law people. "They're only doing their job, Boss," he would defend.

"Oh, I know and I'm grateful to have them around . . . only not right now!" Most governmental officials and some citizens knew of her advocacy towards the homeless but some did not.

Slipping the zipper of the turtle-neck sweater all the way up, her eyes moved to the clock. It was 8:00. She had to get going, but her mind could not help but to reflect on how awkward it had been having a male sibling for a roommate. "That child's adolescence had arrived much too soon!" she thought. They'd encountered more embarrassing moments than she cared to remember. Whenever she suddenly would walk in interrupting his hearty delight in his new-found manhood her biracial face would turn crimson. "Not again!" she would storm back out. Soon she learned to walk loud or knock even if the door was ajar. Soon she was also flung into womanhood and miraculously managed to conceal the cramps and other feminine necessities while sharing the tiny bedroom. She began to realize that a good mother would never have allowed her teenage daughter to share the room with a teen male child. Dassah recalled how odd it was that the old house had no living room like she was use to at her grandma's. But she soon figured out it was really a one-bedroom house—a living room, bedroom and kitchen. She was grateful for the hallway with a window which she would retreat to do her home work on a little shaky table and chair. She watched neighborhood kids play while she read or did homework. She and Jarvis had no friends. The kids hated them for having such a mean mother who never would speak to them in passing. Dassah recalled the living room was her mother's room with the wobbly air conditioner in it. She and Jarvis just had to sweat bullets every summer. That room was the first room to the left of the hallway and front entrance. The bedroom her and Jarvis' room was the middle to the left of the hall. The kitchen was straight to the back of the house. Dassah recalled hearing her mother tell one of her boyfriends she was glad to have her room at the front of the house. "Good!" he had snarled. "Then I won't have to sneak pass those nosey brats of yours!" laughter erupted from both. As a teenager Dassah was disappointed that her mother never stood up against the men who bad-mouth her children.

In the parked limo Dassah' mother's haggard face on her death bed flashed before her eyes. Before getting ill her mother had made it as far as she had on good looks alone. She was curvy beautiful and provocative with vibrant youthfulness at that time. Then by the time Dassah turned fifteen she and her mother could pass for sisters being only 15 years apart.

Dassah having any memories of her mother going off to work would have made her a little prouder of her mother. But all her mother did was to spend hours primping for dates and then stepping out all night sometimes.

Sadness overshadowed her face in the same way the snow was beginning to cover the limo. As a doctor she knows how truly dangerous it was for her mother's boyfriends to hang around her female child. "It's even more dangerous around male children these days!" she sadly thought. Her deep light brown eyes filled with remorse just thinking about all the different men who had visited her house. After all these years Dassah can still feel the pain of a brutal attack which claimed her virginity at the age of only 15. It had caused not only psychological anguish but also physical pain she could not forget. The occasional pain will always be a part of her life and remind her she will never be able to bare children.

There in the parked limo with Step under the wheel and snow falling she tried to suppress those memories, but brashly overpowered, she surrendered. As a skilled psychiatrist she had helped others—herself no such luck even under hypnotherapy. So once more in her mind the attack became vivid. Her earnest vow to wait until marriage had been violently ripped away. Her grandmother had intently taught her mother and then Dassah at the early age of eight to refrain from sex outside of wedlock. "That's fornication!" she would remind them both. Dassah later learned that her disappointed grandmother figured she'd had a watchful eye on her daughter through the tender age of 14. But come to find out her daughter had been lured many times after school to Mr. Desoto liquor store. When her grandmother tried to have the 30-year-old Puerto Rican, White-skinned man prosecuted his money had found him not guilty. He claimed he would never touch an African American girl. So, it was his money against Dassah mother's word—being very pregnant with Dassah. "Even if my underage daughter had been willing wouldn't that be statutory rape?" Dassah' grandmother had pleaded with the all-White court. The God fearing woman refused to believe her daughter had become a call-girl at ever since the tender age of 14. This man had been her first paying customer. Her grandmother had cried that she and her husband had tried to lavish their two late born children with everything they needed. The oldest girl had been very easy on their parents. Thus Dassah' spoiled mother had not known poverty the way she later forced her own children to experience sheer destitution.

As a doctor Dassah encounters ex-virgins both male and female who had lost their precious gift to a rape. When rape happens the victims seem to struggle harder to forget the anguish and shame. So she advises them, "Anyone who gets forced will surly suffer. . . It's just human nature not to like giving up something against your will!"

Dassah cringed in that she also would never bear babies as a result of the unnecessary brutality towards her. Her irreversible tilted womb would be a lifetime reminder. Now she knows that had her mother allowed her to get medical attention the doctor would have repositioned her uterus before it healed. Then the ovaries also would not have fused into her womb. Other abdominal tissue had also massed into the brutal injury. Not only physical but hatred for the rapist was embedded into her as she recalled the event that left her less than a woman—or so she felt useless. "Surgery might be the answer to you ever having children," her gynecologist had in her mid-30s assured her. "But it'll be very invasive and I can't promise any success," he had added. "But I'd be willing to see you through no matter what the outcome. . . You can also go the route of In Vitro Fertilization . . . you still have a uterus, you know?"

"No, I'll just live without children of my own," she had sighed to his kindness. She was not one to go under the knife and was not married anyway. "I'll just help with my niece and nephew!" She had a special bond with Jarvis's pre-teen girl and 10 year old son. Each of his children had their professionally decorated room at Auntie Dassah' house and spent just as much time there as at their own home. "I would really become a murderer if any man ever raped my kids!" she always flat out claimed without any regret. "And without hesitation or mercy, "I would cut his thing off at the very root!"

As a doctor of the mind she knows it made a rapist feel grand to belittle and overpower his victim even to kill most of his victims. One female rape victim on her 'Couch of Confessions' had cried, "As many women as there are who will willingly give it up why had he insisted on hurting me!?"

"Only a very small percentage of rapists do it out of lust," Dassah had said. "There are two kinds of rapist. . . A lust-rapist usually will stake out his particular target for a period of time. And when he's ready she's the only one he will go after." She had softly explained to her patient. "On the other hand, a serial rapist is a more random predator and attacks by the mental urge to inflict physical harm or sometimes death. If physical lust were all he wanted he *would* go out and do just any willing woman. But rather he's sick in the head with the urge to kill!" Dassah had counseled the patient that day. She knew that in her own rape her mother's boyfriend had lusted after the young girl. She recalled how at their house as a girl Dassah would suddenly catch him ogling at her so when the time was right he made his sinful pounce.

Then there in the limo that night of the brutal attack began to flood her mind again, but she was not ready to go back there. Yet she felt compelled. . .

In the limo she and Step almost ready to get out she stared blankly pass faces and into the snow flutter. She recalled when she had just turned 15 and had gotten a job. She had had a very tedious day at school that day and afterwards four hours of non-stop work at the neighborhood diner. She had left the restaurant that Tuesday evening at the usual time of 7:00. Sometimes she chose not to take public transportation for the two-mile walk home—only she wished she had boarded the bus with the crowd that evening. Anyway she needed to use that bus fare to care for Jarvis.

It had been a warn night in Victory, Georgia as she hastened through the early darkness with the usual Styrofoam plate of food for Jarvis whenever she could afford the half price. When she could not afford it he ate whatever was in the refrigerator, which was nearly bare. In deep thought that evening at dusk, "I hope Jarvis did his homework," she whispered into the dusk. It was near school closing and Jarvis was already behind in his exams. That night she was not in the mood to fuss with her adolescent brother who was almost as big as her. However she never felt threatened by him because she knew Jarvis would never go toe-to-toe with her. But he would sometimes obstinately rebel which agitated her. It made her sad that her brother thought more highly of her than he did his own mother. Too many times being the teenager she was she also wanted to just give up on him ever doing well in school. Her self was always hustling just to maintain a B average.

At the restaurant that evening it seemed the entire town ate out. And the thin shoes had offered no support to her young swollen ankles.

She hurried through the cracked sidewalks where very few people were walking that night. Having to lug the plate home she fumed over the responsibility of having to keep her brother fed. "He's not my child!"

she had complained aloud that evening. "But if he's to get anything at all I'm the only one he can rely on!"

While in the limo, Step listening to music and bundling up Dassah recalled that evening and how quickly her countenance had softened as Jarvis's innocent face flashed before her. So she had whispered to herself, "But I love my brother and at twelve he's too young to hustle for himself." She was grateful not to be the kind of sibling that would abuse a younger sibling. As a doctor she often witnessed too many cases of sibling mistreatment which sometimes ended up fatal. And an outsider would get the blame for having killed the child. That abusive sibling's true desire had been to lash out at their parents. However his sibling was more convenient to receive that rage.

In the parked limo with snow collecting on the cool windshield Dassah glanced over at Step coat on sipping coffee and reclined under the roomy wheel waiting for her next move. Instead her mind went back to her unhappy childhood. That anger she held for her mother suddenly flared up again. She recalled how she had at one time contemplated taking out an expensive insurance policy on her mother. That was the best vengeful idea she could come up with at that time. Shamefully she recalled how she had planned to murder her own mother. "Well, she's not too ashamed to make her own children suffer!" she had thought during that depressed moment. "But how will I stage the accident!" she had seriously asked herself. "To sneak up on my mother is like trying to catch a bear by its tail!" And then, there in the limo Dassah recalled the shame of that thought had slapped her squarely in the kisser that day. "Dassah how could you even think such a thing about your own flesh and blood!" she had strongly reprimand herself. But when Jarvis would cry out with hunger again the insurance policy didn't seem like such a bad idea after all.

Dassah ate square meals at the restaurant. But aside from school Jarvis's diet consisted of cold cuts, potato chips, bread and water . . . Very little milk. Most of his nutrition was what Dassah brought home whenever she could afford it. He loved meat but she could only afford to bring meat on his plate once a week. In the summer when school was out he would scrape until she got home. Dassah has now become aware of the function of the government food stamps program. Her mother had not applied for food stamps or welfare because welfare guidelines required the parent to be disabled or actively seeking employment. "No one can ever accuse my mother of using the government!" Dassah bitterly thought. So in order to keep the law at bay her mother had simply pretended to take good care of her children. When in actuality it was her teenage daughter who did all the working on a job. "If my mother would have refrained from her spending the day at Saks Fifth Avenue and Neiman Marcus we would have been able to eat a bit healthier!" she confessed to her sister-in-law who had now learned of the family secret through Jarvis.

Dassah recalled one day her mother was in her own room seated at the small dressing table where she spent most of her time applying gobs of make-up. And in a robe fit for a movie star she had pouted her beautiful full lips, "Dassah, I'll never make enough money working' for other people! She had claimed. "Plus I can't dress the way I want in no restaurant or grocery store!" she had paused, her lovely dark eyes glaring seriously into Dassah' innocent face. "That's the only type of job a Black woman can get around here, you know!"

Dassah was just glad to have her say anything to her that was not in a yell. And the girl longed to tell her of the African American women working there with her just to keep food in their children's belly. These women where Dassah worked did not adore their jobs. Nor did they like getting up a 5 in the morning just to accommodate the early eaters at the diner. But Dassah knew it was in her best interest to just stand quietly and watch her mother primp and gripe. Then, suddenly after having lost track of which makeup to apply next, her mother had become slightly perturbed that day. She finally found her next placement, and snootily continued, "And they always want you to wear those retarded looking uniforms!" she had glowered. Her half made eyes moved to the very vintage uniform Dassah wore most of the time. They both looked down at the yellow and brown, first-uniform-ever-off-the-machine, and then looked at each other—laughter suddenly broke out of the two females.

CHAPTER 3

Doctor Dassah Desoto a psychiatrist and Stephanas Carter her bodyguard sat in her parked limo preparing to get out and find some homeless men for her lucrative makeover program. While in the car on the snowy streets of Neal, New York that Saturday morning Dassah sadly drifted in and out of her devastating childhood. Another cup of coffee and between sips she stared at snowflakes settle on the windshield. They ignored new faces straining to peer inside the car. Then in order for Step not to think she was a living fruit-basket with too many nuts in it Dassah only snickered under her breath. She had recalled what her late mother had said that day at the dressing table. Though Dassah had to admire the humor of her, beautiful smooth brown-skinned mother. Then the two of them had laughed together— an uncommon occurrence. Dassah liked listening to her mother when she was not pitching a tantrum. "But I would be so very happy to have her talk *to* me, rather than *at* me!" she thought for the thousandth time. Whenever she would see a mother and child interacting, that reality would make her fantasize that child was her or Jarvis.

The doctor of the mind and her faithful bodyguard Step bundled up to get out into the snow in search of homeless men that Saturday morning. Again, she began to have flash-backs of the brutal rape that left her both mentally and physically bruised for life. But again, no matter how hard she tried to suppress that thought only with rudeness it broke through her iron wall.

So, there in the limo she recalled how as a 15 year old, around 7:15 that humid night she had hurried to get home. Except for her the streets of Victory, Georgia, was deserted or so she thought. Her mind was on Jarvis. Then suddenly the humongous dark, bare forearm of a man, wrapped around her throat from behind. He had been lurking in the bushes. Dassah recalled how his grasp was so tight she thought her vertebra would surely snap into. "Y-y-you're choking me to death!" she had managed. As an indifferent reply he simply clasped his other mammoth hand over her mouth and nose. Thus from a lengthy lack of oxygen she felt as if her temples would explode. The Styrofoam plate had vanished from her tiny grasp—at what point it flew away, to this day she cannot recall. But what she can recall is her heels. And when the glued shoes tore away as he had dragged her merciless through an open field? And through the twilight she could see that his destination was an abandoned school bus in the field. She had either rode public transportation, or walked that route for the past two months she'd been working and had never noticed the old school bus there. "P-p-p-please, you're hurting me!" she managed another frantic whimper through his thick hands that smelled of fried chicken.

"Just you shut up or I'll snap your pretty neck!!" hatred mingled with a lusty voice.

At that her knees lost all purpose for holding her up. She finally passed out. The next thing she awakened to being dumped onto a seat in the mildew bus. Her fierce kicking only brought out more of the beast in him. Suddenly it was difficult for the teenager to tell which was worse the smelly bus or his mouth clamped over hers. Every muscle in her jaw retracted resulting in a desperate bite to his thick lip. But in return she received a vengeful slap across the face—blood immediately trickled from her lip and mingled with the blood from his bitten lip.

The girl began disgustingly, to spit out the blood . . . some spit was a bill's eye into his face and some landed on the windows. He lashed back with another stinging slap. But, worst of all she felt the shift of her youthful mandible.

"Do that again Dassah Foster and you're, a goner for sure!" he firmly assured.

"W-w-who are you!" she shook out the cob-webs. The fact that he knew her name pumped more adrenalin through her. She could not believe this was happening. "This happens only on television!" delirium set in. The man had not yet raped her but all indications was confirmed when he began to squeeze her breasts as if he was trying to pop the core right through her nipples. After that unreal ordeal the doctor in her still have painful nightmares about the pinching and yanking that day long ago. Then under pressure the uniform snaps gave way, and her bra popped open, bearing her down to the waist. A battle between a bashful virgin and a brute beast began as she repeatedly attempted to cover up in the twilight—him attempting the more to uncover. Cover, uncover was the game of wills, until he finally back-handed her again.

There the young unyielding girl had never known of anyone getting raped in that neighborhood or maybe news of any just never leaked out. "Will this one get out? Will I be able to live this down?" she thought through burning tears and weak struggling. Then he was finally doing what he had set out to do. Even now there in the limo Dassah cringed from that pain.

In the limo staring blankly at snow flurries Dassah recalled that long unbelievable assault as she had drifted in and out of consciousness that early night. For the virgin of 15, he was stronger than Super Man. And upon awakening to the animal abuse, again her screams lead only to the taste of his tongue probing deep inside her throat. There in the limo Dassah smiled at the one thing that made her feel better about what was happening to her that night. With his tongue inside her throat she could not hold back the vomit which was a direct aim into his mouth . . . meat loaf and all. Then she panicked again when he began to swear ungodly. Then she passed out again. As she recall the nightmare went on for an eternity, him damaging her fragile body and her future beyond repair. And to add insult to injury he had devilishly whispered, "Look at me!!" he jerked her head in his direction. "If you utter this to anyone at all, I'll finish you off next time!"

"I-I-Is he going to do this horrible thing to me again?!" she had thought beneath him, her body had already gone numb.

There in the limo, recalling how her little body felt the night. Then a special she had seen on television came to mind. Hungry animals would attack their prey and sometimes would have to eat the animal while it was yet kicking and alive. The attacked animal, until it finally would die, would cease to feel the pain of being chewed alive. That night her fragile body also felt as if it was being, consumed alive. As she recalled the pain started out so excruciating until her brain sent endorphins and numbed the nerves in her body. Then it became only her mental self that grievously pained and she wished for numbness to take over her mind. Plus the thought of him doing that a second time totally devastated the teen. On that rank bus she had passed out again. When she awakened again the springs piercing her back was the lesser of two evils. She had lain helplessly under him in the twilight, gritting her teeth while he sickened her. "A virgin should never be forced to endure that!" she had said to a fellow doctor later in life. "That man didn't even know the meaning of mercy." She had said. "If he had let up just a bit then maybe I would be able to bear it even now . . . But I still pray God will have mercy on him when he needs mercy!" Now she knows how to pray for the enemy rather than to seek hateful revenge. She knew he should have gone to jail for that crime. Instead her hateful revenge would be to kill him. Or to wish something just as horrendous would befall him or his loved ones.

Through the maddening assault that night Dassah was finally able to recognize the man's voice as one of her mother's boyfriends—the one who always licked his thick lips while he ogled at the young pretty girl. "He had lusted until it was time to act upon that craziness!" the above-board-certified doctor assessed.

So, she recalled being on the smelly bus after terrifying and depraving her of her self-respect, he had simply walked away with her pious attribute of virginity and having no regret at all. There in the limo

Dassah angrily recalled the clank of his huge footsteps going down the metal steps. As she listened each rung drove a nail through her heart. Then she sighed of some relief but soon froze again. What had followed was unforgettable and unforgivable for her young psyche. Finally, there in the limo the memories became too agonizing. "Let's go Step!" she almost demanded.

"Okay let's go for it!" He switched off the music.

As they were about to exit the car that snowy morning in Neal, New York, another thought crept into her head. She wondered if the rape was the culprit behind her apprehension about ever getting married. And with one last desolate stare out the windshield, "Am I like those snowflakes?" she silently asked herself. "Will I be frigid forever?" Being a doctor of the mind she knew the answer was that she possibly would be. Dassah was straight in her sexual preference but could not seem to get over the attack that left her permanently scarred. Since then she had encountered men she had been physically attracted to. But she would only give them an occasional movie or dinner date. However now as a Christian and with obedience to God she can earnestly justify having abstained from fornication for many years. Before becoming saved she would blame never getting married on not having time for a serious relationship. Then suddenly, again that nightmarish evening threatened to resurface but she shook her head and it let go. "That was eighteen years ago—on with the new Dassah!" she sensibly thought.

A gentle nudge from Step brought her back to earth in the comfort. "Are you ready Boss?" he playfully nudged again. The older 2010 limousine served only as temptation to make the handsome bodyguard long for his king sized bed.

Dassah always used that limo for scouting trips. Nowadays she got due respect unlike when she sported holes in her shoes as a girl. "Plus, when the homeless are convinced I'm wealthy enough to put my money where my mouth is, they tend to loosen up a bit," she always says. The 2014, Stretch-limo at home was used only during special events. And mainly to pick up the celebrities who attended the graduation of the ex-homeless men. Many business tycoons looked forward to visiting the makeover farm in order to present business opportunities to the nearly graduates. The advertisement about the men's readiness to transact business way before he graduated drew business dealers by the hundreds. "We want to avoid waiting 'til the last minute to solicit offers!" she would warn the men. "Your money has loud voices you know!" She knew that the men's guaranteed investments would draw many viable small-business sellers.

"Oh!" Dassah snapped out of the trance at Step's nudge of her arm. "Yeah let's go for it Step!" She bent to check the 38 caliber in her boot holster. Step likewise checked his in the body holster he never left home without.

They stepped out the crunch of ice under very durable boots. A leaky fire hydrant had created a pool of freeze. With keys in hand she enabled the alarm. And pulling the hood over her shoulder length auburn ringlets she took a deep breath dreading trudging into those damp alleys today. "It's got to be done though," she thought. Her outfit this morning was a downs quarter-length coat flaunting firm knees. The insulated well fitted denim jeans outlined almost perfect thighs with her every move. Step was also set for hours in the weather. A virgin wool hooded jacket stopped at his taut quads. He had his gloved hands crammed deep into his pockets. He also wore insulated pants. They could wallow around on the snow and never get soaked.

Finally, they stood in front of the limo just surveying the shabby storefronts and houses packed tight, co-existing in the little town of Neal. Then memories of her poor childhood threatened but she flipside them. Instead her light brown eyes came to rest on a diverse race of scantily clothed teenagers loitering on the corner that early. The crowd was mixed in that the 2000s had brought about somewhat of a positive race relation. She eyed the billowing cigarette smoke around the heads of the teens, "None of those children can be any more than thirteen of fourteen!" Snowflakes hid her teary eyes as she knew they were also pushing drugs. Those mere babies had been out there all night. "Their pimp must've forced them to sell until the last haul was bootlegged," she said to Step. "But one can't save them all," she sighed.

During her free counseling classes for youths, the younger kids she would put forth an extra effort to convince them to join the YMCA or

YWCA. And the older ones she would suggest the Job Corp. However if they Joined the Job Corp, they had to be at least 21 and had already made a choice to quit high school. As a positive result many had joined and learned stable trades. She also wished the government would take more young Black males into the service instead of hauling them off to prison.

The doctor and her staff tried their best to reach the youngsters before they rolled into a life of crime. "But I'm afraid too many will be raised by this biased judicial system anyway," she sighed to Step, "Some will even be sent to prison for simply acting like any sixteen-year-old act during his adolescent years!" She knew that the hormone years was when most kids got into minor mischief. But handing out jail sentences for minor crimes and some not being released until adulthood, was a bit much. "It's truly a shame before the Almighty that society can't see the pitiful need for those Black children to be rehabilitated!" she sighed again.

"You can't save them all Boss but knowing you, you'll give it a whirl!" Step was unable to stifle a yawn that broke through. It was not that he was unconcerned but was tired from last night. Step had been around a few corners himself, only never to jail. And he barely escaped having to push drugs while living on the wicked streets of New York.

"And how many times have I told you not to call me 'Boss?' her naturally full lips shot a smile up at him, them now standing in front of the limo.

Then they began to walk on towards the alley in spite of gapes from the few people out that early Saturday. Step lifted his dark face to the sky. The glare was bright as fine snow shown through the snow that slid down his thick jawline. The wetness melted onto the thick turtle neck sweater that fit tightly around his neck. And just as he hoped the coolness popped him wide awake. "You sign my pay-check twice a month don't you?" He was finally his perky self.

"Of course I sign your check, who else?"

"Well, that makes you my boss, Boss!" he flashed a white, now even-tooth grin on her as they walked side by side toward the narrow alleyway. The costly dental work he had already paid off had been worth every penny.

The navy-blue jacket was a suitable color next to his skin. The six-foot-four-inch bodyguard's laugh rang loud through the morning. The insulated, slightly loose-fitting jeans were a compliment to his personal tailor. Additionally his religious work-outs had well rewarded the 25-year-old. Also ever since completing the program he has maintained a strict wholesome lifestyle. Hesitantly he recalled that only six years earlier he too had been among the homeless she had sought out. Still in spite of being extremely good-looking he keeps a mental hat-pin to deflate his head. "It's difficult not to toot your own horn when you have everything!" he used the hat-pin to send his big head back to earth. Also whenever Step found himself getting egotistical he would take a long look at the before and after snapshot Dassah gives to the men as a shocking reminder.

CHAPTER 4

I t was 8:20 in Neal, New York. Doctor Dassah Desoto and Stephanas Carter her rugged debonair bodyguard approached the alley they would venture into this Saturday morning. She was glad the snow had let up as they went in search of homeless men to recruit for her successful makeover program. Her ultimate goal for the past several years was to find serious men whose desire was to retrieve their lost souls and lives. So finally as folk gaped after them in that run-down neighborhood she and Step entered the narrow alleyway between two empty graffiti-marred buildings. Step stood aside to allow Dassah to take the lead, their usual formation when entering narrow alleyways. On the way Dassah thought about her yearly income dynasty. "But what if some fatality would happen to me during a scouting trip?" Always the thought of that has put fear in her even now. Then she thought, "Jarvis, even though he has a Bachelor's degree certainly doesn't have the zeal about making my money grow. He wouldn't be thrifty with an inheritance toppling millions!" Dassah' grandmother had died some years earlier. Her grandfather was in a personal care home at his own request. Dassah had an aunt but she had moved out of the country as a young woman and completely stopped communicating with the family. She never even visits her own father in the nursing home. Whether or not Dassah have cousins she guess she will never know. Dassah was most ashamed of her dysfunctional family! Her mother had no other family that Dassah knew of, or wanted to know about. Plus her family had not seen fit to rescue her and Jarvis from the well-known constant abuse. Dassah recalled the sad thing as a child she had not even realized that she was being abused. She simply figured she was being chastised for being bad. Now as a psyche she knows that naivety is the character of most children. If the kid is unable to read the parent's mind they got slapped silly. "You stupid child!" her mother parent may say. "You should know to run and get my house shoes even before my feet hits this cold floor!" her mother had told Jarvis one day. So that deserved a blow to my little brother's head," Dassah wished she could have been brave enough to talk meaner to her mother, "You should have your house shoes beside the bed like everyone else does!" she would fling at her. "If that man had not picked you up out of them, and carried you to the bed, you'd have your shoes beside the bed!"

Dassah was well aware that Jarvis had finished college. And he was now head of her security department. But the makeover business was not a number one priority. "To live and die rich is not his forte!" she thought walking ahead of Step. She knew that food, shelter, old jeans and a plasma TV was Jarvis's definition of heaven. Watching the little 19-inch television as a boy had been his only pass-time. So the habit had taken over his very being. As a boy she had also disciplined him with television. Though now he never neglects his wife Aloma a beautiful African American and their two children. Secretly Dassah wished she could be more like Jarvis, especially when she see his dead-bolted family unity. But unlike her brother she had the unending urge to watch her dollars go through a Chi-a-pet transformation—from airiness to thickness. However, she was always aware that in spite of her financial obsession, honesty and integrity kept her reminded of the impoverish life she'd lived as a child. "And you mustn't forget your needy neighbors either, Dassah!" she would say whenever she felt a stingy attack coming on. "The poor around you may very well be strangers, but they're still your neighbors," she recalled the Bible story about the Good Samaritan. She marveled at how the Samaritan had not known the robbed, beaten man whom he had helped and yet he paid money for him to receive medical attention. Dassah recalled how according to biblical history the Samaritans, mingled in with the Israelites by King Jeroboam, the son of Ne-bat, were no longer a wealthy nation at the time of this story about the Samaritan. See 1 kings 13:32 regarding King Jeroboam. Several times she had read the 12th and 13th chapters of 1 Kings and surveyed the full picture of the dividing of the Northern and Southern kingdoms. It seemed that even the Samaritan woman had become so poor that she had to go out to the well and draw her own water.

Dassah, walking ahead of Step through the snowy alley, Step humming a happy tune, Jarvis's innocent face flashed before her. Other than God her baby brother was her heartbeat. She recalled being only a child herself and was forced to rear a three years younger brother, who had not given her a moment's trouble, "Other than eating me completely out of a livelihood!" she snickered as she walked, an occasional snowflake melting on her beautiful face. Then she began to recall the night of the rape again, and how she had kept it from Jarvis. That was when she had entered her mother's room and miserably tried to inform the unconcerned woman of what had happened to her. With dire apprehension her mind slipped back to that night anyway.

She recalled how the man had left her sobbing on the musty bus. The girl sat on the bus trying to wipe her own vomit from around her neck with apron from the uniform. And sadly from that night on abandoned school buses became a serious phobia. Even with a capable bodyguard she trembles at the sight of an abandoned bus. "It seems that, I the psyche have become an emotional time-bomb myself!" she had exclaimed to a sympathetic fellow doctor one day. "As of late we hear of too many females who had at one time in her life been raped. . . My next mission is to research the number of past rapes on children," she promises herself. Ever since just a few women decided to step out of the closet the number of secret rapes has increased at an alarming rate!" she said through an aggravated huff.

She recalled how back on the mildew school bus alone that early night she had soaked her palms with hot tears and vomit. "Where are all the people that's normally out!" the teenager had whimpered. Then suddenly in the darkness, a weird thing had happened. Through blurry tears she had noticed the approaching silhouette of her attacker. He had returned and was moving slowly towards her. "Oh no!" she crouched into a corner, knees to her chest she pulled the crumpled uniform over her knees. "Please don't hurt me anymore!" the knot in her throbbing throat constricted the scream. Then the twilight revealed him stop in his tracks. His hand moved at a snail's pace to the back pocket of his somewhat baggy jeans. In his eyes were joy at her squirming again. Then with even more fear-antics he purposely took time pulling something out of his pocket. His deviousness had worked because the girl was trembling like it was fifty degrees below zero. "It's a gun!" she had thought. Then boldness suddenly overcame the numb ex-virgin. "So what!" she had thought loosening up. "At least I won't have to live with nightmares about this!" But to her surprise—or to her disappointment, it was not a gun. He flipped out a white envelope. Still she flinched when he harshly slung it at her, a direct blow to the forehead. "Give this to your good-for-nothing mammy!" he had growled through the dimness on the bus. And then he crammed his hand into another pocket and withdrew some loose dollar bills. Cold-hearted he also flung those at his maimed prey. "Now you can't say I took nothing from you!" he had hissed. "Let's just say I paid for you just like I pay your nasty mammy!" And in her ears hateful insane laughter filled the smelly bus. Then finally he wheeled and left. Now, as a doctor she is compelled to research on why rapists seem to totally detest their victims even more afterwards it's over. When, it is only the victim that should be unforgivably infuriated. The doctor of the mind was reminded of a Bible story about Amnon one of King David's sons. After Amnon had defiled his own sister, then it had been he who hated her more intensely than he had once thought he loved her (2 Samuel 13th chapter). But Dassah knew that entire scenario involving Amnon, Tamar, and eventually, Absalom was only part of the curse that God placed on David's household in 2 Samuel 12:10 when God promised the sword (disaster) would not leave David's fleshly house for David's disobedience with Bathsheba. David had taken a man's wife, impregnated her and then had that man killed. Dassah understood there was a spiritual heart in David in that David saw fit to repent of his past sins. And there was also a fleshly side of David which God referred to frequently in His prophecy. After David had repented and was renewed, God then referred to the spiritual side of David as, "A man after my own heart." Nevertheless, David, just like Christians today, have to live with the consequences of our past sins. For example, if a person repents and thus get saved, but had been a drug addict, if those drugs had damaged his body in some way, he still has to live with that deadly illness.

While going through the alleyway Dassah continued to recall the night of the rape. Petrified, she had stared out after the man through the thick dirt on the window and dared not to breathe until he had disappeared into the deserted field of Victory, Georgia. It was only then that she had managed to pull her agonizing bleeding body off the springs. She found herself wishing terribly for the numbness to return to. Then she felt something choking her waistline. She looked down. It was the strap of her tiny shoulder-bag. And her eyes met with all the littered papers on the floor along with the white envelope and the two, one dollar bills. Her tiny hand managed to grab the envelope. Then she dared not touch the dollar bills no matter how desperately she had needed that puny money to feed Jarvis. "Whatever I tell the police about this will be nothing but the truth!" she had bitterly promised that night. "I would never agree to such an animal having me!" With her entire body aflame how she ever was able to pounce off that bus like a sprinter for the gold yet puzzles her. She tried all the while to hold the blood stained uniform close so as not to reveal her bra. The faster she ran it felt as if he was directly on her heels. The girl had run puffing through the pebbles despite the hot blood trickling down her thighs. Finally she was back on the streets. Wildly she streaked, ignoring the concerned inquiries from people who had known her. She lived two miles from work and had made it home under record time. As her eyes were a blur it was only instinct alone that kept her from falling flat on her face. At that point her body had become one big pain, except at the end of her ankles her feet had a weirder feeling. She recalled glancing down only to discover her pale toes. By then every man she passed looked like the rapist. Struggling intensely to catch her breath she finally found herself on the squeaky porch of her house. She was about to turn the knob when she finally noticed the envelope critically grasped in her fist. Blood from her fingernails had stained the white package. Glaring frightfully at the envelope the girl cared less about its content. Nevertheless, under the dim, globe-less light bulb her eyes had come to rest on the accidentally torn envelope. There peeped out some ten and twenty dollar bills. Then hasty fumbling fingers curiously began peeling it open. Dassah recalled how the sight of that money had brought a loud gasp from her. "Why would he ever have me give her money?" she whispered. "And why couldn't he give it to her himself?!" She was totally confused over the entire ordeal. "Why did I pick this up anyway?" she still grasped the bloody package and knew the answer to the latter. He had demanded her to give it to her mother. Though she had not known at the time what it was for. "If I don't give this to my mother, she'll kill me for sure," she insanely thought, all reasoning running amuck. She crammed the bulky envelope into her small purse and stumbled inside. The terrified 15-year-old thought things could not possibly get any worse. However, once inside the rage her mother displayed had given her a double dose of trauma. She began to wonder if this type of thing happened to rich girls since all of this seemed to be about angry people and money.

While walking through the damp alleyway with Stephanas flush on her heels, them stepping over debris, the doctor recalled the undue fit her mother had pitched that night. The girl was so grateful for being able to snap close at least one snap on the uniform. Then she had eased into her mother's room around 9: 30—two hours late from work. And her mother knew that overtime at the restaurant had been absolutely prohibited. The sound of the television in their room alerted her to be as quite as possible. The last thing she needed was for Jarvis to see her looking that way.

She desperately needed her mother to inquire as to why her female child was so late. Dassah now realizes that a caring parent would have even been there to pick her up. The two of them would have assuredly had to take the bus home. "But at least the two of us could have fought off any lone attacker!" the doctor thought going through the damp alley not yet feeling the chill of the weather. And with Stephanas behind her she allowed the tears to go on and swell in her eyes. She recalled how when her mother had laid eyes on her she had been totally unmoved. only She had been dressed to step out that night. It had been as if she sneakily expected her daughter to be late. Dassah recalled her mother sitting at the little vanity staring admiringly into her own stunning eyes thinking how they would also allure her men. Dassah came softly over and fell down sobbing at her mother's feet. Her fingernails were still bleeding and her clothes torn. "Ma-ma!" cries of sheer pity. "Your Jesse just forced me to-to. . ."

No reply only the usual mean glare and picky-ness swiping her child's bleeding hands away from her clean clothes.

Then the child was eager to please her mother and to make her smile. Dassah then pulled out the envelope full of money. "H-he said to give you this," she had sadly whimpered, dumping the contents onto her mother's lap. Instead her mother jumped up agitated. The bloody envelope tumbled to the floor—money spilling out. Then her mother had simply sat slowly back down, but her greedy gaze never left those bills. Dassah was still on her knees searching her mother's face for even a hint of compassion. Dassah then pulled up her ripped uniform to reveal scratches, bruises and clotted cuts on her thighs and legs. Dassah regrettably recalled how at that moment her torture would have moved even a stranger to tears. But her own mother only sat ogling that money. Finally her mother had torn her eyes away long enough to glare at her pleading child. Then suddenly intense rage turned her mother's brown face crimson. "You've just been lying up with some big-headed boy, probably more than one boy!" she shoved Dassah to the floor. "You're just jealous because I'm more popular with the boys than you are!" her mother had insanely hissed. "You've always tried to take Jesse away from me!"

And upon hearing that accusation it had ripped out the young girl's heart. "Who, but you would want an animal like that?!" she had only thought, daring not to talk back.

As a doctor Dassah now realizes that when her mother had made reference to herself as being more popular with the boys, her mother had been under the delusion that she too was still a teenager. And also the younger fashions she had worn were proof that she craved to relive her teen years. Also she had become a mother way too soon. Dassah realized that mothers could be jealous of their daughter's youthfulness.

Then, that day her mother had simply turned back to pampering in the mirror leaving her distraught child staring in disbelief at her tastefully slender back. The young girl was left to try and figure out why she was so hated by the one who was supposed to protect her. And now as a doctor Dassah realizes her mother had had a severe mental disorder. The doctor of the mind had discovered no firm reasons why animals seemed to love their off-springs more than some humans did theirs. Plus she realized there were several factors that may set off a mentally unstable parent. She recalled some of her abusive clients would claim they abused because they were abused by their parents or a parent. On the other hand she had other clients who had undergone abuse as children but had made conscience decisions not to perpetrate that painful torture on their own children. Thus, in order to stabilize her own sanity Dassah would rather think her mother had an inapt mental disorder rather than to think her only parent hated her enough to prostitute her. However, now as a devout Christian, the doctor is convinced that sin plays a major role in child-abuse and any type of battering. She refers many of those abusive clients to read Ephesians 6: 4, "And you fathers provoke not your children to wrath: but bring them up in the nurture and admonition of the Lord." Provocation is to purposely, unnecessarily anger a child. And that in teaching them about the love of God is done with tact and piousness which is the parent's responsibility. When a parent uses his strength to push a child around that provokes the child. That child will grow up one day if the parent does not kill him first. And he will remember that abuse and be bitter towards his now old and helpless parents. Thus kind of revenge can be a deadly weapon in the hands of an angry offspring who has been taught nothing about forgiveness. The parent also knew nothing about forgiveness when the child had accidently spilled that milk as a mere 3 year old!

On the other hand, discipline does not have to be so harsh. To spare the rod is to hate the child. Proverbs 13: 24, "He that spares his rod hates his son: but he that loves him chastises him betimes (early in life)." A concerned parent will not wait until a child gets too old to be controlled by anyone but the prison system. But that consistent positive rearing at home begins at birth. Babies learn to control a parent at birth. When a parent runs and picks up a baby at every little whimper, then the baby has taught the parent who is supposed to be in control. If the baby is not hungry, wet or sick, don't let him control you . . . It's a habitual tool he will use on you throughout life. And using the rod does not necessarily mean a parent must brutally beat the child with a stick. An occasional slap on the butt or punishment may be helpful in most disciplinary households.

Dassah recalled a first-time mother that came to her, tears meeting under her chin. "This baby just won't sleep unless I'm rocking and singing to her!" she had cried with the innocent 6 month ole even then attached to her hip. And, of course she had neglected many house duties, including her husband and him, her. Both the father and the mother was wrapped around the baby's finger like a yo-yo string.

The doctor had gone on to explain to the sobbing mother that other stimuli could nurse the child while the child is in her crib. Then the parents assured Dassah that everything had been tried. "What baby would not rather hang onto his parent's hip all the time!?" the doctor asked with knowing determination. The adorable little darling had taught his new parents to jump through hoops of fire. But the larger picture of this learned behavior was that when the child would grow up, the parents would be expected to continue to jump. Only when the child was older the demands would be greater and more severe. Maybe even to the point of physically forcing them to do her bidding. The doctor in her chair of answers and the patient sitting rocking the babe, Dassah had sadly looked at the weeping mother. Dassah' own mother had been the complete opposite. She'd never even seen her mother carry Jarvis on her hip or even in her arms. It was their grandmother who had held and bottle fed him as a baby.

Then, going through the alley Dassah' mind strayed to that night and how she had dared to lay her dirty self on her mother's back there at the vanity. "Well, Ma-ma will you at least take me to the hospital!" the girl pleaded "I'm bleeding and it's not from my monthly cycle either! My body aches so badly, and I think I'm cut down there!" she had moaned now through a whisper because of Jarvis. Even that fell on a stony heart. Suddenly Dassah jumped up and wheeled on bare heels. She had lost her shoes—the only patched up pair she then owned. The mere thought of having no shoes at all sent double panic through her. "What shoes will I wear to school?" Even though she and her mother wore the same size shoe, her mother would never let her borrow a pair of her costly flats. She had stood before her mother that night, gritting her teeth to keep from lashing out. Then the girl had wheeled around and rushed to the phone. She began to dial.

"Don't even think about it!" a growl worse than the attacker's, and so familiar to the young girl shot out from her mother. It was the 'I'm-about-to-slap-you silly again, voice'. Dassah slammed the cordless phone down so hard it should have shattered into little pieces. As she recalled that verbal attack had, by no means been the first but that night was the most memorable episode. Along with all the other pain so did her heart began to throb. And for the first time in her life Dassah stood tight fisted, openly evil-eyeing her mother. At that point the passive girl had become an insane defender, the rapist's face so fresh in her mind. And for the first time with subtle fear her mother sensed the rage in her child. Dassah had relentless satisfaction just to see that hint of alarm in her mother. That had soothed some of Dassah' pain even until this day. For once her mother had no doubt that her offspring would strike back this time. Nevertheless, Dassah managed to refrain. She had wheeled and stormed out of the room. But for the first time she wished her mother would go on and strike her so that she too could unleash the years of built up frustrations onto her. "I wish I would have gone on and slapped that devil clear out of her head that night!" Dassah thought while going through the snowy alley with Step loyally on her heels. But that night she felt a dire need to get to the bathroom. She had hastened on toward the bedroom door in the little shabby three-room house.

Then her 12-year-old brother had been standing at their mother's door. He suddenly stepped directly into Dassah' path when she came out. His dark face was face to face with her tan face. Jarvis dared not to come into their mother's room and never had. "Where's my plate, Sis and what happened to your hands . . . did you cut yourself at work? You got blood on your dress!" Jarvis stood there with a neat low haircut thanks to his sister.

"Yeah, I had an accident!" Dassah recalled only pushing pass her hungry brother. Getting to the bathtub was all she cared about at that point. She recalled stepping into the narrow hallway and directly into the only bathroom across the hall from her mother's room. "Good thing Jarvis didn't notice this huge rip in my uniform!" she had whispered under her breath that night.

Finally in the safety of the tiny bathroom she poured the contents of the half full bottle of shampoo into the tub and turned on the always low pressure water mostly hot. Instead of slipping the dress over her head the way she normally did she forced her bloody finger tips into the snags and ripped it off—that had also lifted some rage. She had a mind to just snatch down the too short cheap plastic curtains from the high windows. She wanted to just rake everything from the overcrowded counter onto the floor. "Maybe, if I acted like a stark raving fool, then she'd call the police!" But the aching girl somewhat managed to keep her sanity that dreadful night.

As Dassah and Step walked through the narrow alleyway fine snow flurried. Step was dutifully on her heels. Even now out in the cold the doctor could still feel the hot water engulfing her body that night as a girl. The water had really stung as soon as she touched down. The girl jumped nevertheless she eased into the thick suds, tears also plopping into the bubbles. And uncontrollable sobs began to rock her. There she scrubbed her tan skin until it turned crimson. Suddenly the excruciating abdominal pain drew her young body into a tight knot. "I need a doctor for sure!" hesitatingly, she reached under the water and touched herself afraid of what she would discover down there. When she ran her finger across a small tag of torn flesh, she cringed and jerk her hand away. Just as she thought, she had been seriously injured. "How could anyone be so utterly atrocious to a child?!" she had cried. "Somehow I must get medical attention!" Then her young mind remembered his threat to do that again or even kill her if she told. Now Dassah counsels children to go on and tell an adult. Then if the adult refuses to listen, the child should keep searching until she or he finds some family member or a teacher who will listen. In many cases the rapist would be too afraid to follow up on those threats. He then becomes too frightened of going to prison. Dassah also knows that nine out of ten times a rapist's threats are just scare tactics to a gullible victim. However, as a doctor of the mind she knows that most children who are raped by a stranger may not be able to identify him and will be left alive. On the other hand when a child is raped by someone they know, sadly the child may be murdered.

There in the old fashioned claw footed not for beauty, bath tub. "Why won't my own mother protect me?" she had cried bitterly. The rape had certainly been a hard pill but her mother's attitude had been wholly indigestible. Up until that incident Dassah had figured maybe she deserved to be hit as most abused children feel they are to blame. But as she matured, she learned she was raised in a dysfunctional household.

So, that night there in the tub tears plopped non-stop into zillions of bubbles. Jarvis's pecking on the door pleading for food had been ignored by the totally frustrated girl. "How terribly afraid he is to ask his own mother for anything!" she managed to move her mind pass her own pain. Then her weary young eyes wandered over to a little table beside the tub. A pair of rusty scissors lay there enticing her. Then, slowly puckered fingers inched towards them. "Maybe this is the best way." Sobs had rocked her as her fingers finally grasped weapon. With both tiny hands she placed the point between her bruised breasts. Underneath the mound of foam as she was about to thrust . . . "I'll just lie here and bleed to death!" she recalled saying. Then, with a sudden pause, the girl had whispered, "But, what about poor Jarvis? Who will take care of him?" So down her belly the scissors slid between bruised thighs. The clank on the old steel tub only reminded her of the rapist's footsteps on the metal stairs just minutes earlier. She knew it would also be Jarvis to find her dead because her mother would be out for the entire night. Now realizing her mother had sold her, Dassah have nightmares about her mother sitting serenely at home knowing what was happening to her own child. "All she was thinking about was that filthy money!" the doctor has pondered on many times over.

Going through the alleyway Dassah recalled enduring more pain from the rubbing alcohol drenching, which she thanked God they had some kind of antiseptic in the house. Afterwards, she had padded herself from the Girly Cabinet that Jarvis dared not ever peep into, which she once caught him doing.

Then she had finally trudged out of the bathroom that night. Her dark natural curls dripping around a long tan neck. It had not surprised her to discover her mother was gone. Suddenly she remembered the envelope. Every scrape on the bottom of her feet throbbed. She stumbled into her mother's room and looking around—no money or bloody envelope anywhere. At that time the young girl had been unaware her mother had consented to the rape. "Jarvis!" the girl had screamed. "Did you see a white envelope?" She had turned concern to getting food for her dependent brother.

"Uh-huh, the envelope had blood on it and I know who got it," his adolescent voice affirmed while in his room. There in front of the little television, he was busy cramming potato chips into his.

"And where did you get those?" She knew he rarely got food unless she brought it home.

"Ten dollars was on the floor in the hall and I went to the store," he innocently admitted. "Sis, you were in the bathroom for a long time you know and I had to pee, too." Like a little child to a parent, he handed over the change from the ten.

Dassah reluctantly held out a puckered hand and took the much needed money, "Please just say you needed to use the bathroom Jarvis," aggravation. "It's not necessary that you tell *what* you have to do in there. . . And you went out at this hour!?" The girl was too upset to dish out a firmer reprimand. As she grasped the change she knew it would be needed in the days ahead in that she was flat broke until almost a week away. She also knew her mother had accidentally dropped the money in the hallway because she never gave them money even for food.

Dassah recalled how Jarvis had been oblivious to anything but those chips and the horror movie that night. She was glad she'd had enough sanity left to close the door behind her when she had gone into her mother's room. "Jarvis will never know what a mess Sis has become," she had promised herself that, and has kept it from him. She knows that if she were to tell him now he would probably go straight and dig their mother up and kill her. Already any thoughts of his mother he held in total vengeance. He is not a Christian, but she is working on, and is praying for him and his family.

Dassah recalled that though she was a teen, poor and abused she'd still had mega-pride before that night. Before that she had maintained her purity even in the midst of the manager at the restaurant persistent sexual harassments. She considered it a blessing not to have gotten fired for not giving in. But he was aware that she was the most faithful worker he had there. And one day after she had slapped his greedy hand away from her breast, he had snarled, "You know your little butt would've been rolling on the streets if the other workers were half the looker and worker as you are!" Dassah could only sigh a big relief, watching his double wide back and greasy, blond hair walk away.

Dassah recalled how she never saw that white, bloody envelope again. Neither would her mother mention it again. Later, as she matured she realized her own mother had sold her out to such brutality. Additionally, Dassah recalled with intense shame, her rapist had been one of the men suspected of infecting her mother with AIDS-HIV. After her mother's diagnosis and true confession of all of her partners the health department tried but had been unable to find that one. They tracked down most of the other men. Most of those men from different backgrounds and races had names and addresses. Now Dassah knows that her mother had had finances to support her children if she would have just been a caring mother.

Then finally, a couple of years after the rape which her own mother had set up for her young daughter, her mother became totally bed-ridden. They learned that her mother had actually been infected for a long time before it took a toll on her. And another one of her mother's down sides was that ether did she believe in taking herself or her kids to a doctor. But then soon her mother became too feeble to even rule the house. So Dassah was able to have an HIV-AIDS test on her own. With praises on her seventeen year old lips she jumped and stomped for joy. "God allowed the curse to pass over me!" She had the West Nile Blot test to determine if the virus was incubating—it had come back negative. She recalled smiling big at the reporting nurse. Dassah now goes on to testify that, "Now I know how good the Israelites felt when God had put His special protecting over them when He sent those plagues into Egypt!" She was truly grateful that God had been so favorable to her, as an innocent victim.

She recalled the day of the test results how the young, pretty nurse had angrily huffed, "Well if that bastard didn't have it he should get it! AIDS is only fitting for a snake who's low enough to mutilate a child!" It infuriated her when she discovered the healed scar on the then seventeen year old. And how her uterus had healed all twisted beyond repair. Dassah' cervix had totally closed over with scar tissue. Hers had not been a simple rape. It appeared the animal in him was out to damage the child.

As Dassah and Step was almost at the homeless men's resting place in the alley Dassah recalled how learning to forgive that sadistic person was the second toughest thing she ever had to do—the first was to forgive her mother. Now as a Christian she calls on the Holy Ghost to intervene whenever that hatred tries to suffocate her again. "But what if I met him today?" she thought for the millionth time. "Would I have him arrested? And if he gets off because of the time-frame statute of limitation, I can now afford to have him beat to a bloody mess the way he had left me!" Then her conscience poked hard at her. "Having him beaten up would be self-vengeance and God says that vengeance belongs to Him," she thought, going through the alley. "Of course, even a Christian has the right to obtain earthly justice. . . Any rapist certainly deserves to pay for his earthly lawlessness. But God will judge his sins." She had become totally convinced of that. So she decided that if she ever ran into her rapist she would have her capable lawyer see that he got what he deserved at any financial cost. She would request a jury trial in order to present her damages. "But how will they be able to prove it was he that did that to me?" she thought many times over. She knew she would have to bring Jarvis into the mess because he had seen the blood that night. So she would rethink, "I'll just leave it alone and God will take care of that coward!" if only she had gone to the hospital that night instead of going home, this puzzle would be solved and he would have gone to prison. "Apparently he and my mother had planned no hospital thus no police!"

On the way through the alley Dassah looked at her watch. It was 8:35. "We're making pretty good time, Step." a quick glance over her shoulder, "You still with me?"

"I've got the lens, right on you, Boss!" He really wished he could compliment the way she seductively swayed her hips ahead of him. But Step cared too much for his job to put it in jeopardy with a mere flirt. He realized how picky Dassah was and would avoid leaving a bad taste in her mouth about him. "The boss and I simply spend too much time together to be stressed over such am issue as sex," he thought. He was not a Christian but had made up his mind that the first move would come from her if she wanted him. Her bodyguard knew absolutely nothing about her vow of celibacy. Though, she had warned him and all the recruits that fornication was a sin. And upon Step's entrance into the makeover program she had not hesitated to point out that she did not date her employees. And Step was intelligent enough to know that just because he had once been homeless, that did not give him any license to be ungentlemanly. He planned also to someday raise his future sons to be tactful and gentle when it came to the opposite sex. So, simply trudging along behind her he forced out any untoward thoughts from his handsome hooded head.

"I'm a skilled bodyguard not a sex-starved pervert!" Plus Step had such male-magnetism that even without trying he attracted women from sixteen to sixty—not that he felt compelled to act upon all those advances.

That snowy morning Dassah and Step continued the long trek to get deep inside the alley where the homeless roamed and nestled. On the way Dassah' mind went back to her brother, Jarvis. As head of her security department where he now managed one-hundred-eighteen people, 90 percent are ex-homeless veterans and ex-convicts both men and women. The other ten percent of his staff are non-homeless people who had applied for the position before the makeover program began. Ex-homeless women were hired because they were not allowed on the farm in South Georgia. Women were hired in that too many women were forced to be heads of household. As a Christian and doctor, Dassah regret prohibiting females from living on the makeover farm. "But that's life!" she thought, going through the snug alleyway, snow flurries melting on her somewhat keen nose. "I have to protect my interest in order to keep the program afloat. This is not just to make me rich but also affords resurrection benefits for many of the helpless homeless." Overall she never forgot how she had once been burned by allowing women to reside on the farm along with men.

Then, suddenly her thought flipped back to Jarvis and how he had the least bit of interest in being a business owner. And holding any other kind of job was simply out of the question for him. Even with a college degree his rich big sister paid him much better than he could ever earn working for someone else. "Now you're able to run your own business, Jarvis!" she recalled trying to convince him after his college graduation. She had hugged her good-looking, dark skinned brother while they together cried tears of joy. She recalled there at the university that day the two drew stares crying over their lives as children. Jarvis had brazenly thanked her for the food she used to bring from the restaurant and care packages she faithfully sent to the college. "Sis, you sure kept my greedy butt fed!" he had said loudly, deliberately disregarding mentioning their mother. "You have no idea how glad I would be to see those Styrofoam plates of vittles in your hand every night!" They had laughed, and then cried again. At his graduation, staring proudly up at her brother her smile faded as she recalled having hid how she'd lost his plate the night she was attacked.

While going through the narrow alleyway Dassah knew that if anything were to happen to her, Jarvis's wife A-lo-ma would see that he kept the makeover program up and running prosperously. Her sister-in-law had agreed to appoint some doctors from within the firm to keep up the business. She would choose doctors that are familiar with the ropes, because governmental stipulations require that a doctor of psychiatry protocol the mental aspects of the program. "No doctor, no makeover program!" she had said to A-lo-ma one day as they made plans, "Anyone can simply white-wash homeless men on the outside and then turn them loose on society. . . But to stabilize and re-program their lifestyle can only transpire through a doctor." She also knew that without the ex-homeless employees her stores could not thrive. She thought about the impressive exit business plan she had in place if for some reason A-lo-ma decided to turn on a dime and decides not keep the business. But if A-lo-ma did decide to keep the program alive and her being an accountant, she would not have to implement the exit plan in case of Dassah' death or inability to keep it going. She was glad that both A-lo-ma and Jarvis had Bachelor's degrees in business and A-lo-ma also a Masters in accounting.

While walking in front of her bodyguard just in case some crazed homeless man or other robber felt lucky she felt totally secure. Plus, both she and Step were packing guns. As snow flurried before her part Black, part Puerto Rican features Dassah recalled her beautiful sister-in-law whom she adopted as her sister. Dassah finally had someone in which she felt safe confiding. Reflections of being a med student when she had no friend to turn to crossed her mind. Nevertheless, she kept occupied when her childhood ability to earn money came into play—she would counsel the non-psyche students. She discovered that many of them had backgrounds of mental and physical abuses also. Thus the young student discovered that any physical stresses eventually would lead to mental derangement. Yet all the while she advised others, she purposely would avoid any invasion of her own space whenever they attempted to befriend her. The mistreatment her mother instilled in her had become a silent volcano deep in her gut. But she now knows that contrary to popular belief, God can quench the most ferrous volcano. She had heard some doctors say that the lava of hatred would eventually gush out of the client and burn up everyone in its path. As a Christian doctor now she too knows if it were not for her faith, it would be only a matter of time before her eruption would occur.

She recalled hearing other students' cry of abuse and how deep inside her she felt like hers had been the worse of them all. "But I'm too ashamed to tell of how my mother sold her little girl to be mutilated!" Dassah had thought as a student. "She had to have known that man's mean nature since herself had prostituted to him." Dassah knew that he self could have easily become homeless as a teen. "There were many times I simply wanted to turn in the hand I was dealt, but just the thought of leaving Jarvis alone with a mad woman had nailed me to the floor," she sadly thought. And with the illegal, less than minimum wage she made at the little restaurant, she could never have made a decent living. So, in the light of that load during med school her insides exploded from the intense desire to confide in someone. "But I can't trust anyone!" she had thought in anguish so many lonely nights. Then Jarvis introduced her to A-lo-ma his fiancée. A compassionate shoulder finally came available. The Christian in her knew she could always talk to God, but she knew He had also placed humans to help bear each other's burdens. "It just takes trusting in the right human!" Dassah used to say. The Enquirer-type of listener would only recount stories, but rarely accurately. Even back then she was aware that if she entrusted the wrong ears she could be labeled a teenage prostitute who contracted AIDS as a punishment.

Dassah and Step went through the snowy alleyway early that Saturday morning in search of homeless men. There the doctor of the mind recalled how she always solved the woes of others but never having any consolation for herself. Even when Jarvis got married it took a while to let go more than just small-talk to her sister-in-law. "Psyches are not invincible!" A-lo-ma, with a serious stare had assured Dassah knowingly. And then had prompted her to go on and ventilate. Finally able to dribble her agony onto A-lo-ma she was reminded of a Bible verse on which she now meditates. She recalls Ecclesiasts 4: 9-12, which suggests that if your arm is too short to reach the itch then a true friend would scratch it without complaining and vise-versa—and that it was mentally unhealthy to be a hermit. Verse 9 says, "Two are better than one, because they have a good reward for their labor. Verse10-For if they fall, the one will lift up his fellow: but woe to him that is alone when he falls; for he have not another to help him up. Verse 11-Again if two lie together then they have heat: but how can one be warm alone? Verse 12-And one prevail against him, two shall withstand him.

Dassah recalled feeling that she was losing a grip on her sanity when she would talk to herself too much. Then she would rationalize that most people talked to themselves. And in the same breath she would say, "But if one has to always answer themselves back, is the proverbial sign of loneliness." She had noted that once again she had to reply to herself. She acknowledged Jesus as a spiritual Rock but A-lo-ma became the earthly sidekick for which she longed. She was forever surrounded by people yet still had that longing to confide. After finally having a friend she understood why God commanded Christians to exhort one another.

And the fact that the homeless also needed earthly friends was the real reason she developed the out-reach program. But she never dreamed it would evolve so quickly. Her naturally full lips smiled thinking of how many of the homeless she had led to the Lord's body. First a hot meal and then the hungry were receptive to digest the spiritual dessert. She was aware that trying to preach the gospel to a famished person could be compared to trying to teach a hungry tiger to perform tricks. On the other hand it infuriated her to see so many serious homeless people on the streets. Many were there because they wanted to be there. But many had been offered no other choices. They just needed a little help.

While walking in front of Step, Dassah shook snowflakes off her long eyelashes. Since Godly meditation was now part of her daily routine, she recalled another passage in Ecclesiastes, 5: 8-15 where God condemns the stingy rich people for abusing the poor. As a wealthy woman that was one of the lessons that led her to believe when the rich oppresses the poor just because they can get away with it, God would severely judge between that kind of unrighteousness. And sometimes punishment comes even in this lifetime, but for sure eternal punishment happens in the life to come! She remembered the words of that scripture, "If any see the oppression of the poor, and the violent perversion of judgment and justice towards the poor not to worry because in due time God, who is higher than any earthly judge would judge those merciless earthly judges." And on down to affirming how, naked everyone came into this world and naked everyone will leave this world! In this present earthly kingdom money has proven to overpower justice. And Satan is the king who reigns in this kingdom. She recalled one time in a meeting how she had said to the audience of poor homeless souls, "The God of heaven created the earth for everybody to enjoy and not just for the profit of the rich. . . Also taxes, high interest, unbalanced store scales and gas-gougers will assuredly answer to the Almighty!"

"Amen!!" was the audiences' hearty reply remembering their cardboard boxes, while the rich bought mink-lined beds for their pets and fed them steaks for dinner, no doubt.

As they walked in the snow the concerned psychiatrist thought about the impossible gas prices. "Only a few short years ago gasoline was two dollars a gallon," she thought. "Now the jump is nothing short of injustice towards the poor!" Then thinking about gas prices and cars, and feeling the sting of the cold sent a sad mental picture of some women she and Step passed that morning huddled at bus stops. The temperature was close to 15 degrees in Neal, New York. Those women at the bus stops were no doubt hard workers and had left home at five or six in the darkness of the morning—the sun would not rise until about seven in the winter. She knew that some of those women may have had cars. But for many of those mothers it then becomes a choice of should she buy gas, or give her children money for lunch. Dassah recalled how many of those defenseless women had become victims of crime standing at the bus stop. They had to come and go on foot in the dark. And the woman that did not have children the minimum wage that she earned would only get used up on gas if she drove to work. The doctor knew that the scenario of any American working just to buy gasoline, in her opinion, was inhumane. "You talking about the poor being caught between a hard place and a rock!" she had said one day. That morning she had peered sadly out at the women waiting at bus stops. Then inside the limo the warmth and surround-sound music caused her to feel quite ashamed that she now had so much.

While they walked through the damp alley stepping over debris Step was on her heels as snowflakes misted before them. As usual, Dassah' conscience poked her about being filthy rich but as usual God's word became her refuge. Reflections of another Bible passage swiftly came to mind. The scripture was Luke 16th chapter 19-31. The parable was about a rich man and Lazarus a poor man. She had learned that parables were stories told by Jesus to help the spiritual mind understand spiritual things. And while the holy would comprehend the parable the carnal mind would struggle desperately to grasp its meaning. And that was exactly what God intended for a parable to do . . . confuse the devil and his followers. She recalled the scripture for that story in Luke 8:10, where Jesus said, *"Unto you it is given to know the mysteries of the kingdom of God: but to others in parables; THAT SEEING THEY MIGHT NOT SEE AND HEARING THEY MIGHT, NOT UNDERSTAND."* The worldly mind must first yield to the Holy Spirit before he can understand holy things.

While going through the alley she recalled how the parable depicted the poor man after he had died as having been carried into paradise a place of calm and comfort. On the other hand the rich man, after he had died, ended up in flames a place of total torment. It appeared the rich man finally felt the urgency to repent after having received his eternal reward—too late—his fate had been sealed by the life he chose to live while he was alive. This parable could also be summed up as, 'what goes around comes around'. In her earlier years before she was saved, she had known 'what goes around' as an old cliché. But now she knows that as coming from God's word—everyone eventually reaps what they have sown whether good or bad.

She recalled how the rich man's earnest plea was for Lazarus to bring a dip of water because of his torment in flames. During his just reward the rich man failed to perceive that in his lifetime his heart had been hardened towards the poor man's constant longing for only the crumbs that fell from his table. "How many rich people and Lazarus' there are in the world?" Dassah shook her head. Amazement also took her when she learned that people would remember their past life whether in bliss of paradise or in the torment of flames. During a Bible class Dassah had once commented, "And the twenty-fifth verse is proof of a remembrance because Abraham asked the rich man to recall how he had treated the poor man while they both were alive." She recalled how the teacher of that class had sternly remarked that the parable was also proof that poor people also have souls. "Why is it that very few well-to-do Christians ever try to evangelize in poor and homeless communities?" he had asked, really knowing the answer. "I'm talking *really* try to bring them into the body of Christ as opposed to simply handing out meal tickets and then forgetting them! Listen Church! Just you remember all of us will stand before the judgment seat one day, some of us sooner, some later." The aged, sad-faced Bible teacher had sighed.

Then another member had commented that day, that people knew it was simply too stressful to take a homeless person under their wings and help him get on his feet. So they would rather move on to the sinner who have more self-sufficiencies.

Dassah also recalled a scripture in Mark, 10th chapter, how Jesus had rebuked the rich young ruler for not selling his substance and sharing with the poor. And how Jesus' disciples after hearing Jesus had misunderstood that and felt it was simply too impossible for a rich person to enter into heaven. The disciples then became sorrowful because in their loyalty to Jesus they had given up an abundance of their earthly goods. Then Jesus saw the need to comfort His faithful followers by affirming that with men some things were impossible, but that with God all things are possible. Dassah had heard some say that, by God having claimed that *all things* were possible for Him was a contradiction of His own word. But she knew that it was not God's nature to do anything that He had commanded man not to do. Therefore, there was one thing that was impossible for God to do and that was that God could not lie, meaning He could not sin. She recalled reading that in Hebrews 6:18. She knew that 'all things' meant all things that are within His will. And it was against His supreme deity as the first named in the Godhead, to lie—The Godhead being God the Father, God the Son and God the Holy Ghost. She recalled how Jesus had answered his discouraged disciples in that passage. He promised them that their earthly goods would be returned to them a hundred-fold in this world, plus they would have life eternal in the world to come, meaning heaven. Dassah recalled that upon having read that she had smiled big because she was a disciple with very much earthly wealth and had not shunned to help the poor. So she happily looked forward to sharing in the world to come. "The best of both worlds. . . Now it doesn't get any better than that!" she thought. But she realized that just like the well-to-do disciples of that day, not every Christian today have the money-savvy-talent to manage their wealth. "Some Christians," she thought, "just like some non-Christians just aren't faithful stewards when it comes to budgeting God's money!" And she also realized that all good thing came from God. He only allows man to use His money. "One day He will come to us and ask how did we use His money.

Dassah also realize that even with an abundance of money, the rich Christian would inevitably have to suffer persecution. "No pain, no gain is not only for the body but also for the spirit," she thought going through the damp alley. The Christian doctor was aware that famous cliché was mainly intended used for those who fervently exercised their body. Nevertheless she also viewed the sacrificial workout to refer to the spirit. She recalled a scripture in first Timothy 4: 8. "For bodily exercise profits little, but godliness is profitable unto all things, having promise of the life that now is, and of that which is to come." And again, in that scripture she was reminded of inheriting heaven after death. She understands that her riches are not to be used simply for whatsoever her flesh called for. And that alone is the cross of persecution she must bear as a wealthy Christian! She was to have self-control over fleshly lusts. She would just love to lavish her millions on stuff for herself! "But since my goal is to please the Almighty instead of self-indulgence, I must exercise godliness by sharing." She says. She believes that God wants her to live a good full life but also to care for the fatherless, homeless and widows indeed. A widow indeed is a woman whose husband is dead and she has no income and no other family members to care for her. She had read that command in First Timothy 5:16.

While she and Step went through the snug alleyway that Saturday, he trailing her in search of homeless men. She recalled how impressed she had been with the rich vs. poor parable. So much so that she did some research on the term 'poor'. And to her enlightenment, she discovered that 'poor' did not always literally mean physical impoverishment. She had found one answer in Matthews 5: 3. That scripture was part of what Bible scholars call the Beatitudes of Jesus. Jesus had said in his sermon on the mount, *"Blessed are the poor in spirit for theirs is the kingdom of heaven."* She learned that meant the spirit is lacking of essential nourishment. Man's spirit is poor without the Spirit of God. She recalled one day in Bible class how she had joyfully commented, "Now, I understand!" she had said. "When we allow God's Holy Spirit to take control of our carnal spirit, then our poor spirit follows God's— thus we are guided by His written word, the Bible and not by our own worldly wisdom." She was enlightened that she as a mortal without the Holy Spirit could never find her own way to heaven, because the path to heaven was not a physical one. "Flesh and blood cannot inherit heaven but the spiritual soul of man could," she had said that day in class. She recalled having read in First Corinthians 15:50, that flesh and blood could not inherit heaven. And to prove God wants all men to be rich in His spirit she had also read Luke 1:53, where Mary, Jesus' mother had said, "He hath filled the hungry with good tidings; and the rich (rich in his own spirit) he hath sent away empty." This was a spiritual prophecy concerning the coming of the Christ, who is able to give us of His Spirit.

The doctor believes that so much that she counsels her clients and the homeless about the Holy Spirit. That is the receptive ones who are willing to listen. However she knew that just as the Bible also teaches that not everyone would believe there is a heaven and hell. She recalled Galatians 3:22, "But the scripture has concluded all under sin that the promise by faith of Jesus Christ might be given to them that believe." Logically speaking, if some would believe, then some would not believe. Another scripture that caused her to believe in heaven as a real place was Matthew 19:23. There Jesus admonishes that a rich man could hardly enter into heaven. King Solomon in Proverbs 23:14 spoke of chastising a child in order to keep his soul out of hell. So while in Bible class that day she had commented, "And those couple of scriptures that claims there is a heaven and hell are just to name a few!" she had said. Even in a humble effort to save her clients' soul she was disappointed that for the most part her clients still preferred to leave her office laden down with drug prescriptions instead of carrying their burdens to the Lord and leaving them there.

Walking through the damp alleyway with Step on her heels, Dassah recalled the blessed day she was baptized and added to Christ's body his church. She had said to the minister, "I just hope I'm able to live accordingly!" As a new concert she still had difficulty shaking off worldly thoughts. Plus, she had perpetuated the hatred for her mother and the rapist. She also recalled how tight-fisted she had been when she first started to make some real money. No matter, who it was except, Jarvis that needed her financial help she would squeeze that dollar so tight until tears would run down Washington's cheeks. Even though she had been raised impoverished giving to the poor had simply not been on the agenda.

"Sister, you know that the *love* of money is the root of all evil," the minister had seriously said when she asked for prayer for the sin of being too stingy. Her lusty flesh had tempted her to rob God. Then she finally realized the gift of the Holy Ghost she had received when she was baptized could teach her how to loosen that vice on the dollar. And, as her riches began to increase through the makeover program and her practice, she would cry, "God it's really true! I *can't* out give you!" she had beamed looking at her bank statement.

Then Dassah sadly recalled a story in her home town about a woman everyone took for a destitute bag-lady. Then right after the fiftyish woman's sudden death they found her to be a warden of all the money she had begged for years. Absurdly, she had locked up thousands of dollars. As a child Dassah heard people talking after the death of that woman. Another family had found her body in a condemned house and discovered the money in four-layers of trash bags. All the time people thought the bags she lugged around contained nothing but clothing. And Dassah, at that time was such a poor girl herself wished it had been her who'd found that woman. "Even though that dead body would have scared me to death!" she now teases. She recalled what some neighbors had said, "The State is going to take that money anyway!" In the end the family that took the money had gone as friends to the morgue and saw to it the woman had a fairly decent burial. The police had been none the wiser about the money and nobody snitched. After that the young girl wondered daily why anyone would deny themselves a normal life just for the thrill of hording money. "Money was made to be spent!" she had said to her mother one day. But, now as a psychiatrist she attributes that to the woman's state of mental illness. "Stinginess ultimately robs one of a life of fulfillment!" she thought going through the alley, "People like that have to literally be forced into even buying themselves a meal, let alone a shirt to put on their back!" The State had tried to find the woman's family without the faintest clue where she was from. Even with pictures posted no family claimed her. "It was nothing short of utter insanity that she had no identification among all that stuff!" she thought going through the alley.

PART TWO

CHAPTER 5

As Doctor Dassah Desoto a psychiatrist and Stephanas Carter her bodyguard trekked deeper into the snowy alleyway in search of homeless men that Saturday morning in Neal, New York, again she recalled the beginning of the makeover program. And how she deeply regretted her attempt to house homeless women on the farm had failed. Additionally, how she also cautiously kept a suspicious eye on the homeless men that lived on the farm. "Rarely does men cry rape, but it's not beneath the dishonest ones to falsely claim maltreatment in order to sue the shirt off my back!" she had said to Callie her personal attorney. "I'm well aware that wherever there's the scent of money there're also greedy smellers just waiting to inhale it right into their own pockets." She had said, "And they'll do nothing short of pimping their own child to get a hold of money!" Her mother's long since deceased face had flashed before her eyes that day. But by now she has already forgiven her childhood enemies.

As Dassah with Step close on her heels, stepped over piles of snowy debris, Dassah desperately hoped to be taking some men back to her makeover farm today or no later than tomorrow. First she would give them a full breakfast in her limo. Then, if they were willing she would have them clean up in her lavish hotel in Upper Manhattan. Afterwards she would take them to the smallest of her three restaurants which is in Lower Manhattan. The homeless men could get a gut of special prepared goat meat and unique organic vegetables, all prepared by ex-homeless chefs. She only served farm-raised special buffalo meat at her two large restaurants. The entrepreneur doctor-of-the-mind snickered as she recalled not many men turned down joining up once she vividly described the goat dish to his watering palate and insanely growling belly. "Getting the men to believe it's all legitimate is where the work had lain!" she had told Callie one day. But she totally understood the men's apprehension was due to the fact that nothing that good in life came with such ease. "It's really, really true!" she recalled assuring the more mature ex-cons and homeless men. Strangely she had discovered it to be less trouble convincing the younger men to join her makeover team. She recalled one eighteen year old just coming out of prison. He had said he could not wait until he turned nineteen to join up with her. "I had no business in prison anyway!" he had exclaimed. "I was just a stupid kid of fifteen following the wrong crowd!" Sadly she discovered the boy never had a father in the home or any older male for a role model.

At that Dassah recalled a special program on the Discovery Channel. In Africa some researchers had rescued a male baby elephant from poachers. The animal was so tame and cute even growing up among other species of animals there at the rescue haven in Africa. But when the elephant finally reached adolescence he became rudely aggressive and began abusing other animals. He would harm them even to the point of chasing and killing hippos. This raised the brows of researchers, in that elephants were natural herbivores. The elephants had not killed got food. Then after many sleepless nights and close observations the researchers witnessed the teenage elephant suddenly being scolded by the male bull-elephants whenever he began to get disorderly with the other animals. Then the researchers discovered that the male elephants' chastisement kept the young males' hormones in check. This eventually taught them self-control. Amazingly the scare tactics of the older bulls lessened the hormones of the adolescents. Then Dassah marveled how people could so easily assess and then rehabilitate animals. When on the flip side they had not given a hoot about Black human adolescents. But rather researchers would prefer trying human kids as an adult. "I guess it's easier to just toss human children in prison!" she had huffed to Callie that day.

"But with the swiftness other races receives personal rehabilitation in a positive light!"

"You'd better know it, right?" the two angry girls, bumped fists in total agreement.

Then Callie, being an astute attorney, posed, "Why is it that this judicial system in certain cases shuns the reality that Black kids are also simply foolish kids. When on the other hand they never fail to defend other races of wayward adolescents?"

"The judicial system is apparently respecter of persons!"

Going through the narrow alleyway with Step right behind her, Dassah thought of the many young Black ex-cons that she had personally rehabilitated. Though, she would never turn down any race or gender that needed personal counseling. Then she had said to Callie that day, "And as you may know, no other races have problems getting favor from a judge," she had said, "In a courtroom, most judges will even recommend counseling for disobedient kids of other races . . . but rarely will he do the same for Black kids!"

Then Dassah took her thoughts back to her restaurants. She licked naturally full moist lips as her mouth watered about the food those ex-homeless chefs were now preparing for lunch. With the culinary training the men soon was prepared to clink knives with the best artists in New York. Most of the men already had innate talents for making recipes even if the dish was not on the menu. In the finer restaurant everyday customers would randomly bring in recipes, knowing it would be prepared just right. And with another generous gratuity aside from the regular tip the chefs would really put his foot in the dish. Even that extra tip the chefs and waiters earned went towards his upcoming small business and the care of his abandoned children. "You aren't in this to waste money on your fancy whims!!" she had scolded a man she caught trying not to report the fifty-dollar tip he had purposely tucked away in a secret pocket. "I thought I'd just take a honey out this weekend is all!" the now very nourished, polished looking man had pleaded, reluctantly handing over the money to Dassah.

"Are you serious!!?" snatching the bill, marveling at the man who had only a few more months to go in the program. "By now you should know to let the honeys know that they must pay their own way for just a bit longer!" The men were allowed only one weekend per month away from the farm in order to date.

Dassah recalled that soon after she had opened the restaurants how fame traveled around New York about the goat-buffalo dish. And before long visiting celebrities in the two large restaurants became as familiar as the big white Baby Grand pianos that sat in each restaurant. Also a full band of shiny instruments always poised on the wide platform ready for capable ex-homeless musicians and performers to entertain guests. "Let's make a night at Dassah' Super Fine Cru sine," guests would eagerly rush in. Those rich customers knew that when their tummies got full they could burn it off on the dance floor. The doctor seized every opportunity to utilize ex-homeless people for every service that she needed. And she was not surprised to find so many talented people roaming the streets in dire poverty. Some of those homeless people both male and female Black and White had been artists with plenty of money at one time. Unfortunately, they had wound up on drugs or other pitfalls had trapped them in. She was sorry to see that too many Blacks had difficulty handling such magnitude of money during the height of their show biz days. "As you may have learned by now that money and party life just don't mix!" she had later reminded them in their rehabilitation stage. "No doubt, you may have started out drinking beer only," she had said, "Then you may have graduated up to marijuana and then to cocaine and then to only God knows what!" she glared meanly out at the many undernourished races staring back. "When you make that much money with no particular goals in mind, you're able to afford those addictions . . . But then, finally when you become the unpopular junkie, your talent also refuses to shine anymore," she continued to scold. "I've never known a substance abuser to go in and practice on anything, right?!" she recalled heads nodding in sorrowful agreement that day. "Nevertheless, to restore you is what we're here for and not to brow-beat you for past mistakes," she had said as some were being re-taught to sing and play instruments.

Dassah reflected on the huge flourishing fish pond that was on the farm year round. The seafood there was guaranteed fresh and mercury free with nourishment fed fish. Each of the two restaurants had a one acre lake in back for the customers to fish for their own meal. Ten they would have the fish prepared right there in only minutes. The atmosphere was filled with all kinds of trees and blooming greenery. The artificial greenery that was used as fillers sometimes even fooled Dassah. "Our senior citizens will absolutely love this inside lake during the winter seasons!" she had said during its construction. She was right. The reservation list for fishing is never short. With an insect-free environment the wealthy elderly guests are always kept happy. Dassah smiles at how she treats the lake with good fishing water to keep the customers healthy. "This is the best bass I've ever ate!" a wealthy elderly man had boasted while gobbling the special-battered coconut-oil-fried catch.

Dassah recalled that the men understood that working on the farm was part of the two-year training. She was grateful that the sensitive men would go the extra mile while working the farm. Some of them did not mind for putting in extra efforts by raising the animals with loving kindness. His love for them would move him to take care of the animals with zeal. She would hear many of them say to the animals, "Just like us humans and plants so can you feel when you're loved!" The men quickly learned that a happy animal produced less adrenalin hormones during the slaughter. Dassah believed wholeheartedly that what you eat is what you are! And when she saw satisfied customers in search of a healthy lifestyle she praised God for giving her the vision for the program. She sadly realized there were way too many slaughter farms that placed emphasis on making money rather than consumer health.

Then after the program process some of the men just would rather work on the farm instead of owning his, own business. Which, she discouraged so that the other men could have their opportunity on the farm. If she allowed all the men who graduated permanent jobs on the farm then other ex-homeless men would not have their fair chance. Plus the farm would too quickly become over crowded. However she does make a few exceptions. Some men are allowed permanent positions due to severe diagnosed introvert-ism. With this type of mental illness it proves imperative that he avoid the unpredictable rat-race altogether. She recalled how during her search she had discovered most of the anti-social homeless men simply off sitting in a corner of the alley alone as other men interacted with each other. This type of mental illness always filled her eyes with tears, "The poor introvert never would be able to have their mental condition accepted in an outside work place," she thought going through the alley, Step close on her heels. She recalled how those introverts in her program are privileged with permanent jobs. They are not paid but rather room, board and all necessities was compensation for as long as she saw fit. It had been his choice not to let the outside world into his life. A few introverts has been on the farm ever since the program began 8 years ago. She kept them because they were very hard workers. She never saw them standing around jaw-jacking.

While going through the snow flurried alleyway, the buildings were warding off most of the snow. Then Dassah smiled thinking about being the owner of one of the largest malls in Manhattan. The social gym with its huge health bar never closed. The night spot there had an exotic grocery nook which emphasizes herbal products. It has vitamins and all brands of natural heath enhancers. For movie goers and athletes the theatre and school of Martial Arts is famous statewide. The clothing stores with every fashion imaginable, caters to the great demands of movie stars even for personal tailoring. Dassah recalled how thrilled she was to discover many of the homeless people, men and women had been tailors, or had sewing backgrounds. Some had learned certain other useful skills in prison. Her real estate firm is extra ordinary in that she is able to offers below average interest rates. The doctor smiled again realizing all the stores in the mall belonged to her, "And that certainly would not be possible were it not for the makeover program and the small salary I'm allowed to pay them!" she thought, smiling. Though, in some stores many managers were educated, non-ex-homeless females. "I'm a woman myself, so why would I ever discriminate against one?" she had flung at the investigating detective who came to check out the bogus, envious accusation brought against her by a woman. And the under-wage-requirement she paid the ex-homeless workers was because she afforded them room and board to boot.

Dassah recalled how the successful man would have passed both the physical and psychological test before going further into the program. And finding out if he had children was the number one priority. If he had children, then the homeless man would first find his dependent children and sign an agreement to provide according to the letter of the law when he began his business. But as long as he was making progress in the program the government would assist with his children. If he in any way showed that he would not complete the program, then he would be reprimanded by the government, "Would you rather work for yourself or give us free labor in prison?!" would be the million-dollar-question. "Ain't nothin' wrong with me workin' for myself!" one young Black man with five children had answered. "I've spent six years on the streets with no hope . . . now at last one day I'll have my own business and get my family back!"

Going through the narrow, snowy alleyway with Step on her heels, Dassah recalled her business partners and how she had worked independent of any in the beginning. Then the makeover program and practice began to excel by leaps and bounds until it was imperative that she take on a few sincere associates. Her sister-in-law and now second best friend, A-lo-ma was one of those minor share-holders. Jarvis was her best friend and not aware that A-lo-ma held a lavish portion of the dynasty. A-lo-ma had whispered to her the day of signing the agreement, "If I died first, Jarvis and the kids will get a surprise chunk of change aside from the regular four-million dollars policy." she had snickered her pretty brown face lighting up like a school girl with a secret.

"Smart Gal!" Dassah had beamed happy to know someone else in the family was as frugal as herself.

Dassah recalled the day the government replied to her grant regarding the overall makeover program. It seemed they were just as ecstatic to clear the blight of homelessness off the streets of New York. Though it deeply disturbed her to know the government's concern were leaning largely towards the loss of revenue due to all the homeless pestering. Nevertheless, the doctor also was broad-minded enough to know that tourism was necessary for any city to thrive and succeed. It was at the same time that she had submitted her grant proposal that a disturbing pan-handling ban against the homeless was also knocking at the door of the county. To the perplexed officials it had been like a cool drink of well water to have half of the problem licked. During that critical ban her makeover proposal was readily welcome. So with the swiftness their approval for the purchase of farm land was put in writing. And the only retribution the government asked was that the streets and parks of New York be white-washed of homeless folks. She did not have to pay back one red cent, except for taxes on her income like everyone else.

Finally Dassah snapped out of deep thought that Saturday morning in Neal, New York. With her hood off for the moment she glanced back over her shoulder at Step dutifully on her heels. And in return, with his hood over a low hair-cut, he raised an inquisitive brow, "What's up Doc?" through a very appealing lip-line. Most people say he and L. L. Cool J. could be twins—Only Step was the dark skinned twin.

She glanced back at the 25-year old, "Just thinking how you're a success story I'm proud to show-n-tell, Stephanas Carter," she grinned big. She visualized how he has been the main attractions in her male Fashion, Business Readiness shows. Only he had not been seeking business ownership. After only a year and a half into the program and having gotten his high school diploma, she had asked him to become her personal protector. He is now a part-time freshman in college. Yet he is still the main participant in shows for the fun of it and to impress the honeys.

"Boss!" he frowned at the back of her shiny auburn curls, sprinkled with tiny snowflakes, "How many times have I asked you not to call me Stephanas, Step will do?" With respect in his baritone voice, "You know how I simply *loathe* my complete name."

"Yeah, I know . . . forgive me, Step." She pulled up the hood and glanced at the inexpensive watch she normally wore when scouting. Outside she pulled out her cell phone as little as possible. It was 8:47.

CHAPTER 6

There in Neal, New York, walking through the snowy alleyway Doctor Dassah Desoto a psychiatrist was in the lead. Stephanas Carter her buffed bodyguard was close behind her. At the mention of first full name, which was his father's, he reflected agonizingly on his father. They were in search of homeless men for the doctor's depleting makeover program. The doctor had sent a large batch of men into their own businesses. Some had gone back to the church of Christ and engaged in a soul saving profitable work there. She needed more to replace those.

Trailing his boss that morning Step recalled how he and his two younger brothers were torn away from his already ripped apart family and placed in an orphanage at the age of seven. He had loved his father his idol, who had abandoned the family when Step was six and by that age he had bonded with his father. Step was the first born and wore his father's name. Afterwards his mother did not give them up right away but tried her very best to raise them. Finally all worn out she had succumbed to hypertension and deep depression. So, in order not to beat her children to death she surrendered them to DFACS. Step had made

Dassah aware of the toils of his past as all the program participants had to do. But then she could only wish her mother had been so brave as to give up her children as opposed to abuse. She and Step would have had a mouth full to say to each other about that. But then she always kept her past from her clients. "I'm the one who's supposed to be doing the psyche work!" she would think.

Step recalled how he was raised in foster homes by people only taking him for the puny amount of money. By the age of thirteen he had a rep for running away from those families. Most of the foster families had children of their own and older than he was. He got beat up a lot in those homes. When the young child would run away they would only drag him back. As Step recalled his last mad dash was at the age of fifteen—finally able to get lost in the grimiest parts of New York. At the age of fifteen he sometimes dangerously spent several days with people he met along the way. Then feeding him became a burden on them. Plus their utility bill began to soar from his having to bathe and wash what few clothes he had. As he sadly recalled after that street life was his appalling crutch up until he turned nineteen. And without legal identification and no money to forge ID, it had been impossible for a teenager to get a job in New York. But when he turned eighteen and sprouted a beard that got him jobs by standing in line on corners. Construction work became his closest friend. Those cash wages were convenient but not nearly sufficient to get him settled into a place of his own. Occasionally a room at cheap hotels that required no ID provided a bit of refuge from the elements. However in winter construction was at a slug's pace but the lad sense enough to thank God when the seasons of plenty rolled around.

As a homeless teen the embarrassment of panhandling was a serious blow to his self-esteem. Being homeless had not blotted out the typical sensitive-hearted boy he really was. While panhandling on his favorite corners he would pray that girls would not stare at his clothes. But especially he hated sporting those ditty tennis shoes. Air, Jordan and Nikes were merely labels as far as he knew. In fact wearing any name brand were a stretch of the imagination. Those profitable corners just happened to be in downtown Manhattan where all the well-to-do frequented. There he knew he would at least return to his cardboard home with enough to purchase more office supplies to sell. That area was also where the prettiest girls shopped. There going through the snowy alley, Step snickered under his breath, "It's that certain something about teenagers and shoes that make them that special creature!" He looked ahead at Dassah walking through the alley. He recalled how the first thing most girls did was to look down at his feet. And as soon as her eyes fell on his shoes he knew there was no need to even speak to her. "Teenagers can be so superficial!" he thought there following Dassah. Then his handsome eyes went proudly to the 270-dollar Timberlands now on his size 13feet. "Feast your eyes on my feet now you snotty girls!" humorously, he snickered. Then he recalled how dating had only been his nightly fantasies. "I missed out completely on pubescent," he thought, not having his first real kiss until he was almost eighteen—from a homeless, 40-something woman.

Not ever dating girls his own age made him want even more to strangle his father with his bare hands. Even though Step had not found his mother he had long forgiven her. She had persevered for as long as she possibly could and was dealing with her husband leaving her with three small boys. "Some people are simply too weak without a mate to help raise the children," he made excuses for his mother, picturing her defeated face. However he did not look forward to finding and facing her now as a grown man. "Maybe someday I'll get the desire to look for her and my brothers," he thought. His brothers had also gone to foster homes before he did. The younger kids were always the first choice. Deep down Step really knew it was the fear of what he would find out about his brothers—his mind went to the worst case scenario for Black boys. He was now 25 so they were 22 and 20.

He walked on along behind Dassah through the snowy alleyway in search of homeless men. As well he was eager to get the men off the cruel streets of Neal, New York for good.

He recalled being only nineteen and feeling he had lived for an eternity. He felt his life was over even at that tender age. Then one chilly afternoon he and a 28 year old homeless friend had sat sulking on a park bench watching people scurry back to the comfort of the office. And against Step's better judgment not to steal he had huffed, "Let's just rob a store or a bank!" his stomach growling louder than his voice talked. That morning's breakfast at the mission had already digested into his still growing body. Plus he had just pitifully begged a store owner to let him use the restroom. The man finally let him in and shoved some cleaner and a toilet brush at him, "After you've finished you be sure to wash down that stool real good, ya' hear!?"

"Yes Sir!" Step knew he had better be nice for future use of the restroom. So many store owners would not even dare allow a smelly homeless person the use of the same stool they had to sit on. So as a special favor he would scrub that floor and toilet until they shined. That manager finally offered him a one day a week job keeping the toilet clean. He had paid him only 15 dollars but that money was like 150 dollars to Step.

Then Step recalled that day his partner was all game for hitting the little bank across from the park. His friend had eagerly said, "Let's do it man!" in that he had long since given up hope of getting off the streets anyway. So right there on the park bench they began to plot about the bank that had only one guard. They could talk openly not having to worry about anyone overhearing. No one, with their nice cleanness would dare sit beside two dirty ragged men. The two decided to keep the plan between themselves so their peers could honestly say they knew nothing if ever questioned. So, the following day with anticipation they were set to pull it off with an old rusty gun they had—no bullets in it. Then Step on the day of the fiendish heist before the bank opened while in his cardboard bed, was approached by Dassah and her then stone-faced bodyguard. He recalled the day of planning there on the park bench. He had told his friend, "If everything goes according to plan and we hit pay-dirt, then I'll take the money . . . we'll split up and go duck in and out of these alleys . . . then we'll calmly start walking . . . the guard won't dare come after us, because he'll think we have guns that work. . . afterwards I'll bury the money in an alley, okay?"

Then his friend had frowned twisting an unkempt beard, "Now how far do you expect we'll get on foot lugging a bag of stolen money and with these ragged coats!?"

I figured that out too . . . we'll only demand two or three stacks of money. . . several thousand should get us back on our feet. . . we ain't greedy just hungry And we'll get better coats from the mission and have them hidden to change into afterwards!" Step had assured his friend.

"Sounds like a winner . . . but where will we meet up at?"

"We'll have to lay low for a couple of days, and then meet back at our usual boxes."

Step recalled how his friend had begun to scratch his head, confused, "Come to think of it man, it'll be easy for you to lay low for a few days since you'll have some money . . . that's why we're stealin' in the first place is because we're hungry now remember?"

"I guess you're right. . . Well, let's just plan to meet back in the boxes the same night. I'll bring you some vittles . . . what would you like to eat?" Step recalled that at the mention of food that day both their gut grumbled a simultaneous song. He recalled how at the mere mention of fool, there on the park bench, his friend's dingy eyes had lit up, "Man, bring me some barbecued ribs, Brunswick stew, donuts . . ."

But before the list could get any longer, Step threw up a hand to his friend's face, "Whoa, Man if I go bringing all that food then people will surely get suspicious!" They laughed realizing no fancy-food-feasts ever happened up in those alleys.

"Well okay, just bring whatever you can as long as it's hot!" a gust of wind rocked him there on the park bench.

Step had replied, "Then back in our old coats no one would be the wiser. Even if we get caught, then in prison at least we'll eat every day and those tiny cots are more inviting than having to pick gravel out of our butt every morning!" They had planned to sit all day at a shelter just to beg for better clothing for the bank robbery.

Step knew it was wrong to steal what other's had worked so hard for, but at nineteen he was always famished and very weary. Then that fateful morning of the bank heist peeking out of his cardboard box, he heard the four words that changed his life. The sweet smelling woman had bent down in his face and propositioned, "Need a job, Sir?" He recalled how that offer gave him a rope of hope for which he would be forever grateful. But not before the enduring doctor spent the entire morning convincing him she was legitimate. Before that the youthful, lanky lad had been approached by a man with other arterial motives. But being a live-in bed partner was not the "straight" homeless lad's desire. So Step had flat-footed instructed the gay man what to do with that huge amount of money he offered. Finally, that day Step conceded to Dassah' appealing, and what he felt was a decent offer. He and his almost partner in crime and two other men had a hot breakfast in her limo that memorable mid-fall morning there in Manhattan. Afterwards they had taken her infamous blind-fold, three-hour drive to one of her hotels to begin a new life. "That was six years ago," Step thought, trailing her through the snowy alley. Nevertheless, as a depraved 19-year-old, it tickled his dark face pink just to spend the night in a hotel. The video games and cable were always at hand and he learned fast. Also back then he had only *heard* of the adult channels.

As they cautiously walked along the narrow alleyway, fine snow flurries, Step pictured his friend now in his own locksmith business. He snickered at him picking combinations not only for banks, but for fine cars and homes—trustworthily for the past four years.

While walking along behind his boss, flexing his mussels under his coat as an away from the gym exercise, Step recalled the magical transformation he had undergone after just three months of total wholesome discipline. His counselors always advised the men that with abstinence from smoking, drinking and drugs they would soon turn into a superman. Though, Step never had taken up smoking or drugs, mainly because he could not afford any. "It was not that the unbelievable madness of the streets wouldn't drive one to drink!" he had sighed to one of his therapists one day. Even now he only drank an occasional beer and even then he had to be pressured by a buddy. After witnessing the devastating effect alcohol had on some of his street buddies, especially those that could not afford the habit, had stung him. He recalled how the alcoholics would awake each morning with uncontrollable shakes. Then the homeless alcoholics would sadly realize that the last of last night's cheap wine had been his night-cap. Then, later that day when these homeless alcoholics would finally beg enough money again, they would rather buy a bottle than to eat.

Step watching Dassah walk ahead of him recalled how she now proudly poked fun at him about his new addiction to self-empowerment, "If you'd done time for bank robbery, I shudder to think what could've happen to a boy of nineteen in prison," she had seriously said to the new recruit to whom she had grown attached.

Trailing Dassah Step could not help but to take in her gracefulness again. More often, nowadays he found himself admiring his boss. "She really doesn't look any older than me!" he would think, "You're only fourteen years older Boss, so don't be so picky!" he only thought. Again Step recalled the 'sweet' salary deposited into his bank account bi-weekly. "No date is worth tossing that, not to mention my decked-out pad where I can date whomever I so desire!" he thought but still discreetly admiring her natural sway ahead of him.

She, as well knew he gawked. "I'm truly flattered, but I hope he decides to keep things between us just the way they are," she thought. "It would deeply grieve me if I had to fire the greatest bodyguard in the world!"

There going through the narrow alleyway, now stepping over one pile of debris after another, Dassah and Step were almost at their destination—the homeless hide-away. With light snowflakes before her light brown eyes, Dassah wondered if she could ever have a serious relationship as of yet she had not. Only an occasional short date was ever written in her diary of romance. And since she was now a Christian and not married, fornication was out of the question. She recalled how the dates she had told about her celibacy only laughed in her serious face, "Honey thirty-nine is old enough to be a grandma!" one had sneered. Nevertheless, her vow to wait until she was wed was held very sacred. Neither Step nor her other clients were aware that she was not really a virgin.

As they trek through the alley she recalled another one of her dates. She was beginning to have high hopes towards this one. Then one night he had disdainfully said, "You know Dassah, you just might die unmarried," indicating he would never marry before he had sex with her first. Then he had looked seriously into her eyes, "If you died in celibacy, then what?" stupidity sounded in his deep voice.

"What then?" she had snapped, "I'd just be a dead, single, obedient Christian gone to heaven! Many women have died having *never* done it but trusted in the Lord to keep them pure!"

"Those women were nuns."

In the quaint candle-lit café Dassah had stared disgustingly at her date whom she had felt was so good-looking. Now he resembled and talked just like a dummy. At that moment she was grateful she had withheld her past from him. In her opinion she had never had sex before and was still a virgin. Then she recalled that the second willing experience before she became a Christian was almost as horrible as the rape. During that willing act she had visualized her partner as the rapist. Then again the psyche in her had been unable to counsel her-self.

So there in the candle-lit cafe her date had sensed the issues in her and slowed his roll a bit. With more compassion he suddenly abandoned any expectations of her and simply never asked her out again—even in spite of her millions. "Another one bites the dust!" she had thought.

In the narrow alleyway with Step on her heels, Dassah recalled the outcome the night of the rape. That same sleepless night she had figured out that her own mother had sold her. "It wasn't enough that woman would defile her own body but she also did her little girl's," Dassah had madly thought. Dassah recalled there in her house in her mother's room, after her mother had left on a date. "My virgin days are truly over," she had whispered so that Jarvis would not hear, "I'm a woman now!" To add insult to injury the sanitary napkins she wore for two weeks reminded the teen that she also had a serious internal injury. But finally it healed by itself. She recalled how rarely people went to the hospital in her hood. Aspirin, rubbing alcohol, peroxide and band aids were highly favored. Everyone would suffer a toothache either until it rotted out or simply had to be extracted at the free clinic. Sadly the decayed-to-the-gum tooth would only be pulled because aspirin no longer was effective. So, for many reasons her mother refused to allow her to see a doctor—mainly for the rape herself would be arrested. Now in spite of Dassah having the scar checked regularly she yet experiences extreme tenderness in the area. As a doctor she knows the scar will always be sensitive, occasionally, like any incision. Of all of the inconveniences the worse was bearing the mental scar of never being able to have a baby. She recalled one day in her doctor's office. The kind older doctor, that only age she would allow to touch her. He had sat her down and frankly said, "Dassah, now as a doctor yourself you realize that you didn't receive immediate medical attention. So in that case you know that you'll be damaged for life," he had assured, "Your twisted uterus could've easily have been re-positioned . . . and with stitches the tear would've mended without much future discomfort. . . And probably with adolescent mental therapy you would've been almost like new by now," he had sighed.

While going through the snow-flurried alley with Step on her heels, Dassah reluctantly recalled the outcome of the night she finally emerged from the bathroom. The near scalding water had added to the existing pain of her 15-year-old body. "Jarvis!" she had snapped at her three years younger brother. "Where did you get money for those potato chips?"

"A ten dollar bill was in the hall and Mama had lots more money. . . Did you get paid today too," innocent prodding while watching television and cramming hands full of chips. He knew that on paydays Dassah always handed over to their mother what money was left after buying groceries. Most of her money went for food and shoes for Jarvis.

Standing there in her only thread-bear faded robe body aching, suspicion had narrowed the girl's bloodshot eyes. Her mother had taken the money void of any questions. Dassah never saw the money or the white, bloody envelope again and was too afraid to ask. She also never saw that one of her mother's boyfriend at the house again. In the days that followed Dassah began to meditate on her mother getting paid to let him spoil her virgin daughter. But Dassah also realized that something good had emerged from the sordid ordeal. Her mother's apparent mental disorder had compelled her daughter to become the psychiatrist she is. "Had my mother not been *crazy*, probably I never would've had any interest in being a shrink and never to gain millions of dollars," she was able to smile about it now. She recalled her real medical quest was to understand why parents abused were part of their own flesh and blood. She used to marvel that her mother never once verbalized any hatred for Jarvis. "She simply made the poor boy non-existent altogether!" she thought going through the alley. She recalled her mother would leave Jarvis when he was a baby, with their grandmother. "At least he received some kind of affection as an infant!" Dassah thought. She strained to summon a vision of her mother ever fondling Jarvis as good mothers did. And as they grew whenever Jarvis needed something he learned to count on Me-ma or Sis, who was not but three years older. Now, as a psychiatrist she knows that an abusive parent sometimes have one particular child on which to use for their 'battering ram'. But in her mother's case she had channeled both her children using different methods of abuse on each. Dassah recalled the abuse she suffered at the hands of her mother was to get punched, screamed at, and handed over to others to also abuse. As for Jarvis, their mother had displayed openly that he was not deserving of her love. As a result Dassah' own little brother is now one of her most frequent clients—the only psyche he will trust, in that it brings the grown man to rocking tears whenever he recalls. "Why did she hate me so much when all I did was try to get her to hug me just one time?!" he would sob. "I just wanted to be loved by my mother like I'd seen other boys get!"

"I know Jarvis, so did I want her love," calmly assuring him he was not alone in this.

Then from the couch, he would say, "But, thank God I had you, Sis or I wouldn't have been able to deal with those nightmares where you always came to my rescue!"

"Yes, I remember those scary nights when she was gone for the night or in her room entertaining another man," Dassah would comfort him even now.

Dassah recalled learning in med school that a selfish parent was famous for pitching temper tantrums just to get their way. And the silent treatment was also a selfish type of sulking attitude that got them attention. The doctor also discovered that many abuse recipients would give their right arm to avoid having someone they love turn on the silent treatment. And the abuser is keenly aware of how that truly hurts their victim. Her mother knew very well that a silent treatment stung her young son.

The doctor recalled one day while counseling a child-abuser she had insisted they engage in role-play as part of a healing therapy. During those sessions she would force the parent to perform nothing but kindness towards the battered child for a change. "At times it becomes necessary to teach all over again how to love another," she would counsel. In that role-play, if a parent sincerely wanted anger-management, then each day he must say nothing but impressionable things to the child, even when the child made a mistake. Subsequently, though it was a very slow process in some cases each compliment produced a bit more self-esteem in the child. Additionally, in some cases the doctor insisted on role-reversal. As the result of that she had many of the abusers complain that being yelled at or totally ignored, or hit did not feel so good when the shoe was on the other foot. "No one likes that inferior feeling, or to be belittled!" she said to the once abusive now crying for forgiveness parent. And as another result some children had practically become extroverts. "A performance of love is the best prescription I've ever written!" she had complimented the patched up parents, "But the bona-fide answer to love is to acquire the mind of Christ!" she would say, "I'm sure you've heard how Jesus wasn't self-centered at all, even during an unnecessarily cruel crucifixion which the Romans practiced in that day! I've prescribed many a pills for mental instability but the love-your-neighbor pill has yet to be invented!" Then she recalled the day she said that. A male doctor had come into the office as she was talking to her patient. Then, finally Dassah and the doctor were alone. Very neatly dressed wearing a suit tie and a wily grin, he had approached the beautiful, unsuspecting Dassah. "I heard what you said, Doctor Dassah."

Then with surprise in her youthful light brown eyes she gazed up at him from her desk, "Oh, I'm sure you did," she simply shrugged.

"Well I disagree there hadn't been a love-your-neighbor pill invented," he parked a taut buttock on the edge of her desk, gazing seductively into her eyes.

More surprise in hers, "And what's that supposed to mean, Doctor Tad?"

"I've heard that Viagra was the greatest invention since the toothbrush. . . . That love pill you just wished for," he winked a very handsome blue eye.

She scowled, "Once again, Doc, I find it seriously necessary to educate you as to the difference between love and lust!" She whacked his buttock with the prescription pad. "And, again, I order you to get off my desk!" They laughed, hers forced. Dassah was thankful she still had somewhat a sense of humor when the male associates got fresh with her. However, as a Christian, sex jokes were not her cup of coffee. Tad, among other doctors she had hired to partner with, had crushes on her. And, none of her co-workers knew about the rape and its effect on her. She had now become paranoid that every man that made a pass at her was out for either her money or her body, or both. She was not unaware that rape could happen to anyone. The problem she had was letting others know she was raised by an insane mother who had arranged the rape.

Walking through the snow flurried alleyway Dassah recalled that taking the best of care of her mother who laid flat on her back with AIDS was proof that Dassah had forgiven her long before Dassah admitted that forgiveness. Though Dassah had reasons for revenge she had made a conscience decision to make her mother's last days comfortable. Plus, she really loved her mother. The day her mother died Dassah was sure she felt her mother gently squeeze her hand—the first time she actually felt her hand except for a slap across the face. That warm evening in that same hot little house, as her mother had lain dying, Dassah had thought, "Sometimes in life we find ourselves depending on the very ones we've hated and used." But sadly Dassah recalled how she could not get Jarvis to go near their mother on her sick bed. Only when Dassah came home from school at the in-town college would her mother get changed and fed. Jarvis at 17 would be the first home from high school. He sometimes would find his mother struggling to reach a glass of water. But he would strangely and quickly pass on by her sick room. One day as he passed on by he heard the crash of glass on the floor. Then he purposely backed up and peered into the room. He saw her hanging over the side of the bed frantically reaching for the other glass of water on the table. Then she had noticed Jarvis peeping in but refused to ask for help. He simply stood there for a few minutes. They eyed each other for the first time in his life. Then resentment really overwhelmed the lad. Still simply watching her as she was finally was able to pull her body back into bed. Now as an adult Jarvis had confided in Dassah how good it had made him feel to finally get revenge—he'd had a chance to ignore her when she needed him. But there in her office Dassah, the Christian had scolded, "Jarvis, you should never stoop so as to seek revenge on your enemy?"

"And why shouldn't I be pissed at her Doc?" he always called her that in the office. "So should you hate her because of the way she would go up beside of your head for no reason at all!" honesty was in his now deep voice. Jarvis was not a Christian at all as Dassah had since become. And, of course ever since leaving their grandparents they had not even picked up the Bible while living with their mother.

That day Dassah had said, "Here!" shoving her worn Bible into his hands. "Turn to Romans, chapter twelve, and verse twenty."

Fumbling from the front of the Bible to the back in search of Romans he finally looked at the table of contents. "Oh, there the page number is!" he began to read, "Therefore, if thine enemy hunger, feed him, if he thirst, give him drink: for in so doing, thou shalt heap coals of fire upon his head." Frowning, he had paused. "What does it mean to heap coals of fire upon an enemy's head?"

Happily, "By doing well to your enemy, when they need you will shame him for having done you wrong when you needed him. . . Go on and read the next verse."

"Be not overcome of evil, but overcome evil with good."

"Now do you understand?"

Long hesitation and then, "I guess so, Sis! I guess this word is right . . . I do recall Me-Pa always reading the Bible."

"Uh-huh" their professionalism had vanished and she was Sis again. "And I did get very, very angry whenever she'd slap me around! I even hated her and wished she would die so we could be someone else's children." She had paused, taking the Bible back. "Did I ever tell you that several rimes I had contemplated running away from home?"

He sat straight up with a jolt, "No way, Sis! You were just going to leave me with her!?" becoming the frightened little boy all over again.

"No, the thought of you was the only thing that kept me nailed down and enduring that suffering. . . I love you Little Bro!" reaching for him the way she did back then.

Moving into her motherly arms the way he did back then, only him now looming over her, they stood embracing warmly. "I love you too, Sis! What would I ever have done if you had run away? Surely she would've killed me by now! Thank you for getting me through school and college, Ma."

She reached a tiny, brown hand up and rung his dark ear, "And I ain't your ma either, Sis will do. I'm only three years older than you, ya know!" They had laughed away the bad memories.

There in the alley Dassah shook her head, "Sad he did not even know his own mother and they lived in the same house!"

As her mother lay dying, Dassah between school work and caring for her family the then seventeen-year-old girl was always worn to a frazzle. But she was grateful that Jarvis was fourteen and able to finally step up and help himself. But, like any male teens he still needed prodding. "Thank God my mother had only the two!" Dassah would often exhale.

Going through the alley in search of homeless men for her makeover program Dassah struggled to remember something positive about her mother. "At least she managed to keep a roof over our heads. . ." she said aloud, "or was that only to keep a roof over her own head?"

"Huh?" Step asked in back of her in the snowy alleyway.

"Oh, it's nothing," she finally said. ". . . just talking to myself . . . again!" She knew there was no acceptable excuse for her mother not working on a real job to feed her children. She had only paid rent and then partied off the rest of the money she got from Dassah and those men. Dassah recalled the many other poor children in the same neighborhood that had single parents who worked legitimate jobs. As a child she would longingly notice how kindly other parents acted with their children. So like any other findings the doctor ruled out poverty as an excuse for her mother's mistreatment of them.

Then Dassah recalled being a freshman in college. She had attended college there in Victory, Georgia to be near Jarvis and still work nights to support him. She was then nineteen and with her mother completely disabled teachers had appealed to the State to allow Dassah to assume the role of head of household. They finally got a real check from Welfare. "I'm certainly experienced at taking care of the household!" she had said to a teacher that had now learned about her past. At least now Jarvis had plenty of food from the food stamps. At that time as a sixteen year old Black male she would not allow Jarvis to work. In her opinion studying for the SAT and his homework was number one. She had won scholarships for maintaining a 3.9 GPA. "Only God knows how I managed that!" she thought many times. And finally finishing college with all the responsibilities she'd had, she knew it had been nothing short of a miracle from the Almighty. Along with grants and the Welfare check she made it through. Any other income came from her father, Mr. Desoto whom she just had, at the age of nineteen learned he was her father. All the time they lived there he had been the Puerto Rican man that owned the liquor store adjacent to their little house. Mr. Desoto and his wife had opened the store there right after Dassah' family moved in. And right before the death of her mother he would sneak money to Dassah unknown to his wife—or so he thought his wife was that gullible. But that remained to be seen.

Then years passed and Dassah finally finished med school which she had also attended in town. She had sent Jarvis away to college where he had to repeat his freshman year—she could not be there to prod him.

So there she was now a refined 29 year old woman packing to move out of their old house next to her father's liquor store. She would gladly leave the shabby furniture for the next struggling family. "One man's rusty iron bathtub could be another man's golden tub. "I can't believe I'm finally a doctor!" That day she proceeded to whistle as she folded the few nicer things she now owned. Suddenly she was distracted by the back door squeaking slowly open, a very familiar sound. And to her surprise there stood the thin frame of a woman—it was Mrs. Desoto—the first time she had ever set foot in the house or even spoke to Dassah. Dassah and her family had moved there when Dassah was eight. She was nineteen before she even knew the well-to-do liquor store owner, who turned people into alcoholics, was her father. She had always adored his SUV in which she would look at her young outdated reflection on the way to school. Her mother had haphazardly told her one day on her sick bed. At the end her mother had become very feeble-minded. Dassah had been late getting in from work and was pressed to do her homework. "Where have you been!?" was the greeting Dassah had received from a weakened voice.

"What do you mean, where have I been? You know I have to work!"

"Oh, you're just so sneaky like your old lying pappy next door!" she had weakly waved Dassah off. That discovery floored Dassah and Jarvis who had heard from the hall. "And where is my father!?" the sixteen year old had seriously stuck his head in, looking at Dassah—not to ask his mother the only one who could answer that. "Ma-ma, where is Jarvis' father?" Dassah asked for him.

"I don't have time to talk about that!" was a weak reply from the now blotchy-skin woman. All the loveliness had disappeared behind a very sickly appearance. Jarvis had not seen his father since he was a baby at their grandmother's—too young to even remember him.

Walking through the alleyway Dassah recalled how she had been truly startled by Mrs. Desoto that day. She turned around to find the reddish, timid looking middle-aged woman staring blankly at her pack. Mrs. Desoto had known all along that her mother had played the whore with her husband. "You've always been the spittin' image of my husband's mother—only with a deeper skin-tone," she had softly assessed. "When we first moved over there my husband would rush to the window every time he saw you outside. . . So, soon I began to use the sense God gave me!" she had huffed. "That lying cheat denied it on his dead mother's grave!" Dassah recalled how tired and haggard Mrs. Desoto looked that day. She was always in the liquor store busy cutting open boxes. The exhausted woman had breathed, "Too bad I wasn't woman enough to give him children." She even found the need to blame herself instead of accursing the guilty party. "He just couldn't raise anybody else's children by adoption." Then just as quietly as she came she spun around and walked out. But before she would exit, she said, "I should've told your grandmother before she died that it was my husband that took advantage of your young mother!" Mrs. Desoto had not known at the time Dassah was born, but had plenty of time to apologize to Dassah' grandmother when she found out. Then Mrs. Desoto rushed out, seemingly too ashamed to look back.

Without the first word uttered to her Dassah had stood watching her puny back. "How could you just sit quietly by and let such a situation continue for so long?" she was tempted to scream after her. "But that's their business!" the now doctor finally sighed, throwing things into the brand new luggage "I'm just glad to finally be out of here!" Yet it pained her to know she was the product of such insanity. Her father was 30 when he impregnated Dassah' fourteen year old mother. "What a pair for parents, a child-molester and a prostitute!" she thought.

Dassah had also learned that the little run down house in which they lived all those years had belonged to her father. "So my mother hadn't paid rent after all!" anger rocked her again at her mother having money and never using any on her children. And the mystery of why the family had not gotten evicted after her mother fell ill, and then died, was finally clear to her.

Going through the alley she recalled she was 29 when she finished med school and moved out of the house to New York where she started a psychiatric practice. Jarvis, the only part of her past she cared to remember had graduated college and was about to finish accounting at a university out of town. At this point her father, as far as she was concerned, was just as dead as her mother—both being guilty of betraying her. "He should have been there when his little girl was violated!" fine snowflakes before her eyes. "He never even knew I was raped . . . and as a father he was responsible for acknowledging me no matter what the consequences would've been!" A tear threaten to fall but she squeezed it back, "God forbid that I should also allow him to make me bawl!"

CHAPTER 7

S tephanas Carter, Doctor Dassah Desoto bodyguard glanced at his watch while trailing his boss. It was 9:01 that Saturday morning in Neal, New York. He and Dassah, the famed psychiatrist walked deeper into the alleyway stepping over debris. The doctor was in search of homeless men to join the makeover program to benefit both them and her.

Step recalled being a weary nineteen year old, going on forty when the beautiful doctor had also found him on the streets. "Anyway, where else is there for us referring to his friend to go *but* to jail?!" he had snapped at her before she was finally able to convince him to come along. "My teen-hood can never be recovered now!" he had snapped, realizing he would soon be twenty and had been on the streets since the unripe age of fifteen. At the time she approached him he had just the day before seriously mapped out a plan to rob a bank. He had figured all he had left was 'balls' and he would use that gallantry to his advantage. "Maybe robbing a bank just this once could buy us a fresh start!" he had said to his homeless nearly partner in crime.

Step vividly recalled his first couple of years on the streets in strange territory where he was as green as a lawn in late spring. 'Baby Cakes,' they had labeled him on the streets. And as a result of that submissiveness he had wound up nearly freezing most nights. The only flimsy coat he had, had literally gotten snatched off his back. Then one night as he stood hugging the can of fire an older Caucasian homeless man walked abruptly up to him. The slap he laid on Step he never would forget. It had surprised him more than it hurt the tough boy. Step recalled how the man then sternly posed a question as Step glared in confusion about the slap. "Now Baby Cakes," the man had huffed, "Which of these two evils would you say is worse. . ." the dingy-eyed man leaned closer into the boy's face. "Will you settle for a frost-bitten butt or will you proudly walk around with callused knuckles?"

As Step recalled that was the stimulating challenge that transformed him into being just as mean as some of his peers. And with a tall stature to match his new spunk, he began to earn the respect he deserved. In no time 'Baby Cakes' became 'Knuckles'. But his nature had been that he would only fight whenever unduly provoked. Then the old man responsible for the re-birth would get the biggest kick out of watching Step stand his ground by holding onto his belongings even during a fight. Though, at times Step had to admit his temper suddenly became unpredictable. "Where did that scared foster kid go?" he would even ask himself. And now back on his feet he thanked God and Dassah for the makeover program—through it he learned all over the self-control he once had. Thus far he thought he really had a sensitive grip on his anger. He never expected what was soon to follow that morning's outing. The farm had been a grinding test of that self-control. When he was new even there the men would try him but he was happy to report he managed to shrug them off. So none of his coworkers on the farm ever witnessed the uncouth counterpart of him—as of yet.

Though Step was not a devout Christian he listened and took heed to what Dassah said about God affording him a quick recovery from a long life of debasement. "You're a blessed nineteen-year-old, Step," she had affirmed several times. "Some of the homeless and ex-cons never have the opportunity to fully bounce back."

Walking behind his boss though the snowy alleyway Step recalled how elated he was when he completed in only several months the one-year phase of the strict mind and body purification. Another boost to his ego was when Dassah preferred him over hundreds of men to be her personal protector after the 2-year-stretch on the program. And every so often he stares at the framed, first real pay stub he ever earned. Then he stares long at the real high school diploma he also afterwards had earned. "I'm no longer a dunce!" he said to the beautiful girl there with him in his penthouse in Manhattan. He had gone from the tenthouse in alleys to a penthouse in a matter of two and a half years. Step recalled how he had kissed the diploma before mounting it in the exquisite frame. "There! How does that look?" he beamed at the lady that day.

"Nice!" She got up from the couch and wrapped her toned arms around him. Then, pouting luscious full lips, "Why would you want to kiss cold glass when you can have these with no Botox to interfere?"

Step, in dating recalled trying to understand what Dassah meant about fornication being a sin. She had shown him and the other ex-homeless, both men and women, how God condemns that debauchery between two people that's not married to each other. The scripture she would show was 1 Corinthians 7: 1, 2. "Now concerning the things you wrote unto me. It is good for a man not to tough a woman." Verse 2, "Nevertheless, to avoid fornication, let every man have his own wife and let every woman have her own husband." That means God forbids having sexual intercourse with anyone other than a spouse. "I'm working on it Lord!" he had looked seriously towards heaven. "I'm truly working on getting saved."

"Now don't wait until you die in your sins!" Dassah had warned all whom she tried to reach to be saved by God.

Then Step's mind strayed to that day at his penthouse with his lady. The strikingly handsome buffed man clad in a yellow body shirt had wheeled around, pulled her voluptuous body to him and kissed her passionately.

While making their way through the narrow alleyway, Step on Dassah' heels, he recalled how he now regularly visits his street buddies—the ones still alive. "Those merciless streets can brutalize anybody!" he thought. A big sign escaped his thick lips thinking about the high mortality rate among the homeless. He visualized the graveyards in alleys. He had even made some graves for those that died in boxes during the night. His old buddy who had encouraged him to stand up for himself had made Step promise to bury him deep when he died. Being much older than Step he felt Stet would surely outlive him. "And don't let them take me to that morgue and cut me up for experiments!" the tattered weary man had pleaded. "Who knows, even though I may be dead, I might still be able to feel what they're doing to me!" And sadly within a year Step regrettably had to keep his promise. That was when the then eighteen-year-old learned that rats would dig up and then eat un-embalmed bodies. But if a body was buried deep enough a rodent would have a harder time digging. The young lad was disappointed in that the very thing the old man feared had happened to his body. Step figured he had dug deep enough with the rusty shovel. The boy had been digging for hours so it seemed. Only instead of the morgue it was rats and opossums that nearly consumed him. Then once again the young Step with the aid of some other homeless men, found themselves disgustingly burning and re-burring the remains. "No teenager should ever, ever have to see, let alone do that kind of morbid thing!" Dassah had said to Step when he told her about that burial incident. He also marveled how a homeless body could be found dead without any questions from the law. So with all the misery in the homeless community Step felt the least he could do was to pay his ex-peers a bi-monthly visit. And with a load of blankets, socks, coats and thermal underwear over the past six years, they would welcome him with open arms. Most of these were men who did not qualify for the program. Some had a record of being hospitalized or institutionalized. The elderly, aggressive or alcoholics beyond recovery had been regretfully rejected for the program. She finally came to realize it was impossible to rescue every single homeless person. Nevertheless Step had the utmost respect for Dassah and her staff for rendering service whenever and wherever she could. "Just too many of them too far gone!" he had heard her sigh too often. He had seen alcoholics with cirrhosis of the liver, which is called, Jaundice. And of course he has no health insurance. "Even the well-to-do can barely afford medical insurance here in America, let alone these poor souls!" she would affirm.

Step also knew that many homeless only took up drinking just to occupy a troubled mind and to prevent freezing. He had heard some men claim to drink only to sleep away their woes—only to awaken to a hang-over and yet emptier stomachs. The Grim Reaper took to following them biding the time they would drink themselves into his inevitable vice. "Even death realizes that consistent alcohol poured into an empty stomach is bad news!" Step thought. He had also wondered about the families of the men he buried. On the streets most of the homeless decidedly would avoid talking about their past as Step also had not told about his. Only he would talk to his old, now dead buddy. He recalled how the men would boast about any material things he used to own but rarely did he talk about children and family. Step truly had no family to boast about. He has yet taken time to find his brothers and mother. But deep down he realizes it is fear of what he might find out about them. "What if my brothers are drug attics or on death row?!" he would think the worst as usual. "What if my mother is dead?" he recalled how happily she would always smile before his father left her.

That snowy Saturday morning in Neal, Dassah and Step walked through the narrow alleyway stepping over piles of snow covered debris. Since this side of town and its homeless residents was unfamiliar to Step, he paused and tapped Dassah' shoulder. "Wait!" he whispered, checking the gun in the holster under his thick jacket. "I don't know a thing about this alley!"

She also checked the snub-nose strapped securely to the middle of her boot. "Yeah, the homeless can be pretty nasty to strangers," she said. The homeless were aware that they were like sitting ducks and should remain on guard at all times. Whether anyone was homeless or not, Step was well prepared to protect his female boss. He knew first-handed that even among the homeless there were the good, the bad and the irritable. "These men's vitamin deficiency is the number one nerve-bender!" he often thinks after having learned a great deal more about nutrition.

After making sure their guns were set, they began to resume the trek through the narrow alleyway. Snowflakes began to thicken before their eyes. Then Dassah suddenly stopped, and holding up a hand, she said, "Bingo!" She had spotted some cardboard boxes with a dirty blanket hanging out—the homeless way of alerting that box was occupied.

As Dassah and Step went, the opening of the alley widened into a much larger open area. "Looks like a homemade compound back here," she whispered. Then she noticed the alley from which they had exited continued to the opposite side of the yard narrowing into a similar space. The opposite side was just another entrance into the alley from the other side street. "What a strange but cunning setup," she whispered.

"Yeah," Step was flush on her heels, left hand on his gun. "Somebody cleverly constructed a shelter. . . People *will* find ways to survive!"

Her beautiful brown eyes moved to a can of smoldering fire, and then darted to the wall, near the can. Only a few feet away from the boxes her trailing continued to the make-shift tin ceiling in the middle of the yard and there the tin ceiling ended, where only a wide slither of sky could be seen in the middle. "Obviously this keeps the snow away from the fire," she whispered. But she knew the main purpose was for homeless refuge. She noticed five cardboard boxes lined up together also had smaller tin roofs extending over them. "This is the first time in my years of scouting I've ever seen such construction up in an alley," she admitted. "These men surely knew what they were doing!" She knew these were men because women rarely slept in alleys with men. She also knew that when the city decided to demolish those two, dilapidated buildings that would be the end of this haven for the homeless. She uttered a silent prayer that the building would remain for a long while to come. Then she whispered, "If they tear down these buildings then where will these poor people go?

"The saddest thing is who cares!" he sadly sighed, having himself been among people just like these.

Now under the make-shift ceiling Dassah' eyes moved swiftly to a puff of snow blowing in. "They should have just gone on and put up four walls instead of just two!" she chattered.

"Are you ready Boss?" he nudged her.

"Let's go for it!" Then she began to move towards a box as he trailed with caution gun pointing skyward. Finally in front of the box she bent over and was just about to investigate but he suddenly stepped in front of her. He lightly tapped the box but the damp cardboard silently bended under the mere tap.

Dassah stepping back around him firmly shook the box. "Is anybody home!?"

Finally inside movement violently rocked the box. Step pulled her back and pointed the gun directly at the box. Suddenly a hooded dread-locked head slowly peeped out of the flap. "Who is that!?" an apparent young groggy voice growled with wind whipping residual snow onto his tattered hood.

"May we speak with you for a moment Sir?" the beautiful clean doctor smiled down on the dirty man.

"What do you want!?" he squinted up, bloodshot eyes suddenly moving over to Step with the shiny gun. The man gasped and franticly shut the flimsy flap for protection. "I didn't do anything!" he seriously affirmed. "Just go away!"

"My name is Doctor Desoto."

"Nobody called a doctor up in here!"

By that time flaps in two other boxes opened and out of each a tattered man curiously peeped.

Now in front of the box, "You can come on out Sir!" she softly pleaded. "We're not cannibals or anything." Then she used her favorite four words, "You want a job?"

Only dead silence inside. She and her fearless bodyguard patiently waited for him to process that. And then the flap slowly opened again. On all fours the man came wearily out. Dassah nodded up at Step to put away the gun. He only lowered it. Step knew there were more men to confront. "Hey you, there in the other boxes!" Step almost commanded. "If you're planning on trying anything just remember bullets can easily penetrate cardboard!" As a homeless man once he realized street people rarely had guns but they had plenty of knives and was skilled in throwing to hit the target.

"None of us have guns, mister!" the man on all fours quickly conceded, standing up.

Dassah with a smile said, "This is Step." She extended a gloved hand to the tall tattered, a few years younger than her 39 years, man. There staring up at the dirty aggravated man pity shaded her eyes. His clothing was typical of having been on the streets for a long time. The fake London-Fog coat over layers of clothing reeked even in the chill. His tennis shoes had faded to brown, caked with mud. A thick beard covered his mid-thirties face. His red locks concluded that he was a very fair-skinned Black man.

"Hey," the man finally grumbled . . . just call me LD . . . And again, what do you want from me?" He walked off in the direction of the can of smoldering fire. Another homeless man eased out and began to trail LD to the can. Step quickly raised the gun again but relaxed when he saw no threat. Her eyes followed the second man. His dirty hood with long blond hair sticking out the sides concluded he was White. "He couldn't be any more than his early twenties," she whispered to Step. She noticed the young White man was about three inches shorter than LD's estimated six-feet. Dassah had dealt with homeless men long enough to come close to guessing his physical stature. Then her eyes moved swiftly to an older White man that had remained inside his box simply peeping out. "Are there any others inside? She asked

"No just us three!" LD yelled over his shoulder. She sensed none of the men to be a real threat so she motioned for Step to put the gun away. Reluctantly he complied this time.

Dassah sadly noticed the younger White man as he timidly trailed LD. His clothing was also indicative of having been a resident of the streets for some time. Step lingered close by with careful surveillance. He knew a hungry man would try anything to fill the void in the pit of his belly. "Some will attack to get the meager amount of money," he thought.

Dassah glanced at her watch. It was 9:16 as they stood there in the alley. Dassah and Step had finally discovered the home of three men that she would possibly recruit for her program. "I hope all goes well today," she whispered over to Step. "We've already made good timing today." She knew the men would sleep longer on the weekend because of the closing of the mission.

Meanwhile, at Dassah' parked limousine three boys in their mid to late teens were trying intensely to peer into the snow covered windshield first. When they could not see, they moved all around the long car. The boys were literally drooling from lust for the vehicle. The nicely casual dressed boys anxiously went from door to door trying to get in. Two of the boys were Latino, and one was Black. One Latino boy in broken English, said, "I see who get out o' dis babe!"

As he hesitated to tell the other Latino boy impatiently said, in more proper English, "So, whose bad ride is this?"

"A big hombre en a doll wen dare," the tattler pointed towards the alleyway.

"Well let's go get the keys and take this babe for a lil' spin," said the second Latino, who appeared to be the leader of the up-to-no-good pack.

"Maybe ride forever, se?" the Black boy snickered.

Roaring with victorious laughter they hastened on towards the alley.

Back deep in the alley Step, Dassah and the two homeless men now stood around the can of smoldering fire. The older man still was in the box peeping out. But unlike his boss Step had sensed some hostility. Mainly the suspicion was from LD. Nevertheless Step being from the streets maintained his cool. "I know I can take them all at once if I have to!" he thought. He recalled himself having a serious nutritional deficiency just like them. However at the age of fifteen he already was five-feet-ten. His other six inches was gained on the streets of New York in spite of the serious lack of food. "My threatening height kept me from getting stomped into the mud after I finally learned to defend myself!" he once told Dassah.

There under the make-shift shelter Dassah, Step and the two homeless men stood around the can. LD had just returned from a pile of dried twigs with a few and agitatedly pitched them into the can. All the time like a little puppy trailing him was the young White man, who also cautiously eyed the intruders.

"Would you guys like some breakfast?" Dassah broke the silence. She knew that food would be a temporary distraction from their many woes. There were still dead silence from the men. The men only exchanged glances around the now ignited flames. Then Dassah was beginning to shiver. She moved closer to the can and was grateful the tin roof intercepted most of the snow that crept through the slit. "Thank God for these insulated clothes!" she only thought. It was her compassion that prohibited boasting in the presence of the less fortunate. She never failed to be mindful that at one time she'd had only a half pair of shoes, having to glue them together even in winter.

Then sadly her mind went back to the night of the rape. That summer night she had been dragged out of the already raggedy shoes and ran home bare feet. The several days that followed she had to remain in bed with her mother screaming for her to get up and clean house. The sick teen even had to clean her mother's room also. So she had forced her sore body around the house in her threadbare house shoes. Then when she was finally able to return to school she had begged her mother to let her borrow a pair of her expensive shoes. There in the alley Dassah tore her thoughts from that horrible event of trying to persuade her yet unyielding mother. Dassah recalled with repulsiveness finally having to wear Jarvis' dirty sneakers he had outgrown. Finally she was able to buy a pair of cheap shoes which she wore until they fell apart. Back at school teachers had narrowed their eyes at the cuts and scrapes on her arms and face and the boyish sneakers she had on. Dassah cannot even recall what excuse she offered the teachers for that.

There in the snowy alley under the make-shift shelter LD and the younger White homeless man pondered on the doctor's breakfast proposal. Suddenly another voice broke the silence, "Seems they're already full, so I'll have their portion!" the voice assured. All heads turned to the older homeless man briskly straightening his clothing. Step reached for his gun. Dassah threw her hand up and he relaxed. She flashed a welcome smile at the approaching, slightly stocky man whose clothing though dirty, were not as tattered. As snow misted softly into her face Dassah couldn't help but notice the expensive clothing the middle-aged man had on. She had long since developed an eye for finery. "He's fairly new to the streets," she only thought being too close to the men to whisper that to Step. She looked at the older man's nourished hair and skin and knew he had very recently lived a better life. She glanced at his not too unsightly pot belly. "A couple of years out here and that'll be gone altogether," she thought.

Meanwhile, in upper Manhattan, in a Victorian home, a well poised fifty-something Caucasian woman sat at a Baby Grand playing well, a Mozart Favorite. As she played the woman gazed long out the wall-to-wall streak-free window where snowflakes whirled around bare trees. An intense sadness shadowed her sharp features and thin painted lips that drew tight with agony. The woman's clothing was as fine as the sparse shiny furniture in the huge parlor. Then suddenly into the parlor pranced a mid-twenties woman. The young woman's long shiny red hair bounced with every move. And without hesitation she headed directly to the pianist. The young woman sighed, bent over and placed a caring kiss on the pianist's maturing forehead. "Mother will you get out with me today?" she pleaded in a northern dialect.

"I don't feel much like it today Dear," her mother sighed with each stroke of the keys like it was a song.

At that her daughter became immediately perturbed. "How long are you going to sit in the house pining away!?" she demanded. "Daddy has been gone for over three months now."

While still stroking the polished keys, "I know, Dear." another impatient sigh, "Burt I simply must be here when they bring your father home!" She sadly recalled how this was already January. And the past Christmas was the first she did not have her loving husband at her side.

Her daughter knelt fondly at the woman's knees. "Mother, you know that I love Daddy too." she softly reasoned. "But what if something has happened . . . and he won't be coming home, ever? It's an uncertain world out there you know."

"Don't ever say such a thing!" tears now rolling as she took out rage on the keyboard. Mozart became a belligerent bang.

Standing up intolerantly her daughter said, "We must be realistic Mother! You know how Daddy already had one short attack of amnesia years ago." Calmer now she took her mother's hand into both hers. "Mother, we cannot say this is another one of Dad's amnesia episodes. . . The doctor did say there has not been a report where a patient had a second attack."

"But he wasn't gone this long before!" She stared into the eyes of her beautiful daughter. In them she hoped to find even a hint of hope. But she only found that her daughter had sadly accepted the disappearance of her loving 'Daddy'. Angrily she snatched her hand from her daughter as if she suddenly was the enemy. She wheeled around on the fine mahogany stool again. She stared blankly at the window again and began to play again. With pain in her green eyes her daughter gently pat her on the back, and then began the long trip back across the hard wood floor. As she went she glanced over her shoulder. "Don't worry Mother. Maybe the twenty-five-thousand-dollar reward will get him back soon." She walked out.

CHAPTER 8

Meanwhile, back in the snowy alley of Neal, New York that Saturday morning Dassah, and Step and the three homeless men stood around the can of fire. The famed psychiatrist and her bodyguard had just offered the newly awakened men breakfast. Their stomachs growled but even that did not prevent them being vigilant towards the intruders. So hesitantly, LD, who appeared to be the leader, said, "Maybe we *will* take you up on those vittles!" still eyeing Step sharply, "But it depends on what you're expecting in return."

"All we're here to do is offer jobs and make *ex-homeless* men of you," Dassah slowly walking towards LD with Step flush on her heels. Step had his hood partially back for better view of the jittery men. LD and Step had begun to eye-ball each other like two brown Pit-Bulls. There in the alley with Step only four inches taller than LD's six feet neither needed to look down at the other. Dassah stared at the two valiant men. One looked like a pauper and the other like a prince. 'Are you truly friend or foe?' shown in LD's relentless glare. Step had detected LD to be a man of high intellect in this brief encounter. Plus the homeless man's demeanor exuded the awareness he portrayed. However there was no doubt in Dassah' mind which of the two would walk down Victory Lane in this battle. "But, if LD was as fit as Step, it could very well end in a tie," she thought. She also guessed LD to be some ten years older than Step. "With both in top condition the age span might just give Step the edge anyway," she thought. Dassah looked over the can of flames questioningly at LD since he appeared to be the spokesman. Through fine snowflakes and flames she impatiently said, "It would please me greatly if you guys would agree to make up your mind in a warmer place . . . like in my car!"

At that, there were silence and uncertainty again.

Then LD said, "Ok, but no sissy stuff. . . We may be poor, raggedy and stinking, but we're straight and decent . . . all male . . . right guys?!"

The other men gave rapid nods. Dassah oddly eyed the younger blond man in a tattered coat hugging himself as if he would soon die of frost. Yet she sensed he was very used to the cold. "This one has an obvious mental problem for sure," she thought, realizing all homeless people had some kind of mental deficit but this one was unique. Then, raising her gloved right hand, "We promise not to try anything funny, right Step?" Sarcastically she posed.

"Affirmative here, Boss," Step quickly agreed while still eyeing LD back. "I'm also as straight as the subway is from Elm to Tenth Street!" he firmly assured LD.

Then LD took his eyes away from Step long enough to exchange glances with the other two men and they finally nodded their approval.

"So it's okay to leave this God-forsaken place?" Dassah blurted without thinking—not her nature. And through chattering teeth, "It's freezing out here!" she said. Then she glanced up and around at the partial enclosure. "Or should I say it's freezing *in* here! Who built this contraption anyway!? Did they not realize that tin stays colder much longer than wood?"

"It was here when I got here," LD said. "I was the second to move in . . . the first here was a friend of mine . . . he . . . oh, never mind!" His countenance became sad about his friend so he simply said, "Yeah, Doc, we'll go, and compared to out in the snow it's a far cry from being

God-forsaken up in here. It's more like God-blessing to us! And tin doesn't buckle under the weight of ice, Ma'am!'"

Dassah being a Christian blushed over the insult she had just haphazardly hurled out. She had been teaching for years that any shelter from the storm was a God-sent. Disappointment gripped her that it had not been her who testified about the blessed provisions God had afforded these homeless souls. "I'm really sorry!" she sighed. "Come on and I'll make it up to you. . . Is there anything you'd like to take from your, your." She decided to only gesture toward the boxes. She groped earnestly this time for the right words.

"The word you're looking for is mansions!" LD snickered through dingy teeth.

The older Caucasian man also rocked with laughter. "And, no, we don't have any gold or mink blankets to take along. What you see is what we've got!" he spread grungy palms.

Humor created a more relaxed atmosphere. Dassah noticed the younger homeless man seemed to find no humor in anything at all. The jolly older man stopped laughing long enough to enquire, "What time is it anyway?"

"Nine thirty," Step offered, ". . . time for breakfast!"

Dassah began to lead the way to the narrow opening from which she and Step had come. Step pulled the hood all the way over his head since it appeared the conflict between he and LD had a truce. Then he pondered on a method how they all would exit the narrow alleyway. Immediately he began to issue orders. Dassah would allow his taking charge of her safety. Step respectfully ordered, "LD, would you go first, then you next," he pointed to the young man whose name he did not know. "Then you," pointing to the older man whose name was unknown. Everyone fell in file, Dassah in front of Step, who went last. With Step on his boss's heels once again LD began to lead the way out. At the exit of the alley, as they proceeded to leave suddenly everyone was totally startled and stopped in their tracks. The three young men from the parked limo had jumped abruptly in with guns wagging.

With a loud gasp Dassah threw her gloved hand over her mouth not caring that they would be smeared with lipstick. With careful reluctance to go for his gun Step only meanly eyed the three young gangsters. Immediately the homeless men, hands in the air, began to back away. She glared partially mean partially frightened at the youths, noticing the nice hooded coats they had on. "They can't be hungry robbers!" she thought. "I got out of my bed for this stuff?!" she thought. She usually slept late at least one Saturday a month and wished this was that Saturday. But the desperate need for more men to replace those graduating had forced her out. She had thought of hiring a scout to go out for her. But she personally needed to hand-pick the men. "After all, *I* am the psychiatrist and this is *my* livelihood!" she had reasoned one day. "Though I do have qualified therapists but aside from God, I trust only Yours Truly!" Her initial conversation with any homeless man would give her most of what kind of person she was dealing with. Just like LD the doctor in her had him almost pegged as the right man for the job.

Step and the homeless men held at gunpoint were stiff—and not just from the cold. Slyly, Step eased his left hand for his own 38 caliber.

"Don't even go there, Mr. Jolly Black Giant!" The Black boy's adolescent voice halted Step. Step, his lips tight evil-eyed the boy just a few feet away and reluctantly eased his hand back in the air. "Now he's going to take my gun!" Step thought. But the juveniles never ordered him to hand over the gun "For sure theses jokers are still wet behind the ears!" he thought.

Then the well-spoken Latino boy, who appeared to be the leader, said, "All of you, hands higher in the air!" Higher they all reached for the sky.

"How in the world did I let them get in on me like this!?" Step thought. "Some bodyguard!" lowering his eyes from Dassah' frightened gaze. But she realized he had been busy protecting her from the homeless men to notice the sneak-attack. "It's okay," she mimed to him. Then her eyes moved to the trembling homeless men, who had separated over the wide alley. She and Step stood side by side in the alley under the make-shift roof as snow misted in.

Reaching deep into his mind for the cunning he knew was there, Step picked his brain for a way out of that pickle jar he was in. But all around were literally children grasping dangerous weapons. "If I let anything happen to Doc, I would break every mirror I even thought about looking into!" he thought. His angry dark eyes moved over all the guns, and then to the immaturity behind them. Step knew he was only a few years older than the boys but with an advantage of strict sharp-shooting training. With snow misting through the slit before Step's handsome dark face his stomach flip-flopped when he noticed the Latino leader lustfully ogling Dassah. And Dassah with her hands high her jacket had risen to reveal voluptuous thighs. The lead boy ran his tongue over youthful chapped lips while taking in her femininity. As his breathing grew rapidly thick steam billowed out. Suddenly the other two boys developed an intense interest in their leader's hankering. Suddenly Dassah yanked the jacket down.

"No, no, keep those hands up!" the sultry Latino dialect demanded. "So far I like what I see!"

Against all odds Step made an angry advance towards the lustful leader.

"Don' even thin' 'bout dat!" said the other Latino teem in very broken English.

The leader finally made his way to Dassah as everyone gaped. At his unsure advance Dassah began to back slowly towards the can of fire, which was also away from Step. But Step, unaware to everyone was inching along. "I can't let her get too far away from me," he thought. "My sanity depends on her leaving this place alive! Plus, she's just too nice to die out here like this." Ever since Step had known his boss he had seen her do nothing but good for anyone she could. Staring at the guns his terror was more for her sake. He could not recall ever feeling so helpless—even on the battle field of the streets of New York. "This has taught me a lesson to always keep my peripheral vision clear on a scouting trip," he angrily thought.

As Dassah backed slowly from the stalking boy she thought, "I dare not attempt to go for the gun in my boot. . . That would really 'set it off' up in here." Finally as he stalked, she suddenly stopped in her tracks. Greedily he grabbed for her like he had just found that pot of gold. She slapped his hand away like a mother would a child reaching for candy. Having a stranger touch her made her flesh crawl. But he persisted to harshly lure her away from her fuming protection. Now a few feet from Step, Dassah and the boy, her taller, she gazed hatefully into his dark, Spanish eyes. And with all her might she refrained from slapping his taut face. The years of psychiatry had taught her that many adolescents were as fragile as a freshly hatched egg. If he got really angry he could also crack with retaliatory danger. "These boys have guns, and my guess is they'll use them," she thought standing toe-to-toe with the sizzling sinister. She knew that if it were just her and him unarming him would be as light as Angel Food cake. Combative training for all staff in the mental health profession was just as imperative as needing air. "But instead, I want everyone to walk out of here on his own today," she thought, deciding against any sudden defense tactics. She knew that an alternative plan was now in order. She and Step discreetly glanced at each other from the few feet away. He knew her well enough to know something was brewing in that lovely hooded head of hers, as well as a plan was in his. There in the cold both hoped to be on the same brain-wave-length. They were. Step's plan was that he would take the Black gunman who was bigger and closest to him. She would rush the leader who was now too close for comfort. She eyed the third Latino gunman now haphazardly holding the homeless men at bay. With his gun-hand somewhat relaxed he was enthused with watching his leader's wanting. Then Dassah noticed that with amazement LD seemed unafraid. The other men were standing away from the action. LD appeared as fearless as he had been earlier towards Step. Dassah knew that some homeless men prayed for death every time they went to sleep. But disappointed some had awakened to discover it just was not their time. "Maybe LD has just been on these cruel streets too long to care about his life anymore!" she thought. Even in the face of danger Dassah noticed LD evil-eyeing the third boy who stood closest to him. At the sight of LD's audacity her prayer was that he would handle his gunman. "I hope I'm right about LD when the time is right!" she thought with the leader's garlic breath in her face. "How can you stomach such spicy food so early in the morning!" she thought with an open scowl. "Or, maybe that's last night's food on your breath? So please go and brush!" she only thought.

There in the partially covered, tin roof alley as snow managed to blow through the leader finally moved seductively close behind the doctor. And with his free hand he eased off his hood and then hers. Her hair was shiny in the light of the morning snow. He glanced around at his crew, "Alright, you guys!" he ordered, "Stay on the job while me and Doll talk a spell!" But instead of talking he heavily began to inhale her perfumed hair, "Smells like el dinero!" he finally whispered in her ear as she, to no avail, tugged away. Then he breathed, "That your baby on the street?" With their bodies now touching she cringed moving away again only to be harshly hung onto. He lifted the gun to her cheek. "What you say, sexy lady?"

His breath on her neck and having a stranger that close infuriated her. "Yes that's my car," she finally forced herself to loosen up. "Would you like to take a little spin? We can leave my big man here." Then she breathed as sincerely and robustly as possible, "If I humor him," she thought, "That'll bide the time we need to figure a way out of this mess." She shot an assuring glance across at Step who looked outright ticked-off, steam rolling from flared nostrils like a big black bull.

The lead boy was at her back with sarcasm and said, "I plan to take the car, whether you say so or not!" His definite disdain for someone else's property made her nauseous. The night of her rape swiftly came to mind as air was now unable to pass between the boy and her. The other boys only watched with mouths hung in anticipation of an upcoming X-rated antic in the damp alley.

Cunningly, Step only shifted his eyes from one boy to another. He noticed their guns now relaxed slightly pointing towards the ground. Their leader's sins had lucidly lured them away from their intentions. And from across the alley Step and LD eyed each other mutually for the first time. Step felt he and LD had to make telepathy a reality as soon as possible. Dassah with the boy now pressing revoltingly against her, keened her eyes as she had sensed Step and LD had a ploy, "I just pray they won't do anything deadly!" she chattered under her breath. She'd had only a few minor altercations while scouting but nothing as frightening as having a believed-to-be loaded gun rammed into her neck. "And to top that off," she thought, "I could very well get raped right here in front of a crowd of men!" Though she knew neither Step nor herself would allow it to go that far. She had vowed never to submit to rape again. She would rather die fighting this rime.

Amidst the heated confusion she knew she should keep her mind on the issue at hand but found herself hoping LD would agree to join the program. With the boy clasped so close she was grateful for her thick clothing between them, "I can only thank God this isn't summer!" she thought. He had not yet removed any of her clothes but she knew it would be only a matter of time before he would be trying.

Step had also sensed no immediate danger, "But I must think fast!" his panicky eyes darted back and forth.

Dassah managed a quick glance at the other two homeless men, whose hands now hung helplessly at their sides. The other two boys were totally oblivious that their victims had suddenly defied the orders to keep their hands high.

Dassah flinched as the boy began a slight grinding on her backside. Still she knew that calmness was the vital key to her freedom. Again she managed to glance at the young White homeless man. And again she marveled that he had not yet uttered a single word. "Maybe he's just shy," she managed to think. "Maybe he's dumb and can't speak." She knew he could hear in that earlier he had nodded at a question from LD. "What if he gets hurt in here?" She knew that if someone got killed her practice would be under the strictest scrutiny like when that woman had tried to sabotage her business. Even though money was no threat to her millions she could never live down a rep of murder. She envisioned the headlines, "Famous doctor trained to renew lives heatedly takes a young life!" She knew the nature of people was to think the worse whenever things were going too well for a Black business. And making over homeless men had become more than just a job to her. "My mission is to make life more fulfilling for the unable and not to take what life they have left." The doctor of the mind adored the psychiatric phase of her practice with the well-to-do clients, as well as with the ex-homeless. But most of all she relished in bringing the ex-homeless and ex-cons into a covenant relationship with God.

PART THREE

CHAPTER 9

In Neal, New York that Saturday morning under the partially covered make-shift tent in the alley snow began to thicken as some blew through the wide slit in the roof. There stood Doctor Dassah Desoto a psychiatrist, Stephanas Carter her bodyguard and three homeless men. The three hoodlum boys, the boys pointing guns stood fearlessly.

As the lead boy was too close behind the beautiful doctor fondling everything he wanted to, her frightened eyes darted to Step. The Black boy was closest to Step but with the gun somewhat relaxed as he heatedly watched the show. Step's dark eyes narrowed with anger watching her attacker grope his beloved boss. She knew Step would never put her psyche business in jeopardy. But she also knew that keeping her safe was foremost in his mind. Looking sadly at her helpless bodyguard she thought, "I've been through worse than having a sissy little greenhorn fondle me!" Then she recalled her brutal rape, glaring over her shoulder at the lustfully panting boy. "Now it's up to me to put on an exhibition so Step can be the superb bodyguard he is!" Then she forced back the mounting contempt and conjured up some nerves—a silent prayer was lifted up. Then throwing all guilt and chastity aside the woman of God began to move along with the boy's rhythm.

"Yeah, Pretty Lady," he whispered. "Let's give 'um a free show." Ecstasy gurgled from the juvenile's voice.

From a few feet away Step's anger was outwardly manifested as his cheeks blew up like a bull frog. Yet, tight lips he had to applaud his boss for her ploy. Then moving his eyes over at the boys he also knew by now they should have detected her trickery. "But I was once a teenage boy!" he thought, realizing how sidetracked they can get when a pretty girl is present. Then, glaring at the one-track-minded youths, especially the one nearest him, "Now they go pulling guns on somebody and can't even stay focused long enough to back it up!" Having lived on the streets all his teenage life he knew that when a gun was pulled the true intention was to kill or be killed, "Now these teenagers dug their own grave with shovels of teen-ecstasy and foolishness," he sadly thought with a subtle shake of the head. Step knew that given the opportunity he would also pull his gun and shoot to maim or maybe even to kill. "I get paid to protect my boss!" he meanly eyed her busy attacker.

In the alley with now fine snowflakes all eyes fixed on the show— some eyes filled with lust some with repulsion some with anger. Dassah noticed the young homeless man's eyes seemed to greatly delight in the exhibition. His blue but dingy eyes gleamed amidst the snow. The older White man, repulsion in his green eyes could only shake his tatter-hooded head in shame. While staring at the older man Dassah detected much astuteness and wondered—as much as she was able to aside from the boy determinately now tugging at the buttons on her coat with his free hand.

Finally from across the alley Step thought, "If we're going to do anything, it's now or never!" He glanced at LD, and then let out a profuse sneeze. In response LD as much as his mal-nourished brain was able to, sensed the sneeze as a cue in that this was the first time Step had ever sneezed. However Step slightly shook his head and moved his lips, 'not yet'. Dassah sighed of profound relief seeing they had caught her ploy, "I knew I hired a smart bodyguard!" shooting a discreet smile at Step as snow blew onto his dark, handsome face sticking momentarily.

The boy's arm was heavy over her shoulder as the gun now rested on her delightfully full bosom. His other hand was now yanking trying to undo her pants, which zipped in the front. He had already succeeded unbuttoning her coat. Again she cringed having him that close to her backside, his eyes tight with passion.

Frozen with anger, Step thought, "I hope LD puts up the next sneeze as a signal to attack!" Step would hold off moving on the Black gunman until he knew Dassah was ready to tackle her opponent. Also frozen in his spot across the alley LD had decided not to move until Step faked another sneeze, "I just hope that sneeze was a signal and not a real cold!" LD thought, his thick dread locks sticking out around the grungy hood. "If it's just a cold, there's gonna' be five dead people up in here!" the street man knew for sure.

As Dassah hoped, it appeared the hoodlums had lost all purpose of why they came into the alley in the first place. She knew the show of exotica had congealed their puny brains more than the snow ever could hope to.

Dassah had slithered around to face the explicitly assaulting boy, her zipper almost down. "Safe so far!" she thought with a sigh." Nevertheless, as he fumbled she was glad he did exactly what she hoped—she would soon disarm him. The Christian doctor, with rhythm she was unaware she even had begun to move kindling his already blazing desire, "I must act now, because he's ready to take this to its finale right here in this alley!" panic in her thoughts. She fought back the nausea at the things the boy was whispering. And sick reflections of the rapist also flooded her. And, being reminded of that dreadful night caused her heart to palpitate with fierceness. Right then the doctor of the mind realized she should not be defiling herself before an audience of men, "But I must keep up this lewd act until the time is just right!" she thought there in his vice. So she managed to melt the snow on his face a little longer. With snow also on her beautiful face and his hot breath melting the snow, she knew the gun was now pointing at the ground in back of her. As his free hand now tried to finish the zipper, she knew it was only a matter of time before her jeans would be loose. "Now is definitely time to move!" she thought as the zipper eased down. She had no time to wait for Step to sneeze and Step knew that. She knew Step's apprehension was merely for her safety. "I have no doubt my bodyguard is a soldier!" she thought. Then suddenly she, Step and LD reacted at the same time. Dassah dropped suddenly to her knees. She grasped tightly his gun-arm, pushing it high. Her glove made it difficult to grasp but she would hang on with desperation. A head-butt in his ridged groin brought a squeal and then weakness to his knees. Still she held on to his arm with both hands as he was now also on his knees. At the same time Step had lunged readily at his target with insane fury landing a strong blow to his face. Blood spurted from the Black gunman's nose and mouth, his legs buckled, the gun went airborne. The gun hit the tin roof and fired. LD, who had already rushed the other Latino boy yelled and grabbed his thigh with his free hand. Nevertheless he hung on to the boy's gun-arm with the other hand. The under-nourished LD had been shot with the gun that hit the roof. But he managed to unarm the fiercely grappling boy. The other two homeless men had dived under a tin covering away from stray bullets. Dassah with the gun now in her hands was also dodging any stray bullets that were firing from LD's fight. Yet she was able to meanly guard her writhing cursing attacker, who was on the ground having his own gun pointed in his reddish face. She hissed, "Don't even breathe loud you poor excuse for a human being!" LD finally prevailed, took the gun and chased after the boy through the alley. LD, now limping only fired into the air, "It's been so long since I even touched a gun let alone fired one!" the tattered, wounded man thought wanting to get that gun out of his hand.

Step had grabbed his partially recovered boy but the big, anxious youth snatched free and hustled through the alley behind his friend. Step rushed over to Dassah. They glared at her attacker who was now swearing experienced and intensely, still clutching his crotch, now not so rigid. While pointing the gun at him Dassah' mind played tricks on her. In her mind the boy was suddenly her mother's boyfriend, who had permanently injured her reproductive organs. The babies she would never have flashed before her furious eyes. Her vengeful mind told her that if she were to kill this boy she would be killing the rapist, and that would settle the score. Then her gloved finger tried to squeeze the trigger but before she could pull, "What would Jesus do to his many, many enemies? Would he simply shot them all?" she said audibly said as everyone stood holding their breath. Then slowly she relaxed the gun. Then Step instead of blood pumping through his veins it had turned into concentrated adrenaline. Dassah quickly assured him, "That's alright! I'm really okay, Step!" She reached haltingly out to him. But daggers in his eyes told her he was already in a world called, Payback. Step was not a Christian and probably was not as forgiving as she. Then suddenly, and simultaneously Step and the determined boy lunged for the gun in her hands. Also determined that no one got hurt she backed away into a pile of wood that caught the heel of her boot. As she went down the gun fumbled out of her hands. The need to have a gun did not seem necessary to Step as he lifted the fist-swinging boy over his shoulder like a sack of potatoes. Everyone had their mouth hung in awe as the boy must have weighed well over 150 pounds. With his human-prey like a deer Step wheeled around to the can of hot cinders. The self-control he thought he had suddenly become a figment of his imagination.

Dassah, knees soggy was also frozen with fear. The doctor of the mind knew exactly what her bodyguard was about to do. She screamed, "No Step!" But it was too late. Rage had compelled him to dump the boy head first into the can. And regrettably in that temporary moment of insanity he had obeyed that devilish prompting.

There in the partially covered snowy alley the boy's horrid scream shocked Step from that vengeful state of mind. He stood there at the can with the up-side-down, screaming boy and shook the cobwebs out of his head. Then with the swiftness Step grabbed the boy's legs and plucked him out of the can. He dumped the screaming lad on the ground. Everyone moved over to the boy and gaped as even the humidity failed to quench the blaze in his greasy hair. Now Step was attempting desperately to smother the fire in his hair. But the boy jumped up and took off running wildly and blindly. Then a brick wall finally knocked him brutally back to the ground. Step was now standing over the delirious fist-swinging boy. Then a dirty blanket was handed to Step by the older man. And suddenly Dassah' eyes moved to the opposite side of the alleyway where she had heard footsteps. And from there re-entered the other Latino boy. He was just in time to witness his screaming partner in crime. "Som' body put out dis fir' on my co-sin!" he demanded in broken English. Step was doing his best. Finally the flames were quenched and burning flesh stanched the cold atmosphere.

As the scene unfolded LD gawked down on the now calmer burnt boy on the ground. Even LD had forgotten that himself had been shot in the leg. He pulled up his pant leg and checked the wound. "It's just a graze on my shin but it stings like the bullet went in!" he said The younger homeless man was in a corner shaking face as white as the snow-flurries around it. It was then that the doctor of the mind knew for sure he had a deep mental issue. "But what sort?" she wondered.

While staring at the crying burned boy anger rose in Dassah again. Yet she had trouble suppressing the compassion lurking deeper within than the anger was. "In spite of the humiliation he put me through before God and everybody I only wish to comfort him!" she thought. She had noticed the boy was about 17 or 18. "He's young enough to be my son! If the rapist would have impregnated me, my child would be twenty-three!" Then her eyes moved sadly down on Step who held the boy close as he was wrapped in the obviously bacteria-infested blanket. Then she announced, "I have no other choice but to get the police!"

"Yeah," a big sigh of regret came from Step.

The boy's cousin pranced around the alley biting his nails and spitting them out with an annoying sound. No one decided to reprimand him for that. Dassah wished the crime had been so that she could have simply given the boys a harsh tongue-lashing and let them go. "I really wish this hadn't happened!" With an agitated sigh she pulled out her cell phone and dialed 911. She noticed the time, and complained, "Is it nine forty-five already? And just look at this mess! We've only been in Neal for a few hours and now all this! With this senseless scenario it seems more like a few life times!"

"You can say that again!" Step sighed from beside the burned whimpering lad. "I'm really sorry Boss!"

"You're not to blame Step, they are!" Then no sooner than she began talking to the police the boy wheeled and ran back through the narrow alleyway. The determined homeless LD limped after him, "Hey you, come back here and face the music!" he yelled after him. But for the second time LD watched the boy disappear through the snowy debris, his coat tail flapping in the wind. The Black boy was not with him this time.

Over the phone Dassah was giving the incident report. "My name is Doctor Desoto and we have an injured boy in an alley, Ma'am!"

"Which alley are you in, Ma'am? There are thousands of alleys in New York!"

"Hold on," she looked at LD, "Where are we?"

"The front on that building is 774 Crenshaw Way," he pointed, very familiar.

"Thanks. . . Ma'am, the address is 774 Crenshaw Way, and we're a long way into the alley of it."

"We'll get someone there soon . . . and don't leave the boy alone . . . whoever is there now must remain there until we arrive!"

"Yes Ma'am. Thank you, goodbye." When she hung up she could have sworn she saw fear again in the young homeless man's eyes. But so much had happened she simply shrugged it off. Then, placing a tiny gloved hand tenderly on Step's broad back, "How bad is he?" softly.

Step lifted the dirty blanket that now began to stick to the crying boy's charred head. "It looks really serious Boss!" he sighed again.

The three homeless men had eased in closer. LD and the younger man gagged at the boy's face and head. But Dassah marveled that only the older man seemed to stomach the burned sight that even snow sizzled on it.

Staring at the burned boy Dassah knew that even if he survived, he would always wear that horrendous scar. "Most of his face is melted and I'm to blame," she thought, even after convincing Step *he* was not to blame. . . I shouldn't have used the limo this morning!" Then suddenly anger arose again. "Why did you thugs come in here anyway!?" she screamed at the whimpering, shivering boy in Step's arms. Sounding like the doctor she is, only harsher, "You're going to be scarred forever you know!" she pointed an accusing finger down on him, her muddy pants really sticking to her by now.

"No!!" the boy screamed putting his hands over his peeling face. His youthfulness had vanished into a melted mass. "Go on! Kill me!" he begged barely able to look up at Step through the hanging skin. "You might as well," a whisper made it past the hole where his lips use to be. "Or I'm going to kill you for sure hombre!" He passed out, deep breaths.

The homeless men could only gawk. Squatting there, Step's very next thought was no longer to prolong the boy's misery. "I'll just put him out like an injured horse," he thought. But he knew enough about the Bible to know he should not play God. He knew that animals had no soul to abide neither in heaven, nor in hell. He knew that it was acceptable for an animal to receive a mercy-killing by euthanasia. But he also knew that if he deliberately killed a human he would have to answer to God. "I've already done enough damage here to last me a life time!" a tear formed while looking on the heaving boy. "If he had been an adult, I would feel somewhat better about this," Step thought. He also cringed realizing if the boy died that would be the first life he had ever taken. Even on the brutal streets of New York he'd managed not to commit murder. Nevertheless when he became a bodyguard he knew this day was eventually inevitable. "But killing someone is easier anticipated than actually doing it!" And as he gazed sadly on the boy he vowed from now on to work on his temper. "This boy was already partially helpless when I- I," he stammered aloud this time, "Why didn't I just knock him out or something!" He slid his arm from under the boy and still squatting he took out his gun. Then he paused and slowly picked up the boy's gun. "I'll just use his gun," And with a loud sigh he placed it to the boy's raw temple. Step looked at the snow misting on the charred scull. With a trembling, gloved finger he tried to pull the trigger. He was not surprised when his finger was ready but his heart hesitated and another loud sigh was all he managed. Just like Dassah when her finger refused to obey, so did his relax on, the trigger. Dassah along with the homeless men exhaled deeply. The doctor had already decided not to interfere with whatever her bodyguard decided to do about this. "This is his call," she thought nervously watching Step hold the gun to the wheezing boy's head. And she was also grateful that the coroner would not have to discover a gunshot wound in the boy's skull, "And how could that bullet wound ever be sensibly explained except for murder?!" she thought.

There in the partially covered alley as they watched Step the older homeless man in a fatherly tone, said, "You did the right thing not to shoot him Mister Step," his pink dirty fingers sticking out of the ragged gloves gently squeezed Step's shoulder. "Really, Son," he said. "He's not worth it because of what he did to the doctor here. . . Plus, he has third-degree burns, which wouldn't be so bad if he'd had his hood on his head!" the homeless man expertly accessed. He moved meticulously closer to investigate. "He won't pull through the morning. . . It appears the hot cinders went clear through the parietal of his cranium . . . I'm afraid I can see clear down where a coal penetrated and turned the pituitary gland into a total crust. . . Not to mention his left eyeball is boiled like an egg!" he said, and then he stepped back, "By the time you would get him to the hospital the infection would've killed him anyway!"

As Dassah heard the homeless man's diagnosis she marveled. "You've correctly assessed portions of the skull and brain," she said, eyeing him. "And I concur with those findings," she nodded peering at the boy's head. "How did you know that?"

Scratching his tattered hood, "I don't know," a confused far away gaze in his homeless bloodshot eyes.

Meanwhile, back in the lavish parlor in upper Manhattan the lovely trim middle-aged woman was handed a cordless telephone by a woman wearing a house-keeper's uniform. "Mrs. Clancy Doctor Silver is on the phone," she announced in a heavy British dialect.

"Hello," the anticipating Mrs. Clancy spoke readily into the receiver.

"Marie, this is David . . . any word from Blake?" David was also 50- something.

"Not a word. . . I was so hoping this call was the good news I needed!"

"No I'm afraid not," he sighed. "Well Marie, I hate to do this but my pleading is no longer working on the hospital administration. They flat out warned me that if Blake isn't back at the hospital in a week, we'll be forced to find another Chief of Brain Surgeons.

Reluctance, then, "Isn't there anything else you can do David?"

"You know I've tried everything. . . I'm really sorry Marie!"

"Well, I-I truly understand . . . and thanks! Tell the wife hello for me. Bye now."

Meanwhile back in the cold alley Dassah' eyes moved to the 20-something-year-old homeless man. Being the curious psychiatrist she wondered seriously about him. She had noticed he showed no interest in anything except the attack on her. A tear formed in her eye over the abundance of mentally ill people there were on the streets. "This young man is apparently one of those citizens," she thought. She was anxious to know more about him. "Although I'm sure I'll soon find out," she thought watching his now blank glare at nothing in particular. She noticed his mind even seemed to stray from the excitement of the boy on the ground.

As wind blew snow into the partially covered alley all eyes suddenly moved to the burned victim. He had let out a moan, breathed deeply and then with a gurgle, exhaled very loudly. All eyes moved quickly to his chest and lingered there—it never rose again. "He's gone!" the older man pronounced, "No doubt, from the spread of infection of the cerebellum just that quickly! Sorry I didn't have anything cleaner than the blanket in the house!"

Dassah and Step exchanged glances of deep regret. "Well in my opinion he cut his own life short!" Dassah finally huffed. "Sudden death is usually a criminals' fate!" Yet compassion rose in her again, "But he was so young," she choked up. "His family shall surely miss him, I'm sure. What will I possibly tell them?"

"I'll tell them!" Step immediately replied. "I'm the one who murdered him."

Dassah glared fiercely at her bodyguard and stepped up to him, her muddy pants clinging to her thighs, "Step Carter, never let me hear you say you murdered that boy! You do realize there's a difference, don't you?" She stared squarely into his dark sorrowful eyes. She was moved in that even through snowflakes before his face she saw tears glint in his eyes. Nevertheless she firmly said, "I hired you to do a job and I'm proud you've done me well . . . though the law might disagree, but in my opinion murder is when one deliberately kills and not when one does it in a passion of protecting his own!" she gave him a solid pat on the back.

LD now at Step's side, added, "You probably never would've dumped that hoodlum in the can if you knew it was still burning man!" He also gently touched Step's shoulder as Step kneeled over the dead boy. "It's evident that if that boy hadn't gone for the gun when it was all over, he'd still be alive."

Step smiled faintly up at LD, "Thanks man." Then he stood up and looked at Dassah. "Thanks Boss." And staring down at the body Step thought, "Would I have not done it if I had known the fire was still burning? I wonder!" He knew that it was through intense anger that he momentarily lost all purpose of rationale. Plus having a low tolerance for someone taking what others worked for, infuriated him. And he had helplessly watched the hoodlum violate his female boss, which in his opinion was the straw that broke the camel's back. "The car-jacking I possibly could've gotten over!" Step recalled when he was homeless and only stole to keep his stomach halfway full. And that was only when he had exhausted all lawful options. As he recalled, his first choice would be to forget his pride and politely ask for food. And, as a youngster it had shocked him to find some people void of the compassion to help even with a meal. "Get a job!" some had hissed in his already broken-spirit, teenage face. Yet the lad was broad-minded in understanding how people were hesitant to hand out cash. "But food is a necessity that everyone deserves!" he had thought so many times after being rejected. With four years of homelessness in his portfolio he is able now to walk a mile in the shoes of the homeless.

There in the partially covered alley awaiting the arrival of the police, Step had his back on. He recalled how he felt that day when he was rudely demanded to get a job which was non-existent for homeless people. "Yeah, right, I'll take my dirty fingernails, no social security card and bushy head to the unemployment office. . . Better yet I'll just march my stinky self into a restaurant and tell them I'm here to work!" he had hotly snapped at one scoffer.

However, Step now knows that here in the 2000s, unlike then there are governmentally funded agencies where the homeless can clean up in order to seek employment. But he also realize that the down side is that the overflow in shelters forces a first come, first serve rule for baths. "Only the strong survives!" he often says. He sadly recalled that without prior employment references it was impossible to get inside jobs. But in due season construction was a friend to be counted on. And through Dassah' Bible studies he learned that God commands the financially endowed to share with the truly poor. Then the young Step had impatiently replied to the trying to convince him, doctor, "Form what I've witnessed," he had said. "On the streets most who were able to assist financially hadn't kept that command. . . And I'll bet those same well off people sit in church every Sunday and pretend to be purest saints!" he recalled there in the alley.

Then, as everyone watched him with the boy Step said to the dead body, "And God frowns on moochers and thieves!" He vividly recalled how Dassah had told him that God refers to the slothful as less than infidels. Then Step's mind strayed to his father before his father abandoned the family for a younger woman. His father would always say, "Some people won't even work in a pie factory!" As a child Step had trouble understanding that but now knows his father meant that everyone loves pies and should be happy to be employed in that bakery.

Step recalled that as a homeless adolescent six years ago when construction was slow, panhandling would be his choice of survival. He quickly learned how to solicit. Even as a teenager his better judgment was not to harass people. Along with his outgoing personality a corner had been more profitable than trying to twist arms. Pencils, hand-made gift bags, and other small items sold from appealing boxes was his main tactic. But, then, soon after he would move there, he would be forced to compete with other homeless people for his popular corner. Suddenly they had begun to emulate his ideas. He recalled how he had a monopoly on selling because of his artistic abilities and wit. Plus, he made gift-bags and boxes and could draw very well. There in the alley he managed a subtle smile recalling one of the small boxes he kept as a souvenir. The boxes he had painstakingly covered with wallpaper inside and outside. On them were painted all kinds of personalized designs. Some buyers came back and told him they used the boxes as little tables for their children's room. Some were used as waste baskets, toy boxes and for other uses. He also made lids for some boxes. The smaller boxes which he sold items from had attracted more attention than the items itself. His fancy signature on each was his trademark. He had painted an amazing sign declaring he would work or trade boxes for food which kept him partially fed.

Step recalled having to go into service stations to wash his brushes and hands. He also fed some of his elderly peers. While panhandling on the streets of New York he was thankful the National Coalition for the Homeless had convinced the county to pass a law that the homeless could sell small items without a peddlers permit. However if he built a booth he would need a permit. To be exempt from getting a permit the peddlers had to be homeless and a USA citizen. In Step's case only his word and his American dialect was proof of citizenship. Many of the homeless had no identification. Either his ID had been lost or stolen along with his wallet. And Step's mad dash from the orphanage afforded him no time to swipe his from the office. It amazed him why anyone would rob the homeless anyway. But once he got held up he discovered that crack-heads knew that many of the homeless usually kept one or two dollars in his pocket. "If a snake of a robber took ten homeless people then he'd have enough for a hit of dope!" Step angrily thought.

Step recalled his pan-handling and how he even petitioned businesses to print their company name and number on pencils for him to market for them. In return he also would receive a small fee to advertise. Mostly coffee mugs were in demand in winter. And downtown Manhattan it seemed that office workers always needed pens. Step recalled how he had purchased one cup for a dollar and sold it for a dollar-seventy-five or two dollars. He would fancy-paint the buyer's name on the cup as extra. He would buy a hundred pens for five dollars and sell them for a quarter each. "A twenty-dollar profit is excellent for any homeless person!" he thought while counting his earnings for the day—money he learned to guard with his young life. He was always packing a switch-blade knife and practiced passionately on how to hit the target. He learned to nab a mosquito before the nasty little blood sucker could take to the air. He made sure his peers knew he was strapped with the trusty blade.

That Saturday morning in the alley the partial tin roof was the only cover they had. Doctor Dassah Desoto shivered, glancing at her watch. It was10:02. Then she sighed big again having a good mind to just leave and take that two-block trip back to the limo. "If Step and I were to leave the police would never find us in upper Manhattan anyway!" she thought. But her Christian heart urged her to do the just thing. "Plus, they would only blame this on these poor homeless souls!" The police over the phone had flat out demanded that they all remain at the scene until they would send help.

CHAPTER 10

S tephanas Carter the bodyguard stood beside LD one of the three homeless men, who LD appeared to be the spokesman for the three. The other two homeless men also stood warmly around the rekindled can. The dead Latino lad, attempted rapist lay on the ground covered with the homeless man's filthy blanket, his charred flesh filling the air. Doctor Dassah Desoto had come out early this morning in search of homeless men for her makeover program. When they ventured out in the snow neither she nor Step expected someone would lose his life during the desperate scouting trip.

Now standing up a subtle smile crossed the hooded bodyguard's strong face looking through the flames over at LD. It had pleased Step that he and LD wee communicating on a more positive note. He recalled how LD had just minutes earlier fought along-side of him to apprehend three hoodlums. LD had also stuck up for Step having dumped the boy into the fire. So from across the can they exchanged subtle smiles, snow whipping into the make-shift tent. Then LD limped around the can and extended a tattered gloved hand to Dassah who was snuggled up to Step for warmth, her muddy knees chilled through the insulated jeans. "My name is really Leon Davis, Doc," he revealed.

The hooded doctor smiled up at him. She noticed Leon favoring his leg. "What about your leg, Mr. Davis!" she reached to examine.

"Oh it's just a scratch!" He shrugged. "It barely broke the skin. . . It's nothing compared to that one!" he gestured towards the covered body slowly gathering snow. "And please call me Leon . . . I'm not that important!"

"In the sight of the Almighty, every human being is somebody special!" she assured.

"Are you sure you're okay Leon?" Step asked also pleased to know his real name.

"Yeah, man I've faced worse," a far away, painful look glinting in his dingy eyes, locks sticking around the hood.

The older man also offered his hand and then frowned struggling to remember, "Just call me . . . Pops," frustrated, he finally gave up trying to recall.

Everyone's eyes moved to the younger blond man and waited as he never offered any information about himself. Then disappointment showed in Dassah' eyes. "But at least I know the other two," she thought. "Well, Leon's name!" Her eyes narrowed about Pops.

Finally sirens sounded in the distance in the tattered town of Neal, New York where houses and storefronts sat side-by-side. An attempted theft, rape and a death had just taken place in the partially covered alley. It seemed to Dassah it all that happened in no time flat, which it had in a matter of minutes. She gazed sadly at the snow blowing in through the opening and wished they had not ventured out that day. She, Step, Leon, Pops and the other young homeless man stood around the can, Step very close beside her, afraid to let her move an inch away. Finally Step had time to realize how cold it was even near the can and a warn body in the fine frame of his boss. However he was not sure he was shaking because of the cold, her body close to his or having just took someone's dear life. He had the strangest feeling in the pit of his stomach knowing the stiff body on the ground was the result of his unusual lack of self-control. Then moving his eyes to his boss, he said,

"I'm sure glad you're safe!" His well-nourished dark eyes full of remorse moved to the dead body again and he let out another big sigh, now thinking about the boys' folks.

When they heard foot-steps, all heads turned in anticipation of seeing the police so quickly. Then they gasped, in that the other Latino boy and a Latino man, the man dressed warmly. With rekindled anger Step lunged hotly at the boy. But the man, low in stature, hastened into Step's path and stood his ground glaring up with disdain at Step.

"Dare he is in the groun', Popi!" the hooded hoodlum pointed to the lifeless body gathering snow. His dad immediately ran and eased the stained blanket off his face. With a sickening gag he threw his hand over his mouth and turned away. Then the man's squeal suddenly filled the morning. After a tender moment of grief the man jumped up and advanced intently towards Step, who defensively yanked Dassah behind him. The man's son, Leon, Pops and the other homeless man moved clear of the commotion. The Latino man reached under his expensive over coat. But Step and Dassah both had beaten him to the draw. "Don't do it!" Step warned both he and Dassah skillfully pointing guns with both gloved hands. The Latino man froze but fearlessly still glared at the gunned duo. Dassah thought, "Police, please get here before another blood-bath occurs up in here!!"

Suddenly as the three stood cautiously eye-balling each other, two quilted-jacketed police hustled in, a White male and beautiful, copper-skinned Black female, also pointing guns with isotones-gloves and loudly demanding everyone to drop the weapons. Dassah and Step immediately complied assuring that they flip the safety so the guns would not fire. All they needed now to put the icing on the cake was to shoot a cop by accident or not.

"You too Hombre!" the police said to the man, who still had his hand cautiously inside his coat.

With his free hand in the air the Latino man slowly eased the gun out and reluctantly dropped it hard.

"Now, don't nobody move or we'll shoot and ask questions later!" the big red faced, but good looking male police warned.

The young Black policewoman hotly demanded, "All hands high!" as she moved guardedly in.

Then the big red police took off his glove and frisked all the men his very white hand not as red as his face. When he finished he directed his partner to frisk Dassah. Afterwards they cautiously collected six guns. "What is going on up in here!" hooted the male police. All the while he collected the weapons, "You've got enough guns to supply Iraq! It's exactly people like you who should be over there fighting . . . seems they've got the wrong people over there . . . my son for example, who had never killed anybody until then. And here you are packing like you own the dad-blasted world!"

Dassah sadly eyed the angry police understanding how he must miss his child and was not sure he would see him again neither dead nor alive. In this war too many young men were blown to pieces and scattered all over the place—not to ever be recognized except for hot teeth. Dassah thought about how before the war broke out so many young White boys had been given the opportunity right out of high school to join the armed forces. She figured that was simply for the benefits the government afforded. They never expected a real was to break out. When on the other hand too many young Black boys right out of high school had been racial profiled and given jail fines or jail sentences. "Now sadly most of the White boys are dead in an utterly senseless war and most of the Blacks boys are institutionalized!" she had complained to a fellow doctor, taking in some very young Black homeless ex-cons one day.

"Hi officers, I'm Doctor Hadassah Desoto." Dassah extended her hand after the officer finally had the guns in a pile and he calmed down. The male police only looked in her light brown eyes momentarily and disregarded her hospitality. He then stormed directly to the body on the ground. And lifting the blanket, "Who is this and how did he get this way?" moving irate eyes to everyone while his pretty partner stood beside the pile of guns holding everyone at bay. The boy's father finally cried stammering for English, "Dat's my el sobrino (nephew) in the groun' en somebody gonna pay for kill him." He managed. "Look how he burn up!" he gestured through a sincere sob.

Dassah spoke up again. "Officers, it was I who called nine-one-one . . . the dead victim attempted to car-jack and rape me . . . My bodyguard here only did what he was forced to do . . . we're obviously licensed to carry these guns," she quickly interjected before the police could interrupt again.

"You got righ to kill child!?" the uncle cried understanding English better than he spoke it.

"Quiet, Sir!!" ordered the pretty police as she was on the walkie-talkie giving the ambulance directions. Afterwards when the big red police had his gun pointed she pulled out a pad and began writing. She began to ask questions after reading rights. Dassah was glad to observe that the police asked questions only after reading the Miranda Rights. Dassah had been told many sad stories by the homeless ex-cons about how they had never been read those rights. Even having been incarcerated numerous times they never heard their rights. Dassah wanted to believe the men had been arrested by unlearned police as opposed to a law enforcer flat out violating the constitutional rights of an American citizen.

The pretty police looked up from her pad. "Whose guns are these?" she pointed to the pile gathering snow.

Dassah and Step identified theirs. "The others belong to the boys who attempted to car-jack and rape me," Dassah, trying to control anger, repeated her earlier claim. She fingered the hoodlum now huddled close to his father like the scared kid he really was. "This one was with them and there's yet another boy that has to be caught," Dassah added . . . The dead one was the leader of the vicious dog-pack!" she angrily pointed, making the attack sound just as serious as it indeed was.

In spite of Dassah' rightful justification of what Step did the dead boy's uncle and cousin never let up eye-balling her and Step. The homeless men, Pops, Leon and the younger White man were only answering questions. Dassah was disappointed at being unable to catch the name of the younger homeless man. He had purposely and very guardedly answered the police causing the doctor of the mind to again wonder about his mental status. "He certainly seems crafty enough to conceal his identity," she thought. "He can't be *too* crazy!"

Dassah stared blankly at the corpse gathering snow. The police were guarding everyone. The hooded doctor's thoughts strayed to her mother's boyfriend and the night he had dictated whether or not she would ever bear babies. A tear clouded her beautiful brown eyes. She hoped that if tears were to fall, they would be obscured by snowflakes. Being a psychiatrist she always advised her clients that a woman could bawl like a baby and not look stupid. Yet she managed to stifle her own emotions. As a doctor of the mind she knows all too well that by repressing tears that would run the risk of stress elevating. So she diligently counsels herself to allow the flood-gates to occasionally open.

So, there in the alley with the crowd she managed to briefly recall a lecture in med school. A student had confessed to an incident where he had 'broken down' and cried. That innocent statement had caused the student to receive a sharp rebuke from the strict professor, "Never use the term 'breakdown' synonymous with an occasional cry!" the professor had reprimanded. "Now on the other hand, if you cried too often you could probably benefit from professional mental therapy."

"And what would you say is a lot?" Dassah, also a new student had raised her hand that day. She could not recall once crying since a few days after the rape. Not even when her mother passed. Her last cry was when she figured out it was her own mother who had allowed her body to be brutally mutilated.

In the snowy alley with the police checking out the murder scene she recalled the professor as saying, "Okay, let's turn to page one-hundred-twenty," the middle-aged man in vintage clothing to match had astutely instructed, "There you'll find a paragraph which describes how when one cries excessively there's either an external or psychosomatic issue which will undoubtedly require professional consideration. That's whether the person willingly seeks help or not. That treatable and sometimes curable illness is known as Manic-depressiveness." The professor had said to his class that day. "That illness is sometimes temporary but can become invasive. What with today's rapidly evolving and callous society. . . Then after the true problem gets diagnosed and confronted, many patients can be cured. . . So never more than today have certified psychiatrists been in demand. . . But you must be vigilant of this one thing, and that is, some people will literally place a psyche in God's stead . . . And if you fail to cure them then they will become down right belligerent!"

"So what do you do about that?" a student had raised.

"Well, I let them know up front where I stand in my faith. . . Nevertheless, some of these people are hopelessly deranged you know. . . You just treat that illness just to keep them above water," he had forewarned.

Dassah soon learned that in some cases mental conflict set in when a person would refuse to shed a few tears like she holds back tears. She recalled the professor's warning of how tears were merely the mind's way of ventilating to relieve pressure, "If we did not cry then God's handing out emotions along with tear-ducts and laughter-boxes would've all been in vain!" he had begun to suddenly burst out in roaring laughter, causing the class' tickle-boxes to also turn over. They all laughed until they cried. When the class was at last calm again, "Oh, that felt good as heck!!" one Black student had admitted, slapping his desk.

"So, what are some other reasons God gave man tear-ducts, other than for cries of joy or pain?" he had added.

At the blackboard the professor slowly picked up two erasers and smiling wryly, he walked to the student, "Just you let me slap these together into your eyes! Your tear-ducts would responsibly defend by trying to flood the foreign enemy out!" Then he asked, "In the case of tear-ducts defending against foreign matter which human emotion would be used to provoke the production of tears?"

Dead silence in wonderment.

Then, he finally said, "And that discredited emotion would simply be panic by physical sensation! When the brain knew that its eyeballs were under attack by a dangerous substance it responded sending synapses to the brain demanding the tear-dusts to go into action. . . As you know all of the human reactions originate from the brain," he had added. Then as all the new med students of the mind looked puzzled he had gone on to explain, "By discredited, I mean people tend to un-expectedly *perform* panic, rather than *think* about panic. Thus panic is rarely thought of as an emotion, because panic usually catches us off guard. . . In fact, in an upcoming class we'll discuss the physical ramifications of a panic-attack," Dassah recalled him saying to the class that day.

Dassah took her thoughts back to the snowy alley. The police, Step, three homeless men and two sobbing Latinos bent over the dead body. Then Dassah recalled how now she would only tear up but the tears never seemed to leave her lids. Even the painful thought of her mother being paid to let the rape occur and go un-reported stopped producing tears anymore. "Most of my clients look forward to the day they can stop crying. . . I seek for the tears to begin again," she thought.

There in the snowy, partially covered alley with the policeman and policewoman, Dassah surely had no problem getting angry. She glanced impatiently at her watch. It was 10:20 that Saturday morning. Then her beautiful eyes narrowed as they moved to the Latino boy. With his father beside him he still was brazenly evil-eyeing Step. Dassah knew the boy had returned only to get his cousin. If his cousin had escaped along with him, none of them ever would have lost a night's sleep for what they did. She wondered how many times they had gotten away with this sort of thing. "Time's up boys!" she angrily thought, "Its harvest reaping time!" the cold getting through her insulated, muddy jeans

"Okay!" the big red police growled. "The ones responsible for this boy's death step forward!" Step stepped out from the crowd, and then Dassah stepped out at his side. The pretty police had stopped writing, her dark brown face well made as she looked steadfast on. The big red police said, "The ones responsible for attempted carjacking and rape step forward!"

With his arms stubbornly folded the boy simply stood his ground there at his father's side. Then suddenly his father gave him a full shove forward. "Din you hear la policia?" he growled. "If you should not try to steal, Greco be aliv'! Why you need steal, huh!?" he slapped the back of his son's hooded head.

But he only poked out his mouth and grumbled in Spanish. Dassah was glad to know the father had better understanding now that the police's inquiry was out in the open. And she was grateful the police had heard her even though he acted as though he had not. The big police stared suspiciously at Step and Dassah standing close to each other. "Did it take the two of you to handle this one puny boy!" he snarled.

"No officer," the hooded bodyguard said, "I handled that one alone . . . and there were three gun-toting-gangsters up in here!"

"Then you're the one I want!" he almost as tall as Step, wheeled the compliant bodyguard around and snapped on the handcuffs. Then he harshly handcuffed the much shorter, reluctant boy. He looked at his Nubian, curvy Amazon of a partner, "These two need to go to the wagon, please?" he politely suggested.

Her gun skillfully drawn, "Come on you two!" she immediately beckoned them towards the exit where Dassah and Step had earlier entered. With fine snow dropping through the ceiling slit and blowing into the un-walled sides of the tent the law enforcers agreed that the policeman would remain with the body and the others until the arrival of the ambulance. Slowly on the way to the exit, Step glanced hesitantly over his shoulder at Dassah, "Will you be okay Boss?" as if she had a choice in the matter. "Oh yes! You know me," she tried sounding braver tan she really was for his peace of mind.

On the way through the alley Step thought, "Never in my wildest dream did I ever figure I'd be coming back this way in handcuffs . . . having killed someone, and leaving behind the one I was supposed to be protecting . . ." He said audibly, "And the dead boy was merely a child of seventeen!" The dead boy was only eight years younger than himself. "But, he committed an adult crime!" he huffed going through the snow drizzle narrow alleyway. He was in the lead, the boy trailing and the policewoman behind with gun in hand.

"No talking up there!" she ordered. "And if you decide to run, I was one of the best marksperson in my class!"

CHAPTER 11

They silently took the long trek through the alleyway to the streets. Step, the Latino boy and the policewoman on was finally on the street. Heads turned and eyes gawked at them. Then the policewoman gun drawn ordered the hand-cuffed Stephanas Carter, Dassah' bodyguard and the hoodlum boy into a white police wagon.

That Saturday morning inside the cold yet warmer wagon, Step and the boy were seat-belted, somewhat uncomfortably on stiff plastic seats. Those plastic seats felt as if they were made from roofing material. Then Step sat interestingly watching through the wire screen as the police's dark curl fell seductively into her face as she climbed into the driver's seat. With snow also before her eyes she only blew the curl away with full tangerine lipstick on. Her copper-tone skin glisten a hint of perspiration even in the cold. Step though he had just killed a boy couldn't help but to admire her striking beauty, even with all the clothes on. She began to write as she listened to calls over the radio. The boy across from Step was in a state of childish sulking.

There in the patty wagon on the short seat with his arms cuffed behind the long legged bodyguard shifted from side to side. The mildew mixed with urine made for a stifling sauna. The scent of alleys was the best he could think of the odor. He thought, "Having been a street person one would think I'd be used to stench!" a frown. "Only this wagon had also been mixed with some sort of disinfectant!"

He stared out into faces of different races, mostly of Blacks. They strained to see in and unlike the limo they had no trouble this time. Step knew that on any given day in the ghettos of New York a patty wagon was not an unusual sight. He also knew that some observers were concerned whether that was their loved ones as a passenger.

Then suddenly anger flared up inside Step again when he noticed the boy's dark Spanish eyes piercing daggers through him—again. "This stupid kid has justified what they did was okay!" he thought. "He just doesn't get it that any defenseless woman needs to be protected from dogs like them!" Step could not understand that kind of insensitivity coming from a Mexican man, in that they were usually so family-oriented in culture. For the most part they deeply respected their women. "Nevertheless, in every culture sin knocks at all doors!" he thought, hood off, glaring across at the fuming youth. Step moved his eyes over the boy's well-dressed frame. He had noticed that the boy's father showed genuine concern. "Why did you make me do that?" Step's guilt finally exploded in the boy's fuming brownish face.

"Hump!" the boy turned his face to the roof.

"Now you're going to spend the rest of your teenage years in jail behind some stupid stuff!"

"I din' burned up my co-sin, you did!" he lashed in very broken English.

"But it was you punks who rushed in on us with guns. . . Remember?! We were simply minding our own business!" the bodyguard felt his blood pressure elevate off the chart, even though he was not hypertensive.

The pretty police had stopped writing and had cocked a listening ear. She shot a glance through the protective screen at Step with new-found respect in her dark eyes, "Hum-m-mm he's not only handsome, but honest and decent as well!" she thought. Then she huffed, "That's enough back there!" Still, in spite of the reprimand she shot him a subtle smile. He caught it, wondering what took her so long. The ex-homeless man dated but had no exclusive girl in particular.

After a moment of commanded silence Step more calmly said to the boy, "You seem like a smart boy so why did you mess up your life with attempted rape and armed robbery?"

"Wha' you care 'bout my lif, hombre!?" he shrieked. "You in you grande coche (big car) say to me 'bout my lif . . . you don' know 'bout me!" Hand-cuffs and seatbelt restriction all he could do was head-bang the back of the seat in a fit.

Now it was a little clearer to Step why they intended to hi-jack the limo. These young boys had no car and desired one even down to taking someone else's. Plus it seemed the boys had a Robin Hood complex—steal from the rich to sustain the poor. "Sad to think some poor folks can be just as prejudice as some rich folks!" Step thought. "Sheer spite has compelled these kids not only to risk their own lives, but also the lives of others!"

"Alright, you!" the policewoman warned but all the time interested in the conversation.

"You're right young man!" The also young Step whispered now. "So I don't know you, but I do know you committed a crime!" Step strained forward while his broad chest pulled against the seatbelt, "Do you really think its right to rape a woman!?"

"I din rape!"

"But your cousin was doing off limit things to the doctor and you did nothing to stop him!"

"Righ', wron' . . . wha' is righ'!?" he cried loudly. "Is it righ' som' people be so mucho el dinero (much money) an' other be so muy pobre!?" (Very poor) he glared intensely at Step.

Silence in the patty wagon. Then again Step whispered, but loud enough for the policewoman to hear, "Would you believe I was once so homeless I had no bed at all like I'm sure you have . . . mine was a cardboard box under a tent, and sometimes the big friendly sky was the only roof I had?"

In the driver's seat the pretty police suddenly stopped writing again. The boy simply nonchalantly cut his eyes at Step. And in a serious tone

Step continued, "When I was your age . . ." staring into the boy's fuming eyes. "How old are you anyway?"

The boy only gathered more wind in his youthful cheeks.

Step went on in spite, "I became homeless when I was fifteen years old, probably a year younger than you are now." The boy, like his father also understood English better than he spoke it.

In the rear-view mirror two beautiful eyes caught Step's. The four locked momentarily. He noticed pity in her dark eyes and was impressed. His gaze was sincere. "I've just been off the streets for six years now," he said, directing mostly to her. "I was blessed to have Doctor Desoto rescue me in the nick of time. . . I was about to do something very stupid just like you when she found me in an alley." His eyes moved back over to the boy. "But then the doc offered me a better life and that was exactly what we were doing back in that alley . . . trying to rescue those poor homeless souls."

Silence in the patty wagon again except the static-radio dispatcher.

Step took his eyes off the boy long enough to glance in the mirror again. Now she was outwardly smiling softly. Their eyes tenderly fused longer this time. Suddenly she snapped out of it, blushed and quickly resumed writing.

Step smiled at her bashfulness, not running across many women with that type of innocence nowadays. "What a true turn-on!" he thought. "Plus, if she looks that good in a uniform, she must be the bomb in regular duds!" he thought. He also noticed that even her sternness was done with tact. She had not been excessively nasty though he felt she could be if provoked. "A softie certainly wouldn't be given a beat on the streets of Neal," he thought. "Only a seasoned cop would dare patrol in this neck of the hoods!"

"What's your name and address young man!" she had already asked back in the alley but used extra precaution to assure consistency.

"I tol you one ti'!" he snapped.

"Don't you answer the officer that way Do-Do Head!!?"

"I can handle this mister Carter!" she insisted. "Now, let's try this one more time, and only once . . . what. . ."

Juan Mendes!" he hotly interrupted. "I liv Cassidy Street.

"That's way on the other side of town," she said. "What are you doing here trying to hi-jack and rape somebody!?"

"You hav' hear of visit som'one, hav' you!?" sarcasm in his juvenile voice.

Step's size thirteen, Timberland's landed a blow to Juan's shin. "Watch your manners I told you!!"

"Oh-h-h he brake' my leg!!"

The pretty police sighed and arose, "I see now that the only thing to do is leg-shackle the two of you!"

"No, ma'am you don't have to do that!" Step, in a softer tone assured. "I'm sorry."

Sitting back down, she said, "Alright, but be quiet unless I ask a question!"

After a while when she asked Step's information, she purposely dug deeper than usual. He saw the curve-ball coming and batted it clear out of sight and divulged the extra info, especially his marital status. Finally, with respect, she said, "Yes, I've heard about the famous Doctor Desoto and her program." Then she informed her suspects that they must remain there until her partner with his detainees would emerge from the alley. "Is it too cold in here?" she asked. "But, if I turned up the heat, the smell would only smother you!"

"No-no, we're okay!" Step was already gagging from the week old urine stench.

"Speak fo you-self, Hombre, I col bak here!" Juan hissed the contrary.

"Well, you'll just have to button up, won't you!?" Step hissed right back.

Meanwhile back in the alley that Saturday morning, again sirens sounded in the distance. Dassah' heart shouted of joy knowing the ambulance was near. Not only had she become nauseatingly annoyed with the red-faced police's gripes but the moisture had managed to penetrate her insulated jeans. Snow came down more densely as she and the three homeless men stood under the tenthouse quietly close to each other. She had long sense ceased to notice any smell from homeless people. Her eyes moved agitatedly to the partially covered tin roof that offset some of the snow. And also the boy's uncle was bawling and kneeling over the body. Though she had compassion for the uncle her eyes then moved to the shivering homeless men as well. Then sympathy over their plight out-weighed the compassion for the boy. Guilt also overshadowed her as she realized a Christian should not be partial in handing out consideration. "But, at least these homeless men tried to help us instead of violating a woman as the weaker vessel amidst so many men," she thought.

The fire in the can was almost quenched and the meticulous policeman with watchful eyes refused to allow another fire to be kindled. Then the doctor mildly shrugged it off by convincing herself that the homeless men were used to the elements and famine all at the same time, "But this boy will never come back to his family!" Then she looked across the can, "In just a few minutes you guys will be in my car having the wholesome breakfast I brought along!"

"Golly, I sure hope so!" Pops breathed shifting impatiently from foot to foot. He was also rubbing his pot belly.

"You said a stomach full Doc!" Leon also rubbing his growling belly under tattered clothing. The younger man similar to a child was stuck to Leon's side.

Then suddenly the Latino man jumped up from kneeling, and wheeled to face Dassah. "How ya' talk abou food wen ya' jus kil a kid?!" he wagged his head in very broken English. She wondered if he was really a legal citizen with that kind of ignorance of the English language. "Even some Latinos who've never been to America speak better English than you!" she thought in his face.

The police immediately stepped between the man and her, yet remained impartial in taking sides in their quarrel.

The refined, Christian doctor glared vehemently at the angry man. But in a defensive mood she tried her best to move maneuver around the policeman. She'd had about enough disrespect for one day. So, the 5 foot, 11 inch doctor, over the policeman's shoulder, "I'll tell you how I can easily speak about food Hombre!" she screeched, not even recognizing her own voice, which she rarely raised. "When was the last time you had a hot meal . . . or even a cold meal!? Maybe just an hour ago!?" she firmly accused, "And you probably even gave your dog a steak and a soft doggie-bed or does he sleep with you?!" She waved her hands around the policeman, who yet remained neutral barricading both. Nevertheless she went on, "Well, for your information these humans here possibly haven't eaten in days. And, furthermore they sleep outside in all kinds of weather. . . The last time I read the Holy scriptures humans normally sleep in beds and animals sleep outside . . . even though some people die," she gestured toward the body on the ground, "the ones still alive have the right to survive!"

"Das too bad they nee food," the man sputtered back, "Wha' I gona tel my sister 'bout her boy?" a frantic but sad sob escaped his chapped lips, "She already lose her husband depor' to Mexico." Then he stumbled sobbing back to the body.

"Well Sir, it just appears everybody's got a sad story to tell today!" she huffed. It was not the doctor's intention to sound insensitive toward the death of the boy. And she really loved animals—she has two well cared for dogs, two cats and five birds of her own, "But if I had a choice whether to feed a truly helpless human or an animal well . . ." she thought there in the alley. But as always she would make sure the human was truly helpless and willing to work. "Way too many moochers are certainly out there preying on the compassionate!" she always says.

With the wide-eyed homeless observers of another melee in the alley it became quiet again, except for the uncles' sobs. Then the policeman finally chided, "Now you two, may I go back to being the boss up in here!?" He moved to a big rock and propped a thick-boot on it, while listening to his busy radio. Dassah had softened, but had begun to pace back and forth. But then she had moved too close to the body and the uncle.

Leon reached out to her with caution. "Doc, I wouldn't get so close if I were you!" he advised. "Some people can be unpredictable in certain cases, you know."

"Oh, yes I know!" immediately beginning to pace in another direction. "Thanks, Leon!" She began to feel safe with Leon there in that her mind frequently wandered too far off for her own good.

Dreaming the impossible dream of stamping out homelessness altogether had almost consumed the doctor of the mind. Nevertheless she knew the poor would forever be a sad part of society—some of them preferring the streets and some not being able to do any better. And assisting the latter was her Christian quest. There in the alley now standing by the cool can she recalled a scripture where even Jesus himself attested to the fact that the poor would always exist. And she found that prophesy to be visibly real. Because many rich or whomever, can has refused to share with the truly poor. She know that statement by the Lord was sure, but maybe not so many should be homeless. Maybe the lengthy war and down-spiral of the economy has frightened many citizens into hanging onto their money for an unsavory day. Therefore the poor and jobless suffer the backlash of those penny-pinchers. "Although, many rich people will selfishly hesitate to let go of the all mighty dollar for any cause other than stuff for themselves!" she had once said to another benevolent doctor. There in the cold alley Dassah recalled that scripture and knew that since it was inevitable that the poor would never cease from society. She also realized that if the poor were inevitable then that also means the rich will always be among them. But she was compelled to smile about the wealthy citizens who had done so much for the poor. "Not all of us financially blessed capitalists are heartless!" she managed to snicker even in the mounting gloom there in the alley. Other than God's word the thought of her dynasty always put a smile on her beautiful face. Then she recalled how even some of her wealthy co-partners had invested in many women's shelters. And those independently owned homes were available for women with children. But that lovely smile vanished like the snowflakes on her perfect nose when she thought of the few men's shelters that remained packed until they were forced to turn away too many. Thus the alleys kept its jaws wide for the gobble-down. And once the jaws clasped some men were eternally trapped in an invincible web. Dassah was not surprised to learn that some had been on the streets too long to remember what a real bed felt like. "Anyway," she had said to a fellow doctor that day, "After about ten years of street living he probably won't make it through the dangerous exposure of the elements here in New York!" She knew that longevity would never became bragging rights for the chronic homeless.

In all of her public speeches the doctor pleads for contributions towards legitimate charitable organizations. The United Way, American Red Cross and Salvation Army are usually at the top of the list. She also advises citizens to keep abreast of pertinent articles generated by the Substance Abuse and Mental Health Services Administration (SAMHSA). SAMHSA is a vital organization designed to assist in supporting community centers that assist with certain drug abuses, mental disorders and other crisis. In speaking, she exposes how UW and the American Red Cross render aid to the homeless only through other smaller private benevolent avenues such as church ministries, etc. She was not surprised to discover that too many citizens needed to be informed about the real purpose of the UW. Some seekers of assistance were under the impression that, if they became delinquent in rent payments then all they have to do is appeal to the UW. And that assistive program would automatically go to bat for them. The doctor recalled having to sadly warn people that the UW is solely to assist in disasters and dire emergencies, like homes destroyed by fire and other devastating natural occurrences. However, the Salvation Army is funded to help with legitimate utilities, rent and food. Private donations provide smaller organizations with monetary assistance from private donors in order to issue aid in many desperate situations. The UW is a non-profit connection to other agencies that may assist with rent, food, drug and substance abuse disorders. Also family counseling, and boy and girl scout services and other life-survival necessities are included. Dassah was happy to inform that the employees of UW are paid from donations by citizens of the country in which they live. She would boast about the UW's merciful efforts. Though, some of those volunteers donate free hours of work. Dassah informs needy people to contact the UW by dialing 211. Though she was totally disappointed to learn that 211dialed from a pay phone by the homeless were unable to connect to assisting agencies. Thus the desperate needy caller has to deposit a phone fare after talking to an operator from a free 211 dial. And for the homeless seeker it may have already taken numerous phone-fares to finally get an assisting agency. Sadly that homeless person may have spent a day's panhandling earnings. And then he had to spend another bus fare to get to the pinpointed agency "It's no wonder the homeless are so mentally irritated!" she had said one day to a fellow psychiatrist. The doctor of the mind realized that in certain cases it could have very well taken him asking 20 or more compassionate people just to get the three dollars he just used up on the phone and bus fare. "Well, there goes his food money?!"

"But if they can make it into the UW office in their neighborhood then they have a free phone the homeless can use to contact assistive agencies." He had informed her.

"Oh, that's right! I wondered when they would install those free phones!"

Then her light brown eyes moved sadly to the hungry men with her and the policeman in the alley. The boy's body, his uncle and the policeman was no doubt a sight that added to the men's torture. "That ambulance should be here by now!" she huffed loudly as she stopped pacing. "By now I could have run here on foot!"

"You ain't just whistlin' Dixie!" Pops' added in a raspy voice, "I need to use the little boy's room, but there's a lady present . . . may I go just down the alley, Officer?" he asked the policeman, who so avidly kept his hand on his now holstered revolver.

And only a cold condescending glare at the tattered older man was the reply. "Well if you must!" he finally huffed, "But, if you try anything, remember I always catch my man."

"Now why would I try anything? I haven't anything to ran away from. . . I just have to take a piss!" wagging his hooded head, "Or I could just whip it out right here!" going for the zipper.

"Oh go ahead!" an impatient wave.

Dassah watched Pops hustle and then disappear into the mist of snow between the buildings.

While in the alley waiting for the ambulance Dassah looked at the other two shivering men in hole-ridden hoods. Pops joined his companions and they all huddled by the cool can under the short-shaft tin ceiling. Then her eyes moved over to the red-faced police. He had his thick boot propped on a rock, the guns in a pile behind him. Clad in a durable jacket, gloves and fur-lined cap the weather seemed as only a joke to him. Her eyes then moved to the Latino man sobbing over his nephew's body on the ground. Dire sadness gripped her even for the criminal teens. Then her lovely brown eyes moved back to the tattered men. "How truly starved they must be by now?" she thought, knowing she and Step had been there for almost two hours. She glanced at her watch. It was 10:45. "Odds are they had no dinner last night either!"

Leon noticed her irritability and went around the can to her. "Doc, I would offer you a seat in my penthouse," he gestured towards the soaked box from which he had earlier emerged. "But the furniture I ordered from the Gallery hadn't arrived yet," he snickered. Pops snickered, but the younger man simply remained poker-faced.

Dassah noticed how funny Leon looked with his locks sticking out around his hood and wanted to outright laugh a bit longer, but then refrained. "I don't know what kind of demeanor he really has just yet," she thought. "He might revert and think I'm laughing at him instead of with him. Of course he'd be right!" As a psychiatrist she took heed not to offend the homeless so she simply chuckled with them, "How nice of you Leon, but I'm fine . . . really." She looked at the men who had gathered close to her around the can as if the can contained any heat. Though Dassah had no child, but looking at the men her motherly instinct kicked in. Sincerely longing to give them a hug, she thought, "Everyone can use a, somebody-do-care touch ever so often." She reached over and touched the younger man's hand ever so gently. He jumped as if she had just given his hand a bolt of lightning.

Dassah recalled her own apathetic upbringing where she and Jarvis had received, much needed hugs only at church. "Parents especially should frequently hug their kids," she thought, recalling how her mother never touched her except with a slap across the face. She pictured the bumper-sticker she saw just yesterday, "Did you hug you child today?" That simple question had almost brought hot tears to her eyes.

While in the alley awaiting the ambulance that sounded in the distance, she said, "Shouldn't that ambulance be here by now?!"

"Could be on the way to one of the other millions of emergencies in Neal," the policeman flatly pointed out. "There are way too many of them here you know."

"And if there were not then you'd be out of a job!" she was compelled to scoff.

Then he simply eyed his homeless detainees with more snobbish suspicion. And as if he had nothing else to do his deep blue eyes drifted to Dassah' firm thighs. She tugged her jacket down as far to the knees as it would go. Hooded and gloved shooting a subtle but sultry glance at the 40ish cop she thought, "Nevertheless, I'm flattered," embarrassment crossing her stunning face for being so muddy around the knees. Then the police's eyes met hers and both feeling that was inappropriate bashfully turned their gaze away. The homeless men seemed none the wiser to the mutual exchange between the doctor and the law-enforcer.

Suddenly her eyes moved to the dead boy's uncle occasional weeping over the body. With all the dolefulness in the snowy alley her mind longed to just draw a blank. But then her mind was blank only when it was asleep. So she recalled her inadvertent church going as a child, "At least I can thank my mother for that," she thought, "Up until I was about fourteen, I figured the cunning way she had forced Jarvis and me out of the house on Sundays was for real." Now Dassah realizes her mother only wanted to be free to entertain without the kids interrupting. "Off to Sunday School children!" she would shoo them to the only little neighborhood church of Christ in Victory, Ga. "My mother really accidentally left me something positive that would last for an eternity!" she always now says. Even though Dassah had not obeyed the gospel call until later in life, she was glad when she did.

Then she recalled that little church a couple of blocks away from their house. It had only a handful of members. The little white stucco building was immaculate and the pews smelled new. Her fondest memory was how the people were not afraid to hug each other. And they would hug strangers also. She recalled how the minister would read from the scriptures about the church of Christ being the one true church. But before she learned better she thought he meant that building was the church instead of the people an obedient group of believers. She later discovered there were numerous churches of Christ in every county, city, state and country. The church is a spiritually called-out body of believers that God removed from the devil's spiritual realm and placed them into His saving kingdom. She also learned that 'called-out' basically meant that God called one from worldliness (whatever they felt like doing was alright to do). Then God places the saved into holiness (whatever King Jesus says is right is lawful). She was equally as amazed to learn the church of Christ was established in 33 AD in Jerusalem on the first Pentecost Day after Jesus' resurrection. She recalled the preacher having said, "The first gospel sermon was preached after God raised Jesus Christ from the dead. . . That was when God the Father through God the Son planned for Jesus' church to begin," The preacher had said. Then he had declared, "God knew it was the Jew's custom under the law to be at the Passover during the day of Pentecost to celebrate the Old Testament feast day. Thus God wanted the Jews to hear the New Testament gospel message. . . That day was the era in which God had planned to transition Israel (the Jews) from under the Mosaic Law (Old Testament) and into Christ's New Testament rule." Dassah recalled how the preacher had proved that Jesus was sent to the Jews first. Only Jews were gathered on Pentecost. And to prove that the gospel was first to be preached to the Jews, he had shown Matthew 15:22-28. A woman of Canaan (a Gentile, not of Jewish Israel) had begged Jesus to heal her child. Then Jesus had said to the Gentile woman, *"I am not sent but to the lost sheep of the house of Israel."*

And even with Jesus' apostles insisting that the sad woman go away, the woman persisted to beseech him even more to help her.

But Jesus said to her, *"It is not meet (suitable) to take the children's bread (Jews-Israel) and to cast it to the dogs (Gentiles, disobedient, heathen nation)."*

Still the Gentile woman insisted and declared that even the dogs ate the crumbs that fell from the children's table. Then Jesus upon seeing her faith, said, *"Oh woman, great is thy faith: be it unto thee even as thou wilt."* He healed her daughter even though she was not of the lost sheep of the house of Israel. And concerning Gentiles receiving entrance into the church, Dassah read that in the 10th chapter of Acts after the Jews' conversion, God also sent redemption to the Gentile nation. Thus all people who would obey God would be part of one spiritual body. There in the alley Dassah recalled how the preacher had said, "I want you to study the four gospel books where Jesus had preached, preparing the Jews for the establishment of the church to begin on Pentecost. . . And then read the first and second chapters of Acts to learn how the church (kingdom which Jesus had preached about) had its origin as prophesied by many prophets of the Old Testament. God through Daniel, in 2:44, had confirmed that in the days of those reigning kings of the coming Roman empire, God would set up His kingdom. . . And we know that the kingdom is the church, because in First Corinthians 15:24, upon Jesus' return he will deliver up his kingdom (church) to God his Father . . . thus, after that, Christ will no longer reign as the King the way he presently rules over the church (kingdom)," she recalled the preacher having said to the church that day.

With fine snow blowing into the alley Dassah recalled when she was first added to the church of Christ. She had vowed never to forget one of the numerous scriptures the preacher had used to refer to the church of Christ. It was Romans, 16:16, "Salute one another with a holy kiss the churches of Christ salutes you." The preacher in his usual articulation would alert his audience that 'churches' did not mean all of the denominational institutions claiming to belong to Christ are actually his. But rather, Jesus has only one body declaring the same gospel message and doctrine that the early church had declared. The preacher had read Colossians 1:18, "And he is the head of the body, the church." He also used logic that Christ having only one body meant he also had only one church, "The church and the body are one and the same—Thus Jesus Christ, like man has only one body!" he had reasoned. And again the preacher rationalized, "Why is it that man would give Jesus more than one body (church) when man himself has only one body?!" He became slightly agitated, realizing that man always thought carnally while Christ is spiritual—one Spirit, Father, Son and Holy Ghost. Some nay say that makes 3 Gods. . . One plus one, plus one equals 3. However, they have the math all wrong. The real equation boils down to, one divided by one divided by one equals One! After man fell from grace, God the Creator went in search for a man that was perfect enough to redeem man back to Him. That sacrifice had to be pure in order for his blood to be accepted by God In God's sight, blood is always the redeeming medium. So in Revelation 5:4, 5, the Apostle John's pen dictated what God told him to say. "And I (John) wept much, because no man was worthy t open and to read the book, neither to look thereon. (5) And one of the elders said unto me, Weep not: behold the Lion of the tribe of Juda, the Root of David, hath prevailed to open the book, and to loose, the seven seals thereof." Thus Jesus goes on to open the seals and the book and to read the revelation that God had commanded him to.

Dassah also learned in Ephesians 5:23 that Christ is also the head and savior of his body (church), "For the husband is the head of the wife even as Christ is the head of the church: and he is the savior of the body." She had to also bear in mind that it was God the Father who authorized Christ the Son to be the head of Christ's church when God raised Jesus Christ from the dead. Again, she recalled Ephesians 1:22, "And hath put all things under his feet and gave him to be the head over all things to the church (body). God gave Jesus Christ all authority. And in Acts 4:12 there is no other name whereby man can be saved—no other authority.

There in the snowy alley with three homeless men and a policeman Dassah recalled how it is biblically sound that God's single and overall salvation process was designed for all of humanity. That process was the beginning of how get into His body the church. And that universal pattern is outlined by the God of heaven. A pattern is usually made the same way every time. One pattern was designed to put the obedient believer *into* Christ's body (church). She recalled before she stepped out and obeyed the gospel-call. To prove God does the calling only through His word to which she took heed, the preacher had shown her Second Thessalonians 1:7, 8, "And to you who are troubled rest with us, when the Lord Jesus shall be revealed from heaven with his mighty angels (8) In flaming fire taking vengeance on them that know not God, and that *obey* not the gospel of our Lord Jesus Christ—the calling, Second Thessalonians, 2:14, "Wherefore, he *called* you by our gospel to the obtaining of the glory of our Lord Jesus Christ." The apostles that carried out the gospel-call were given that authority by Christ, through the baptism of the Holy Ghost, given by God. Matthew 28:19, 20, Jesus said to the apostles, *"Go you therefore and teach all nations, baptizing then in the name of the Father, and of the Son and of the Holy Ghost (20) teaching them to observe all things whatsoever I have commanded you: and, lo, I am with you even unto the end of the world."*

The preacher had told the audience that the apostles being led by the Holy Ghost wrote that same pattern in various passages in the Holy scriptures for future generations to read and obey. He had also warned the unsaved that God does not call people with an audible voice in these latter days, but calls by His written word (gospel) according to Second Thessalonians 2: 14.

There in the snowy alley, the doctor recalled how she had sat with her mouth hung listening to the preacher that day. Before that sermon she had been under the impression that all the churches out there had God's approval. But then the preacher had proved from the scriptures how one must be added to the one true church. To the packed church-building the preacher had carefully assured the unsaved visitors that the first step in God's salvation process was to HEAR the gospel. Romans 10:17, "So then faith comes by hearing and hearing by the word of God." They should understand the gospel as being the truth and good news of the death, burial and resurrection of Jesus Christ, 1 Corinthians 15th chapter outlines the gospel as the death burial and resurrection.

The preacher had informed that the second step in the salvation process is to BELIEVE that true gospel. Hebrews 11:6, "But without faith it is impossible to please God: for he that comes to God must believe that he is, and that he is a re-warder of them that diligently seek him."

The third step is to REPENT. Acts 17:30, "And the times of this ignorance God winked at, but now commands all men everywhere to repent." They was to understand that to repent meant they would abandon their old idolatrous ways and follow the new path, and that they were truly sorry for having lived alienated from God in the past.

The fourth step is to CONFESS with the tongue, Romans 10:10, "For with the heart man believes unto righteousness, and with the mouth CONFESSION is made unto salvation.

Then Dassah being the curious doctor before she was saved had asked a teacher, "And what must one confess?" The answer was to confess that one believes Jesus Christ to be the Son of God. That teacher had shown her Matthew 10:32, 33 where Jesus said, *"Whosoever therefore shall confess me before men, him will I also confess before my Father which is in heaven. (33) But whosoever shall deny me before men, him will I also deny before my Father which is in heaven."* She understood that was to be a verbal acknowledgment before others. And other scriptural text also proves that once saved, one must continue to confess Christ by living a daily life of holiness or do all you can not to commit sim. But when a saint falls because of weakness, then you must truly repent.

Then the preacher had gone on that day to tell them that fifth step is BAPTISM. First Peter 3:21, "The like figure where even baptism does also now save us, not the putting away of the fifth of the flesh, but the answer of a good conscience towards God." They were to understand that baptism puts one into Christ's body (church). "Galatians 3:27, "For as many as have been baptized <u>into</u> Christ have put on Christ. (28) There is neither Jew nor Greek (Gentile) there is neither bond nor free, there is neither male nor female: for ye are all one in Christ Jesus." The sinner is to understand that the passage, neither male nor female is speaking in the spiritual sense. We all realize that there certainly are male and female in the physical sense.

Then, after one's act of obedience to God's salvation process, God gives that believer the gift of the Holy Ghost. Acts 2:38, "Then Peter an apostle said unto them, Repent and be baptized every one of you in the name of Jesus Christ for the remission of sins, and you shall receive the gift of the Holy Ghost." Dassah recalled how when she obeyed, she was overjoyed to claim that Holy gift and indeed to be saved by the blood of Christ—to have his mind (Spirit-Word) and not go to hell was an imperishable gift unlike man's mind which is corruptible.

Then she was shown how God ADDS the obedient to THE (singular) church. Acts 2:47, "And the Lord added to the church daily such as should be saved." She understands that one cannot *join* the true spiritual church of the scriptures, only God does the adding. And also, those that should be saved, meant that only God knows who are sincerely honest about being saved. Some of those who were baptized were not honest about their belief. Thus God did not count the dishonest ones into His addition. She had also learned that baptism was an immersion under water and not just to be sprinkled or poured upon. She had found that in the book of Acts 8:36-38, where the Ethiopian eunuch and Phillip the deacon\evangelist came across water in the desert. As she read that she definitely viewed that as another miracle from The Creator. Deserts were normally just that, deserted—void of anything but dirt and maybe a few cactus for the desert animals. Thus Phillip had gotten into the chariot and taught the eunuch about Christ. He had begun with the book of Isaiah the Old Testament. Then the eunuch said, "See, here is water, what does hinder me from being baptized? (37) And Phillip said, 'If thou believe with all your heart, thou may. And he answered that he believed that Jesus Christ was the Son of God. (38) And he commanded the chariot to stand still: and they went down both into the water, both Phillip and the Ethiopian eunuch; and he baptized him. (39) And when they were come up out of the water, the Spirit of the Lord caught away Phillip that the Ethiopian eunuch saw him no more: and he went on his way rejoicing. At that Dassah knew that she too must be immersed in water-baptism God's way. She also viewed Phillip's getting caught away by the Spirit as another of God's miracles in order for the Ethiopian eunuch to see the miracle. So the Ethiopian eunuch went on rejoicing that he had been saved. God worked special miracles in the Apostolic era to confirm the word. Mark 16:20, "And they (apostles) went forth and preached everywhere, the Lord working with them and confirming the word with signs (miracles)." Unlike special miracles were back then, nowadays in the post-apostolic era, man walks by faith and not by sight (2 Corinthians 5:7. The preacher had reminded them that at the time of this statement the apostles had ceased to perform miracles, in that gifts were in the process of being phased out after the death of the last apostle.

The apostles were the only ones who could transfer the gifts to others. (First Corinthians 13: 8, 13, "Charity (love) never fails: but whether there be prophecies, they shall fail; whether there be tongues, they shall cease; whether there be knowledge, it shall vanish away. (13) Now abides faith, hope and charity, these three; but the greatest of these is charity." Of course, God can work a miracles if He so pleases. But He did away with the laying on of the hands of man to impart gifts and healings.

There in the doleful alley Dassah continued to meditate on pure things that made her happy. She had learned that even before the church was established Jesus prophesied we would walk by faith rather than by sight. In John 20:29 he had told Thomas one of his unbelieving apostles, *"Thomas, because thou hast seen me, thou hast believed: blessed are they that have not seen, and yet have believed."* During his doubtful moments of disbelief, Thomas and the other apostles had not yet been baptized with the Holy Ghost as only the apostles were the only ones to get the Holy Ghost baptism on Pentecost.

Again she recalled the preacher reminding them the true reason man changes God's word concerning baptism. They turn the word around just to fit his own conveniences. Because it was much less bother to sprinkle or pour than to get undressed and then dressed again! It was convenient for some so-called churches to schedule a date to baptize all. That practice is certainly unlike the true church of the saints. The early church baptized the same hour one completes the first four processes to be saved.

While there in the alley awaiting the ambulance Dassah recalled that even as a teenager when her mother sent then to church just to get them out of the house, she was confused about First Peter 3:21 as it related to the baptism of today. But later when she became a Christian she learned the '*like figure* in that passage refers to Noah and his family, who had been saved by their obedience of getting aboard the ark. God had constructed through Noah—thus God had saved them by taking them through the flood of water. He and his were buried in water. Likewise (the like figure) is when man and woman obey by going through the watery grave of baptism. Then he adds us to Christ's body.

But God only accepts man after obeying the other four commands. She studied the story of Noah and discovered Noah also had heard God's commands, believed it, and worked his righteousness (obedience) before he and his could be saved. His family obviously also obeyed and went into the ark. It was through that event that Dassah realized God was no respecter of persons. Through her intense search of the scriptures she concluded that God has always demanded obedience prior to anyone being saved. As a young adult when she performed her faith by hearing, believing, repenting, confessing and being baptized, only then could she relish in the hope of heaven if she remained faithful until death. Her prayer now is not to become selfishly judgmental but speak only as God have written in His word. "If God says adultery is a sin then surely as a Christian, I can advise someone not to commit adultery," she thought. However, she understands that she should not rebuke someone else for lying if she steals. "So that's what 'judge not lest you be judged' means?" she had asked in a Bible class. Also from studying she found that an unsaved person does not have the blessed privilege to approach God in prayer. Only the saved has that right because all spiritual blessings are *in* Christ and she was now *in* Him. As a wealthy woman she felt there was no better gift than to have the right to petition the Maker of heaven and earth. Like whenever she gets greedy and enticed with unlawful temptations just to increase her riches. But, thus far she has managed to turn down Satan's luring persuasions. "If that crafty serpent tried to no avail, to tempt Christ, one of the Godhead, he certainly will try his tricks on me!" she always says.

Then suddenly, in the snowy alley of Neal, New York, her thoughts were cut by louder sobs from the Latino man over his dead snow-covered nephew.

CHAPTER 12

Meanwhile, out on the streets of Neal in the patty wagon, Stephanas Carter and the Latino boy sat across from each other both cuffed and having an evil-eyeing contest. With the policewoman in the front and light snow pelting the windows that Saturday morning Step was disappointed with the day's grisly mishap. His eyes moved to the lovely young Black police writing while carefully keeping an ear on the dispatch radio. She had to wait for her partner to exit the alley along with each suspect she had left him with. Nevertheless, both cops knew the man was well capable of handling a woman, a mourning uncle and three puny homeless men.

There in the smelly wagon Step could not help but take in the dispatcher's loud trouble-shooting of all manner of crimes in the little city of Neal. He recalled how he once wanted to be a policeman. But instead through no fault of his own he had succumbed to homeless and then Doctor Desoto happened along on one of her trips of mercy. "Now I just can't give up this superb job to become a cop!" he had thought.

Then, all of a sudden, "Hey Senorita!" the uncouth boy yelled, "I need to bafroom,"

"Just sit back and it'll go away!" she immediately snapped.

Meanwhile, in the snowy alley waiting for the ambulance Dassah was now chilled to the bones. The big red policeman was impatiently pacing but kept an eye on the pile of guns on the ground. She looked at the three malnourished men hugging the cold can. The Latino man had on a thick coat as he hovered over his blanketed dead nephew. Dassah became upset and was about to simply walk out in spite of the strict confinement. "Can we at lease start up another fire officer?" she finally asked and then pointed to her knees. "In case you haven't noticed the mud here!"

"It's against the law to have a fire back here!" he knowingly informed. "And these men know that!"

"Well in my opinion, what should be against the law is for humans to freeze to death!" she breathed unafraid. What was he going to do, beat her up?

Leon and the men only gawked on the conversation. They had the utmost respect for law people.

Then with a loud sigh the police walked impatiently to her, fine snowflakes on his jacket. "Don't you think having a fire up in here has caused enough grief already, Doctor?" he gestured towards the smelly singed body, the dirty blanket soggy with snow and weeping flesh. The police had warned it was against the law to move the body under the tent. "This body should remain in the spot where he died!" he had earlier demanded. The uncle was now standing beside the body in the drizzle, staring blankly down at it. "Dat's righ!" he finally perked up, agreeing with the police. Then the uncle glared at Dassah and the poor homeless men with enough ice to chill the nippy air. "Dey kill my el sobrino!" he shouted again.

"Calm down, Sir!" the policeman ordered, his burly body blocking the guns on the ground.

Leon had quickly stepped close to Dassah at the man's outburst. "Are you okay, Doc?" he asked brazenly eyeing the angry man.

With fine snowflakes before her hooded head she could only sigh of total frustration, "I'm okay Leon . . . what about you? And you, Pops?" Then she looked at the younger homeless man hugging himself as his blue eyes stared at nothing in particular. "And you young man . . . are you alright?" she asked wishing she knew his name. He finally, unhurriedly nodded. Being a patient psychiatrist she was yet relieved to get even that much feedback from someone so mentally disturbed. "At least he's able to respond reasonably," she took mental notes.

"I guess I'm holding up!" the middle-aged Pops responded. "But my belly could sure use something hot!" Again Pops' air and character impressed Dassah. The real reason she was in the alley in the first place dawned on her and she thought, "Pops would be a good candidate for the makeover program." She needed more like him to give wisdom to the abundance of younger men on the farm. As of late it had amazed her to find so many young homeless, ex-cons from 19 to30. Most had been released because of minor offences. As long as the judicial system knew the men could find shelter and work they felt safe releasing them. The doctor of the mind understood that the judges could not loose ex-cons on society without some assurance. And that's where her program would come in. With regret she was only allowed to take in 18 years and up. For the younger homeless she sought other means of assistance. They were ones who were earnestly seeking to be re-mainstreamed. As a psychiatrist she had encountered way too many run-away youths with little desire to be discovered. And the dangerous fact that any child would choose street life broke her heart as she pleaded with them to change their mind about being homeless. Some of those youths had fled homes worse than the streets. Thus mental instability set in along with his evolving hormones. As she had plead with them, some teens felt that if they trusted grown-ups, then that was like swapping the devil for the witch. And which was the worse of those two evils . . . a parent abuser or a police abuser? Whenever Dassah did find a child that sincerely longed to be rescued and not get sent back home, she would quickly offer him a safe haven with her until he at last would trust and go again into foster care. The twelve-bedroom house on one of her properties was a serene temporary respite for troubled teens. "We should build more rehabilitation homes for our Black teens, instead off more jail houses!" she had huffed to a fellow doctor one day, "We surely don't have to worry about rehab homes for teens of other races, because they have plenty!" As a doctor of the mind she had seen her share of Black teens sent to prison while other teens are sent to rehab.

There in the alley she managed a slight smile silently thanking God for giving her the gift of compassion. Her heart was light just to see most of those teens go back to school and on to success. "Unfortunately, too many children don't even know how to get themselves off the streets," Dassah had said to a youth counselor one day. "Little do they realize all they have to do is go to the police and if he's seventeen and under, he can get legal assistance." Nevertheless, the smart doctor was aware that most African American teens were petrified that the police would arrest them by claiming they caught their man, a very usual story. She had heard too many stories of racial-profiling being taken to juvenile instead of foster care. Praying for the day when everyone is treated equal is another one of her fervent rituals.

In the alley waiting for the ambulance to arrive, Dassah looked over at Leon with his dread-locks sticking around his light-skinned face, "I really want him in my program," she thought. "Less than an hour ago that frail homeless man had proven his bravery in the face of danger and danger may occur on my guarded farm" she thought, "Tough men will be rough men!"

She turned to the police, "May I at least go to the car and get some food for these men?" pleading. "Plus, I can use something hot too!"

"Sorry Doc, nobody is going to leave this crime scene unaided!"

Having been a psychiatrist for years, every opportunity she gets to solve a puzzle gave her a buzz, no matter how basic the problem. "Well let's *all* of us go to the limo!" she quickly suggested. "And then we won't be unaided."

The police firmly eyed her, "Now do you think this poor man care to just leave his loved one that your bodyguard killed, up in here alone?" he contemptuously asked. "I don't think so!"

There with fine white snow blowing in Dassah saw red. His insinuation that Step just up and killed an innocent boy ticked her off all over again. "He seemed to have totally ignored the true story though I've told him time and again!" she only thought, not wanting a confrontation with a lawman. Then sighing big, the love-connection she'd had, suddenly dissipated like the steam rolling from her full moist lips. "I'm very tempted to sock him one, but no sense in Step and I both sitting up in jail!" Then she knew it was best to get her mind off the miserable issue before her. Groping desperately to find spiritual inspiration she walked away and vividly to meditate on a Bible story. Leon and the other homeless men simply and sadly watched after her feminine back. She stopped on the other side of the alley. Her eyes moved to the body and then the more intense sobs from the uncle blasted her nerves like an H-bomb. "Will he ever stop!!" she muttered under her breath. Then she softened. "He must really love his nephew." She began to detest even more what had happened. "But he brought his own death on himself!" she thought. Then the thought of death caused her to stare forlornly across the alley at the body. Wonderment of the inevitable event which everyone must succumb to, hit her squarely in the face along with fine snow. Amid the woefulness and the police's walkie-talkie her mind strayed to a Bible story about the event of death. She glanced impatiently at her watch. It was 11:03. The three homeless men had retired on a big nearby boulder.

As her mind strayed, the famous parable about the rich man and Lazarus came to mind once again. When she had first heard the story she was not wealthy and knew she could easily have been the poor person in the story. Though, she had not been as destitute as Lazarus, who had sat begging every day. "Now the table has turned," she thought. "Now I can say I'm the rich person, though I pray not like that selfish rich man in the story!"

There in the alley waiting for the ambulance to pick up the burned to death body, again a tear almost fell from the strong-willed doctor's eye as she watched the homeless men. Them being so ragged and the Latino man, policeman and her, so warmly clothed. Then comparing the parable scenario to the truly homeless in America, she sadly shook her head, "That parable reminds me of the near ban of the homeless to stop them from asking alms in the confines of the only home they had, the streets!" That made her wonder what the homeless would ever do if they were banned from begging for help. Where else would it be for them to go if they were also run off the corners? "I'm sure they'll simply end up like that low IQ-grown-up I once knew, who had died in the streets," she sadly recalled. As she got angrier she inadvertently said aloud, "I guess some people feel its good riddance if the poor went on and died of starvation or something!" The mere thought of some old homeless person being found deceased under some bridge gave her chilled face a heat-rash. And she knew that God would not hold her guiltless if she turned her back on their cries. She sat down wearily on a huge rock. Snowflakes make their way through the slit in the top of the tenthouse and before her eyes.

"Are you alright? Leon asked from sitting on the other rock beside his other two peers. The dead boy's uncle had calmed down with only a sniffle ever so often. Not far away Dassah was able to hear the fierce growling of the men's stomach. While he kept an eye on his suspects the big red policeman listened closely to the walkie-talkie strapped on his side. "Are you okay four-seventy-one . . . over?" concerned voice.

"That's a big ten-four!" She shot a quick, teasing glance at Step through the rear view mirror. Then she turned attention back to her partner, "Eight-zero, are you okay . . . over?" a soft voice.

"That's a ten-four . . . over and out!"

Again, Dassah glanced at her watch. It was 11:16 that Saturday morning in the small city of Neal, New York. Then the doctor assured Leon she was alright and sunk back into deep thoughts, where her overwhelmed mind retreated to another godly meditation. She recalled how it had taken some time for her to figure out that God did not need man, but rather that man needed God in order to stay out of hell. "The God of heaven is already in a joyous place and only invites us to share in that glorious magnificence," she thought, now with more peace overshadowing her almost perfect face. "Heaven's going to be an eternity of pure spiritual passion without the presence of any carnal bodies!" She smiled. She realized that heaven and hell were places of feelings that everyone would experience after death according to the parable of Lazarus and the rich man. Each of these men felt what was happening to him at the time. In Isaiah 66:24, God passed judgment on Israel for their continuous transgressions against Him. That scripture is proof that the *soul* and the *worm* were one and the same. And that the fire was also linked to the soul as mentioned in that passage. The passage reads, "For their worm shall not die, neither shall their fire be quenched. Another scripture she recalled that Jesus said in Mark 9:44, *"Where their worm dies not and the fire is not quenched."*

Dassah had wondered if the soul of a person was merely their state of awareness mechanism. She still had a lot to learn about death. And about heaven and hell as they relate to the soul. And in order to prevent spending all eternity in hell fire she would try to do whatever it took. And she hoped to do all she can as a wealthy woman here on earth. "All I have to do is obey God's commands through the holy, scriptures," she thought. It had been the parable of the rich vs. the poor which motivated her reaching out to the homeless. "Contrary to popular belief rich souls can abide in heaven also!" She always defends. She would strive not to be like some narrow-minded rich people who viewed the poor as less than human. There in the alley, she recalled another Bible passage in Mark, 10:17-30. As Jesus was talking to the rich young man, Jesus' twelve disciples were also present with Jesus. The young rich man had enquired how he may receive eternal life. Jesus' reply was not to commit adultery, steal, kill, bear false witness and not to defraud, but honor his mother and father. And upon hearing just that much, the young man was happy and immediately admitted to having kept those commandments all his life. But then the young rich man was distraught to learn that just doing all those things were simply not suitable to win a pass to heaven. Jesus, knowing the man had many riches, challenged him to sell his substances and feed the poor. Suddenly the rich man's face became saddened in that parting with his wealth was too much to expect of him. Jesus' disciples had heard the conversation and marveled. His disciples knew they had given up much to follow Jesus. And if it was easier for a camel to go through the eye of a needle than for a rich man to enter into heaven, they were done for. It was apparent they hoped to one day become wealthy on earth again. They did not realize Jesus stated that all who **trusted** *in riches, not all who had riches,* could not be fit for the kingdom. Then further in that same chapter Jesus informed the disciples that, if they had given up lands and families to follow him, they could as Christians, also acquire lands and families here on earth and still have eternal life when they died. The forsaken family members were the ones who would butt against the disciples' decision to follow God's will. Thus the disciples made a choice. Would they choose Jesus or would they rather hang on to their hindering family members. And then a loving Christian family would be adopted from within the church. With a church family they would all work toward the same common goal of loving Jesus through serving others. The bottom line was the disciples were commanded to trust God as their savior and not let money be their commander in charge.

There in the alley awaiting the ambulance she recalled one of her constant prayers is that she can remain a good steward over God's money. She would not allow her money to strong-arm her into a lack of wisdom. "Though, sometimes my money can get pretty strong, like around tax time!" she snickered. But she was thankful for all the charitable contributions she could legally itemize. "The more you give, with the eight heart God gives it right back!" However, giving freely and expecting nothing in return was a solid vow she'd made, gladly bearing in mind that it is possible for the rich to live a godly life also. The rich doctor thought of how heaven and hell were as real to her as her millions. Glorying in heaven as her final resting place she recalled Hebrews, 9:27, "And as it is appointed man once to die, but after this the judgment." It was that very passage that alerted her that everyone had that appointment to keep with their works testifying either for them, or against them. She knew that this scripture proved that even some homeless people would end up in hell fire. The thought of that caused her to recall an incident with a homeless man as she was out shopping one day. That day she was standing outside of a department store in Manhattan. Suddenly she was approached by a tattered middle aged man because it seemed the homeless popped up everywhere when you least expect them. On this particular occasion in passing by her he had struck up a conversation. And instead of her confronting him the way she normally did the homeless, she had planned to go on her merry way with her shopping. And what had prompted him to say what he did, amazes her even to this day. Because, at that point, she had not even, mentioned a word about religion to him. While offering her a sad sob story he had whimpered, "Do you know what I want when I get to hell?"

Her being had absolutely fainted at his affirmation that he would eventually go to hell. So at that she had answered, "N-no . . . what would you want Sir?"

The man still pretending he was crying, he uttered, "I'd want a naked woman to wheel in a barrel of ice and dump it on me, then I'd like for her to jump on me also!" Then his pretend sobbing abruptly turned into mocking laughter as he took off with lighting speed across cars in the street while he still was laughing. As Dassah had stood looking dumfounded after him she could only shake her head, "Now I can truly say that I've seen Satan himself!!" As an intern, in many insane asylums she had seen outlandish patients. "But they should be put in jail for letting this one out!" she had declared out loud that day.

She realized there are sick minded homeless people everywhere. However she felt that when one mocks God that took his madness to another level. "God is the absolute last one a homeless person should ridicule!" she had thought. She wondered about the man's past and dreadfully feared for his soul if he did not repent and obey the gospel call. And he had not even given her the opportunity to say anything to him about his soul. Then, that day she had to calm herself by trusting God's word that the road that led to hell was broad and wide and many would go in, but the road to heaven was narrow and straight and few would find it. So she resigned even now that she cannot convince everyone to save his soul.

In the alley the compassionate doctor truly mourned witnessing the poor in such horrendous destitution while she had so much. But during those moments of sadness she yet knows that any able-bodied person can work. She recalled second Thessalonians 3:10, which states, "If any would not work, neither should he eat." And to teach the homeless worthiness was another thing that motivated her to create the makeover program.

She brought her mind back in the alley under the homemade tent. The policeman, three homeless men and sad uncle was freezing. The uncle was hovering over the dead body. The weary psychiatrist recalled those among the homeless who had persevered through the rigorous program. Those were the ones with strong desires at another shot at the bull's eye of life. Another group of homeless men had to receive assistance from the appropriate resources before they could enter her program. They had been on the streets for so long until they required short-term institutionalization, or short-term hospitalization, all from state funding. A smile crossed her face when she recalled another successful group of moderately mentally disabled. These were able to comprehend and had received special training for work purposes. These individuals would work mainly for food as opposed for material excessiveness. They were content just to work, eat and watch television in the supervised housing—just like the child they really were. In their mind, their working awarded a cold soda as opposed to gold. They were able to perform housekeeping and did that well. Of course the doctor saw that they were recompensed more fairly than giving them a mere coke. "Instead of the government giving them a handout, they can also earn their way while living in semi-independent housing," she had once said. "The men and women that are not disruptive can be productive if for nothing but to sweep floors, keep napkin dispenser and wipe tables and window sills." Of course she knew there were some programs for the mentally challenged, but for the ones who were too smart to be retarded and too dumb to be normal. "But I'd never deliberately refer to anyone as retarded or dumb in a negative sense," she had apologized in her notes.

There in the alley she recalled her capable, close-knit staff in the homeless effort. "When anybody's paycheck is livable it helps them to render quality service without much murmuring!" she had smiled thinking about her staff which consisted of 10 part-time psychiatrists and a therapist under each of them. All of the doctors also had their own practices. Another one of her goals for the makeover program is to make citizens aware of the homeless plight by publicizing this dire distress. Some of the financially able citizens were more than willing to provide monetary and physical assistance. "Deep down it eases most people conscience by giving," she thought. A smile crossed her beautiful snow moistened face as she recalled how America came to the rescue of thousands in the Haiti earthquake. "God truly blessed Haiti with much needed everything from other countries," she thought. But what troubled the Christian in her, was that folk tended to underestimate the power of God when it comes to natural disasters. As soon as a disaster occurs human nature is to point a finger at another human. "Nailing down things is of little effect if God sees fit to uproot it!" she had commented on all the blaming during Katrina in 2005.

Then the miraculous parting of the Red Sea came to her mind, "Also God had seen fit to destroy two cities by raining down fire and brimstone!" she thought. "He flooded the entire world once, so how in the world do people feel that man-made, steel levies could ever prevent the forces of the Almighty!" Though, she realizes that it is in the best interest of man to use caution and build as securely as possible. "But in doing so man should expect the unexpected from an all-powerful God!"

She recalled how it moved her to see people hasten to love the victims of all these disasters. As she, along with the world, had watched the Katrina victims in disbelief as the news had unfolded at the Super Dome, In New Orleans, she concluded that one was a poor vs. rich issue. It just happened that more Blacks were impoverished at that time. "Had more of any other race been the poorest citizens, then, they too would've been left behind!" she had said. After Katrina Dassah discovered that many, many Blacks who had vehicles had made it out in time. "Only the strong survives in a dog-eat-dog-world!" she had said to the doctor who had watched along with her.

"Yeah, it appears more Blacks were at the dome because over fifty-five percent of Louisiana's residents were poor and homeless," was his solemn reply.

As a fearful Christian Dassah dared not speak in the place of God. However, after these disasters she wondered if that was God's way of exposing the severity of the plight of the poor. "Here in America we're just too rich a country for anyone to suffer long-term unemployment, hunger, no medical assistance or no housing!" she had said. "Now the world is leaving it up to President Barrack Obama to solve all of these long embedded issues! But God has allowed the President to do plenty in the few years he's been there. . . He's even flushed out Osama Bin Laden!" she thought.

As a psychiatrist she knows that many of the older homeless epidemic, is the result of the Vietnamese war. Many vets she had encountered were grandfathers who had lived with grown children until the children no longer were able to take his post-war syndrome behavior. They had either kicked him out, or he just up and left home. "And the beat goes on!" she sadly sighed. After that war long ago, soldiers had returned to America with mental and substance abuse disorders. And in all fairness she never failed to overlook there were all races in that outcast group. Then back in America the addiction to heroin and cocaine became the epitome of cripplers. "They've escaped the devastation of bombs only to yield to a sneak-attack from crack!" she thought. "And sadly they needn't even travel outside of their hood to find those deadly drugs . . . now, where did cocaine which makes crack, come from!?" she knowingly thought. "Surely no one in higher standings deposited it in the hood where there aren't any other jobs available but to sell drugs?"

The doctor knew that before crack some of these people owned homes, the few jobs there were and families, but begging shamelessly on the streets was now their life-time job. And crack babies were surmountable among the women. "The mother's drug use while pregnant could very well account for the low school grade average among many impoverished kids," she thought. Then she found herself thanking her mother for not doing drugs. Aside from her mother's critical addiction to fine clothing, expensive hairdos and plenty of fine jewelry she rarely saw her even drink a beer.

Suddenly, there in the snowy alley Dassah' thoughts were broken. The cold had also broken through her thick fur-lined boots numbing her toes. Then, suddenly and gladly watching the paramedic rush in with a stretcher, she took a deep breath and jumped directly up from the rock. She said to the three homeless men who also had made their way to her side, "Now, maybe I can get to my car!" Her head began to spin and to the doctor it all seemed like an unreal dream. She cringed watching the young paramedics pry the uncle from the dead burnt corpse. "I'm responsible for this," she thought. "And apparently the uncle is going to give me a difficult bout in court," she glanced at the cold stare he shot her way.

Then the policeman matter-of-factly, pointed out, "Since we already have the ones responsible for this, all of you are free to leave." Then he quickly jutted out his index finger, "But stay where we can contact you!" He looked at the homeless men, "And I guess this hole is your home until further notice!" sarcasm.

"Yes Sir!" Leon saluted, "I'll be right here in Tenthouse number 3," pointing to the rickety, very used damp box.

Laughter filled the alley for the first time in hours. Even the policeman found snickering humor, but the uncle saw none at all.

"May I speak to Stephanas Carter?" Dassah confidently asked, knowing without a doubt she would clear him. "He has done no more than the norm for a bodyguard," she thought. All she had to do was have him produce his license. Dassah pulled out her cell phone for the second time. This time she called her personal lawyer who was always just a call away—and she was. "Hello Callie," sheer frustration in the doctor's voice.

"Oh! Hi Dassah," the 30-something voice on the other end yawned, nestled between red silk sheets. Her dark, long tousled hair gave her chubby face seductiveness, even only half awake.

"I wish I also would've slept in this morning for all that's gone down out here!" Dassah immediately complained, and then proceeded to unravel the story.

"I'm sorry Boss," Callie now sitting on the side of the totally extravagance of a king-sized bed. The black silk very low cleavage revealing gown boasted that she was all female. Her meaty, but very shapely legs hung over the side of the bed, again flaunting the reality that she was all woman, for the man who loved a plus sized package. "I'll surely be on stand-by . . . or should I go on down to the jailhouse?"

"Naw! I don't think there'll be any problem getting him at this point . . . in court might be another scenario!"

"Well, okay. Oh! I didn't realize it was already eleven-fifty-one!"

"Bye Callie. Get some rest. I have a feeling you're going to need it!"

Dassah hung up and glanced around. The paramedics had left with the body. The Latino uncle had followed. She now was exiting the alley with three homeless men trekking ahead of her—the way she had instructed them. As the foursome made their way through the alley from which she and Step had come, she thought about how glad she was to have Callie Langley on her team. Callie was an aggressive, smart Black woman and had proven to be one of the best in her field. Between eating she had won most of her cases. Callie was a divorcee and was always in the market for Mr. Right. Her weight, which certain parts were all in the right places, was on a consistent, unpredictable roller coaster. Just when she had planned to wear that dress for a weekend, she discovered the zipper would not budge, even with the Spanx. And she knew her weight variations were not all contributed to food—being Amazons truly ran in her family. "I know some really skinny women that can win an eating contest over me on any given day!" she had once huffed. Nevertheless, she declares she was cursed with the talent of being able to cook exceptionally well also.

Walking back through the alley, now thick snowflakes, Dassah stared sadly ahead at the three weary backs ahead of her. As she had done all morning, another big sigh escaped—this time a sigh of relief. "Finally the total grimness of that alley is behind me!" she thought. The only dreaded thing was that Step was not on her heels the way they had arrived earlier and she did not fully trust having Leon walk behind her. "God indeed is my right hand and Step is my left hand . . . and foot," she thought with a subtle smile. They had never been separated on a scouting trip in years. On occasions they had returned home without homeless men but always together.

Leon, directly in front of her, "Are you alright Doc?" he turned his hooded dread-locked head around.

"Yeah, I'm fine," she smiled over the concern. She realized that in any alley anything could happen to a woman—and nearly had. Even though she had had a gun in her boot at the time and a trained bodyguard, danger had crept into the picture anyway. She thought of how she could hardly wait to get her favorite gun from the policeman, the gun she used for sharp-shooting, but could only retrieve it after she produced the license and registration.

Finally with the few people on the streets, Dassah never thought she would be that glad to see the shabby stores of Neal once again. With the homeless prospects now trailing her she aimed directly for the patty wagon parked just a few feet from the alley, behind her limo. "Wait there by the limo," she said to the hungry men ogling anxiously at the limo. Then she went to the big white, early model police-lettered patty wagon. As the now fine snowflakes drifted into the wind the few people out that Saturday morning gaped wonderingly. A limo and a patty wagon at the same time was a rare sight to behold.

Dassah at the window politely asked the pretty police for permission to speak to Step. The police already had the window down to a crack, glanced curiously at the shivering, warmly hooded doctor. Her dark eyes moved authoritatively down at Dassah' muddy clothing, and then she slowly nodded, "Okay, but only for a moment," she directed. "Oh, by the way, I've seen a lot of you in the news lately . . . good work!" her dark loveliness glistened through the respect in her eyes.

"Oh, thanks! I didn't think you recognized me." Then with a smile she went and peered in at her handsome, grinning bodyguard. Her eyes moved partially sad, partially angry to the fuming boy across from Step. Then back to Step, she breathed, "I'll come get you as soon as possible okay?" she placed a gloved hand assuring on the window.

"I know Boss." Then he thought, "It seems like so long ago since I last saw her kind eyes!" Step too had become used to their arriving and leaving as a team. As she walked away, he stared intently after her with worry. His gut clued him that she was about to drive off with three homeless strangers. "Maybe you should just call today's work off!!" he, straining against the seatbelt, yelled after her.

"Not on your life!" she yelled challengingly over her shoulder.

The pretty police quickly rolled up the window. "You can't just yell out the window like that!" she said. "You're in police custody for the moment. . . Now sit back!"

Her reprimand drew hearty laughter from the Latino boy in with Step. "You don' own ever-thin' ya' know!" he sneered.

Step glared daggers at the young hoodlum and then simply slid back. Solemn with worry he stared at Dassah now letting the grungy strangers into the limo. "I hope you know what you're doing, Dassah!" he thought with a sigh of deep dread. Then he thought again, "Lighten up Step! Don't underestimate the doctor's ability. . . After all, she is a psychiatrist with years of experience," somewhat relaxing. Still he felt that in her desperation to save the world, especially the poor, she did some pretty risky things. "Like today being alone with some possible murders!" panic again. He knew the streets better than she did, even though she was a doctor. And he knew that not all of the homeless indeed were what they pretended to be. He realized that some were there for the mere purpose of taking advantage of whomever they could. "There are crooks in every crack and crevice of life," he thought. "Some are blue-collar crooks, some are white-collar crooks and some are no collar crooks!" He had even heard some of the homeless men claim that if they took two hundred people for a dollar, that would make them rich in no time. Why would they work a 9 to 5 job if they could make that kind of free money? Being from the streets Step knew some homeless men would use and abuse lonely women, given the opportunity. Then he recalled a story someone had told him: Once upon a time there was a woman who ran across a snake almost frozen to death on the ground. She felt so sorry for the little squirming critter that she scooped him up in a blanket and carried him to her house. She put him in front of the fireplace and lit a fire. She also left some food out for him. Then she went off to work. When she arrived home that night, the snake was all thawed out, had eaten all the food and was reclined comfortably on the couch. She ran over to him and grabbed him to give him a hug. But suddenly he reared back, hissed and sank his fangs into her. As expected she immediately fell down, and as she was dying, she cried, "But I took you in when you were dying!" He hissing over her, replied, "You silly woman, you knew I was a snake when you took me in, didn't you?!"

CHAPTER 13

O nce Doctor Dassah Desoto left Stephanas Carter her bodyguard in the parked patty wagon that snowy Saturday morning, in Neal New York, her immediate plan was to go on to the jail and bail him out. Yet she knew that she should allow enough time for them to book him. "For sure he'll be charged for suspected murder," she thought with regret. "I just pray they set a bond! God forbid that he remain in jail until the hearing, whenever the judge decided one. I pray the judge and his wife aren't having a fight!" she unintentionally sighed to the three homeless men climbing into the limo.

They simply looked oddly at her left-wing comment. Dassah, Leon Pops and the younger White man were at last in the welcome warmth. Those homeless citizens she would try to recruit for her program. The limo was specially designed for the purpose of transporting the homeless. It had one seat directly behind the driver's seat. The other seats were around the walls and another in the far back. In its design she assured there would be room enough to move about. Her therapy chair sat lavishly on one side of the car. And now from the driver seat she turned to the grungy men looking extremely misplaced among all the cleanliness.

For the moment being able to put the alley behind her, she silently prayed of thanks for having so much. She turned up the heat even though the car was not that cold but the wet pants clung to her like a second skin. "It's unbelievable how much has gone down this morning!" she breathed aloud, intentionally this time.

"I'm sure," Leon responded choosing the seat directly behind her. The other two chose side seats—their coats still on.

She turned around again to observe her human prey. "Well, this is my home away from home guys!" she tried sounding perky, "You just feel at home . . . you may rest your coats." She did not worry about the funkiness ruining the car. And simply flipping a switch she turned on the built-in fumigation system. As always the special seat covers were in place.

"You were not lying about being able to help a body!" Leon said, looking all around in awe. "So, this is how the rich and famous lives?" pulling off the tattered coat. Pops and the young homeless man also seemed relieved to get out of their coats.

"That is, if you want to call me famous . . . but the first I will admit to!" Dassah got up and went to the back out of sight, slightly crouching. She pulled out a coiled partition and immediately began stripping off the muddy clothes. The men sat jaw-dropped as they knew what was going on behind the top to bottom car partition. The doctor of the mind knew that was a bad move but felt that Leon had proven his respect back in the alley. "Pops appears to be nothing more than a father-figure," she thought, speedily changing clothes. "But the other man has me puzzled." Not being able to stand completely up she strained to hear their muffled conversation. "Sorry guys!" she finally yelled. "I simply must shed these duds!" Then it suddenly hit her, "I don't have my gun!" panic set in. The policeman who had it was still back at the patty wagon.

As Dassah quickly changed an unfamiliar voice stunned her, "Don't mind us, Doc!" it was the young man now grinning, gawking at the partition as if he could see right through it.

Dassah' heart skipped whether for fear that she had made the wrong choice or from happiness over knowing he was not as out of it as she had thought—she was not sure which. "So the cat don't have your tongue after all, Young Man?" she managed to tease hiding the panic in her voice. "I just figured it was glued to the roof of your mouth or something' Do you have a name to go with that nice voice?" she yelled, peeping around the partition, hair now pleasingly ruffled. With crushing disappointment she watched him become silent and forlorn again.

Then finally the doctor emerged all redressed and staring into faces trying to peer into the limo, with snow blowing pass them. Now in different jeans and sweat shirt she looked girlish. Still slightly bending for maneuverability she busied taking food from the warmer in the back. "If these men do have negative motives then this food is sure to counteract that," she whispered with a smile. Then from the side seat Pop's tired voice rang, "He'll never tell his mane, Doc," he informed. And, in the same breath, "Is that sausage I smell?" his red nose sniffed like a Saint Bernard.

"It's okay if he feels like keeping secrets . . . we all have secrets," she humored the young dirty-blond seated beside Pops. "And, yes that's sausage and bacon . . . are you guys ready to eat!?"

"I could really use some vittles!" Leon chided, rubbing his hands together.

There in the parked limo in Neal, New York as snow flurried the windshield and new faces tried peering in, Dassah moved to another part of the car and pulled out a coffee pot that had freshly dripped. The smell of food put a long overdue smile on the men's smutty faces. And it put a song in the doctor's heart just to see the wide smiles. Then she suddenly reflected on how Step had burned the Latino boy to death right before their eyes earlier. But with a sigh she could only helplessly shake her head. "There's nothing I can do about that for the moment. Both she and Step had never run into such trouble before on a trip. "In fact this is my first witness of anyone being killed," she thought with another sigh.

Dassah handed Leon a packet of antiseptic and a bandage for his leg. He quickly treated the four-inch bullet graze on his thigh. After the men eagerly washed their hands in a little sink they lit into the food. As for the doctor of the mind, she simply sat in the front seat with a cup of coffee, and searching through papers for the registration to get her gun back. She also relished in the food-orgy on grits, sausage, bacon, oatmeal, fruit and biscuits. She switched on soft music for them to dine by. "If God called me home at this very moment, this is the picture I'd want played back to me in heaven!" she thought, looking at the dread-locked Leon who seemed oblivious to anything else around him. She was not sure he even heard the music. And she did not have to be sneaky about staring because they would never notice anyway. Then Dassah smiled, "He ain't that bad looking. . . And if his zeal to get rescued is anything like his appetite, I can sure use him in the program." With a cup of coffee and watching the men Dassah recalled how she never forgot her promise to someday be wealthy. But she had vowed not to trample on anyone else while making it to the top. Her personal decision was to mow the path for others to easily follow. She knew each individual had to seek that road to become productive citizens just like they were commanded to seek salvation. She felt blessed in pointing the groping ones to the pathway that led out of poverty. They could have their own businesses. "Nothing can convince me otherwise this is the reason why God led me to the gold at the end of the rainbow!" she thought as she watched the famished men binge. There in the front seat she sniffed the warm air and was pleased the expensive fumigator did its job well.

With snow sticking to the windshield and the men now full the mood was ripe for conversation. Dassah glanced at the clock. It was 12:10 that Saturday morning. "Will that cop ever bring me my gun?!" she finally remembered. She opened the door as passersby still tried to see in. And ignoring them she peered back where the patty wagon had been. "Oh, no!" she said, starling the now relaxing men. "Can you believe they've already left!? Did you guys see them pass by?" lovely, retouched face frantic.

"No, I didn't see them pass by this car!" Leon declared, sucking his teeth. Pops shook his grey head with hood off. At the time the wagon had passed them they all probably had their eyes on the partition where she was changing. She realized she would have to wait to get her favorite piece back—the only gun she had with her today. Then she thought, "Maybe that was the wrong move to let on I haven't a gun." Now she began to eye her quests more guardedly.

Then Pops finally said, "Just like the IRS the cops take their own sweet time when it's something they owe you!" He leaned back, rubbing the food down his round middle aged gut.

"Yeah, don't worry, Doc," Leon said through the serenity of soft music.

Upon hearing words of comfort she began to loosen up but yet eyed the younger man sitting blank-faced again.

Meanwhile on the snowy streets, in the patty wagon on the way to the station was the red faced policeman. He was driving, and the pretty police was still writing. Step and the Latino boy were still cuffed in the back. The big red policeman pulled over, "You should go on to the station," he said to the pretty police. "I've been assigned to go along with Mike on his beat," he pointed to the police car that pulled alongside of them. "Will you be okay?"

"Of course I will!" she frowned. "I work this high-risk beat don't I?"

"Okay," he climbed from under the wheel of the wagon and onto the snow. Now under the wheel she carefully pulled off and kept in the direction of travel.

Step shifted in cuffs, dreading the 20 minute drive to the other side of Neal. He pictured his female boss all alone with three homeless strangers and a shutter rocked his buffed body across from the forever sulking boy. The boy's father had gone with the body to the city morgue. Helplessly, Step could only hope his boss was safe.

Back in the limo sipping coffee, Dassah prepared to allow the men the opportunity to question her. She got up and went to the side, pushing a button where up arose a red therapy chair in the middle of the floor. As the men gaped with interest, she sat down. Suddenly the chair and note pad stirred up innate professionalism in her, "Would you like to know more about why you're here gentlemen?" she asked, passing a trash bag to them who marveled at her sudden new self. Like most psychiatrists the therapy chair became her security blanket where nothing slipped pass her probe. She confidently breathed, "Now that you trust me not to be the big bad wolf!" humor with tact. "Let's hip-hop to it!" crossing shapely legs, jeans contouring just right.

Then Pops across from Leon sat at attention, "Just how old are you, anyway Doc!?" he frowned. In his voice was the sound of not being use to taking orders from someone so much younger than himself. Though, the homeless man was not sure why he felt that way.

"First of all," she side-stepped the age question. "Since you know my name, I deserve to know your real names. Leon Davis I know, but you two," She glared out at Pops. His dirty suit and hairy, white face stood out.

"Well, Doctor Dassah," Pops shifted, and then hesitated. "I . . . I really don't know my name," he sighed. "And that scares the dickens out of me!" he choked up, "About three months almost four months ago, I woke up in that alley. My wallet, ID and all was gone," he shook his head.

Silence stilled the atmosphere as she had turned off the music. Though she felt deep compassion for Pops, but when she doctored she placed any crippling feelings on hold for the moment. "Listening and making rash decisions is critical in this line of work!" she always says. Her light brown eyes then moved to the young man who now had his arms folded across his chest. He was perspiring, seeming to dread any upcoming questions from her. "Okay," she cut through the quiet. "What's your name?" she pointed the pen at the tattered young man with his arms wrapped around him-self. At that the blood drained from his face, and he claimed, "I didn't do it!" He began to shake fiercely while offering that unsolicited information. Suddenly transforming from one personality to another, solemnity overshadowed him again. But the doctor of the mind was not at all surprised. She had seen it all. His homeless peers also seemed to have adapted to his unpredictable behaviors. "He came to us a few months back all clean-cut," finally spoke up. "As usual we were about starved the day God sent him to us—our angel." Leon gestured towards the once again quiet young man. "Then our buddy here came and started handing out money like it was candy! So we named him Candy Man," Leon reached over and patted Candy Man on the knee.

Dassah could not help but to let sadness in about Candy Man. She realized she had inaccurately assessed that he was simply shy. But now knowing his actions went a lot deeper than that. "No one in his right mind would take up to living with the homeless in this unsuitable climate!" she scribbled in her notes. Also, a notation of how sorry she was that Candy Man displayed symptoms of autistic-schizophrenic would not qualify him for her program. But maybe he could be tested for some other program. His short attention-span would hinder his ability to attend to any task of what she would require in her rehab or employment. Neither could she be available to institutions for treatment of the non-homeless clients. Ever since the makeover program began, all of her psychotherapy has been performed on an outpatient basis. With Candy Man's mental status it would hinder his ever becoming totally independent. "Most patients like him if left alone for some time, would go idle until prompted to do otherwise," she wrote, noting that one-on-one client-staff in a work setting was not feasible in her type of program. She wondered dubiously about how and why Candy Man had wound up on the streets of New York. As a rehab specialist she saw very few Caucasian, young men in her program. Older Whites were not so rare because of the Vietnam War. When her eyes moved away from Candy Man, she heard a soft sigh escape his very thin lips, which proved he had the mentality to be purposely evasive. She observed that he slid relieved back in the seat like a child just let off the hook.

In the limo out of the snow that Saturday afternoon Dassah was writing in her notes and Leon anticipated being next up to bat. He realized he could simply walk away and back into the alley while they were yet close to his home. The smart homeless man knew she would soon ask him if he wanted to go along to whatever she had to offer as she had not fully explained yet. Leon then suspiciously thought, "This deal of hers can't be too legit, because there just ain't that many honest folks nowadays!" Then he recalled how, ever since she appeared and awakened him from the only thing he loved—sleep, he had seen nothing but attempted rape, fighting and gruesome death. "I even got shot!" he cringed at the fact of having to go to court as a witness. With his stomach now tight he figured that to take off would be for his best. He would resurface in court and act crazy. "It's tough enough being homeless, let alone being chased by the police for contempt of court!" he thought. Then, peering around the limo again at its finery he relaxed and leaned back. "I think I'll just hang around for some answers to this mystery," he thought. "I might just wound up liking the set up. . . After all I *have* prayed every day that I would soon get back on my feet!"

Dassah from the chair eyed Pops, having deep doubts about him joining the program. Unsure if she should waste time with a man who might come to remembrance in the middle of the program and bail out was not what she needed. "That could be a spot that a serious man could've had," she thought. Then, looking at Pops' expensive, but tattered suit she sensed that his true past needed some delving into. "Where ever he worked before, surely by now he was about to retire." Then she figured maybe she could just let him hang around for a while without signing up. He would allow him to teach the other men. She glanced up at him as he nonchalantly was picking his even white teeth with a colored toothpick. "Nice teeth for a man his age," she thought. "No doubt well living before amnesia beset him." Suddenly it occurred to her that when she would pick up Step, she would also check the missing person's board. Right then the cautious doctor decided not to inform Pops of her intention to do that. "It seems pretty odd he hasn't tried to find out his past," she eyed him suspiciously. As a psyche she knew that many amnesia victims were petrified of what they might run across about the past and had found some pretty terrible news. So most of them figured that, 'out of mind out of sight to deal with', was fine with them. She recalled having encountered patients who purposely forgot the past. "By erasing the pain one must also displace their existing mental being. However, the doctor of the mind knew that the major cause of amnesia was head-trauma or a brain tumor, aside from age related dementia. "But with dementia the victim usually did not forget everything about the past as dose amnesia.

Sadness overshadowed her to think of only getting one good catch out of today's, fish-net. Fifty men was her goal for that month of January. "This is already the tenth and we're thirty men short!" she thought. She knew the current June graduating men were anxious to get set up in business, and would fuss if asked to tarry a few months. Plus, Dassah would never request any to remain even if it meant hiring someone through regular avenues to work the farm and stores. The graduating men would be released in a few months so she found herself getting desperate.

Dassah thought of how she preferred recruiting ex-cons and the homeless men that had been on the streets for some time. Although she was unable to pinpoint why that was so, but she found ex-cons to be number one at yielding more positive results during rehabilitation. As for street veterans, she discovered that they were more subject to follow instructions than the newly homeless men. "The beginner street-people haven't time to feel true hunger!" she had said to a fellow doctor. "You offer 'them below minimum wages plus housing and with the swiftness they'll tell you where to go!"

"Could be that the newer homeless person has recently known higher wages and a better life," had been the logical reply. "Taking a look at what wages were ten years ago, it's logical that the long time homeless haven't known anything but low wages, so your wage offer is a fortune in his sight."

There in the parked limo with the three men she finished jotting notes. The patty wagon had not yet arrived at the jail with Step so that she could go get him. She could go before them but she would bide more time. Since she had warmed up from the chill she got up bending and walked pass the relaxing men. Before she went she used the remote to turn off the heat. Then peering out into faces still straining through the snowy windshield, she realized she had a slight headache. Even with the fumigator on the heat had allowed some of the stench to break through. "I wonder how long it's been since they had a real bath?" she thought, knowing the shelters only allowed quick tepid showers. and even then, only if space would allow. "There are just too man," the shelter workers would sigh. "It would be so nice if there were no hot water restrictions!

Now who in the world would hire these people smelling like that?!" the workers would say. They knew that only hot water would remove that smell.

There in the limo, with the homeless men's eyes curiously on her, the tactful doctor simply averted her attention to the snow. She dared not fan her nose the way she wanted to, but said, "I understand now how the Eskimo stays warm in their little igloos. . . I guess the ice keeps the wind-chill from penetrating," she smiled, moving back to her chair.

"That's exactly what the ice does for them," Pops sleepily said from a reclined position on the side seat. "The Eskimo live more snug than it actually looks . . . and due to a heavy consumption of fish-oil they rarely catch colds either!"

"Is that right?" Of course she already knew that but anything to make conversation before she explained the dos and don'ts of the program. Now back in her chair she turned professional again. The skinny jeans contouring long shapely legs, she crossed them, while shooting a speculative glance at Pops. Before she would get involved with business, her light brown eyes moved to the clock. It was 12:50. It seemed almost impossible for her to shake the thought of Step. She figured he was probably just now being booked. "How long does it take to get booked down at that jail anyway?" she asked her grimy guests.

Dead silence.

Suddenly Leon sat abruptly up, matted locks around his face, knowingly he eyed Dassah. "Look Doc," he suddenly huffed. "I'm homeless not stupid!" His voice was stronger from the meal. "If you want to know if I have a jail record, you should just ask me. . . It would be just that simple!" At this point the men were not aware that the doctor also took in ex-minor-offense-convicts.

As a psychiatrist Dassah had learned not to marvel at anything a client said or did. Yet she was cautious that they were not in her guarded office. In the limo with three possibly desperate men and Leon's irritability, suddenly became a scary scenario she had not anticipated when she and Step came out this morning. "But I'll not succumb to another rape for certain!" she stubbornly thought. "Before that happens someone else will die and it won't be me!" anger setting in.

In self-defense class she had been taught a method on how to suffocate someone with just the strength of a finger, or a sharp object through the trachea. Grasping the pen, she would use it as a weapon if necessary. She recalled when she had learned the wind-pipe technique she could only wish she had known it at the time of her vicious rape. "But as a mere girl would I have used that kind of aggressiveness?" She knew that children tend to be so submissive towards adults and knew that was why some adults took advantage of them. In her counseling she would never advise a child to try and fight back, but rather to run given a chance.

As Dassah sat in her chair looking at the irritation on Leon's face and the other two men gaping she wished she had listened to Step's warning to let today's find go. Even at that, after Leon had displayed such caring in the alley, she had not the heart to abandon the hungry men. Then she thought, "Leon Davis risked his life but now all I hear is hostility . . . Has everybody gone stock raving mad!" she wanted to scream out. "But psychiatrists just don't lose their cool in front of people," she sighed and then counted to 3. She knew that a psyche's timing had to be cut shorter than 10. From the security of her chair she uncrossed her legs, "Well," she managed to veil the increasing anguish. "Leon it wasn't my intention to insult anyone's intelligence. . . I needed the information and simply figured one of you knew something about these police procedures. . . This is your hood, right?"

Leon only glared intently. "Doc, I don't work for you, so don't go treatin' me like one of your flunkies!" he huffed.

Pops looked across at Leon with surprised in his dim eyes. Dassah noticed Candy Man had moved to the back seat and was rocking with his eyes shut tight. She glanced at him knowing there was no cure for autism but medication could help keep him calm. "If that's even his diagnosis," she thought. But of the three she preferred Leon for the makeover program. "No matter what, I refuse to let him get away!" she thought as she picked up the durable cordless phone. "Maybe I should just call the station and. . ." She was about to finished by saying, 'and find directions or an address'. But what happened next, neither her, Leon nor Pops, expected. But Candy Man suddenly screeched, standing everyone's hair up, "I told you, I didn't mean to help them do it!" He lunged for the phone in her hand. "Don't call the police!" He landed on top of her as the anchored therapy chair reeled back and forth. The cordless phone shot out like a missile and hit Pops with a sounding bop, on his ear. The older homeless man crouched in the seat as blood spurted. Suddenly Candy Man's smelly, tattered body was all over Dassah. "Get off of me . . . you, you. . ." she kicked at him, not really intending to do very much harm with the thick boots. She realized that she had the ability to hurt him if she wanted to. He had put one hand around her throat and with the other he began to grope her. The doctor knew that most homeless men rarely had close contact with a woman, especially a beautiful clean one. She wondered what daunting devil was lurking in Candy Man's closet that held his young mind so captive. There in the parked limo among the confusion, as Candy Man mauled Dassah, Leon once more came to her rescue. The bigger Leon grabbed Candy Man's frail shoulders and tried heartily to pry him off. "Get off, Man!" he repeated several times to his senseless, homeless comrade. The limo rocked like a boat against angry waves. As a psychiatrist, Dassah also knew when a mentally disturbed person lost control it usually took several others to restrain just that one. So pinned, not hopelessly under Candy Man's determined torso, she wished she had chosen another profession. "A Pediatrician maybe!" she thought, kicking harmlessly at Candy Man. But she kept the pen grasped as a last resort. At one time she wanted to be an actress, but changed her mind when she knew she could hardly be a leading lady in any movie. For some strange reason Hollywood hired leading Black men but rarely any Black leading ladies. "God has blessed me with the talent to be a leader of people, not a follower!" she had said.

Then there under Candy Man she managed to think, "On second thought, if I had become anything else, chances are I wouldn't have the farm and this limo to be fighting for my life in!" Then finally, a loud bam on the window froze everyone except for Candy Man. "What's going on in there!" a man's voice demanded. "This is the police, open up . . . Right now!"

By that time, Dassah had gone on and landed a light knee between Candy Man's legs. He yelled, dropped to the floor and grabbed his crotch. "This seems to be my day for cracking nuts the hard way!" she thought, recalling the hoodlum in the alley holding his crotch. Suddenly Pops sat up in a daze and was rubbing his bloody ear. Leon hurried and unlocked the door. There in front of a crowd stood a jacketed, hooded police wide-legged in the snow flurries, gun pointed at the door. "Okay!" he ordered. "Whoever is in there, come out with your hands up! And if I even *see* anything metal, I'm firing!"

Dassah stepped out first, adjusting her sweater. Leon stepped out next, hands in the air. Pops next, still rubbing his ear, still looking totally dazed. Candy Man moaning still lay on the floor coiled up. Another crowd had gathered so soon after this morning with a different police forcefully ordering them to move back.

The shamed doctor glanced around at the curious crowd in the snow of Neal, New York. "What must these people be thinking of me!" she thought. "An obviously well-to-do woman alone with three homeless men, whom they probably knew, all locked inside a limousine . . . now they really have something to talk about around the dinner table tonight!" she shook her pretty head at her Murphy's Law day. "What else can possibly go wrong!" she complained aloud. But for the most part she knew some of those people had heard of her makeover program.

The confused police ordered the coatless men to glue their palms to the wall of a storefront where he roughly frisked them there. Dassah looked in the direction of a second police that stepped from the store carrying a small brown paper bag. "What's goin' on out here!" authority sounded.

As soon as Dassah heard his voice, she sighed, "Oh no!" It was the same police in the alley earlier. He had gone only a block with his pretty partner and then got in the car with this policeman. Now he was back on this beat.

Dassah stood in the cold with only a crumpled long alieved sweat shirt and jeans. The very furry Fat Albert house-slippers also caught everyone's attention as they gaped. Still she looked beautiful and sultry with snow misting around, and then sticking to her newly mussed hair—thanks to Candy Man. "Officer, this is my car and there's another man inside!" she interrupted.

"Are there any guns in there!?" the first police cautiously pointed his gun.

"No there aren't," she impatiently sighed.

Then the big red police eyed her disheveled hair. Suddenly, without another word he immediately dropped the bag and grabbed Leon slamming the homeless man against the wall.

"Hey!" Leon cried. "I didn't do anything to deserve this kind of treatment!"

"Are these scumbags trying to force themselves on you, Doctor Desoto!" he asked, looking at Pops who was also coatless. Dassah eyed the way the police had unnecessarily roughed up Leon. "Aren't these the same maggots that were in the alley this morning!?"

Dassah was impressed he remembered her name but detested his uncouthness. She finally said, "Yes, these are the homeless *citizens* from this morning! And everything's okay. . . May I put my hands down now?" she huffed, putting them down anyway. She had a mind to report it to the police that Candy Man had attacked her. "They'll only take the sick man to jail," she thought. "Incarceration with other men is the last place a mentally ill young man should be . . . but it happens all the time!"

Finally the big policeman harshly let go of Leon and then again eyed Dassah from head to Fat Albert feet. His countenance softened as they momentarily locked eyes. His eyes moved to her figure now in full view with jeans and a sweat instead of a coat. She in turn noticed how nice-looking, but not handsome, he was. She took the red-face policeman to be mid-40s. Then, looking at Pops and Leon, she became angry again. "I'm on a mission to assure the public sees the homeless as human beings and not *maggots*, Sir!" she simply said. But she had a mind to harshly tell him off right before the crowd. But as a law abiding citizen she realized that law enforcers deserved respect. "They already jeopardize their lives to protect us." But she had been around enough corners to know there were too many corrupt cops in America. In her opinion, arrogance and respect of persons had no place in law enforcement. Too many law enforcers had replaced the aggressiveness they need, with unnecessary conceit. "Law enforcers must be assertive in order to do their tough job effectively," she thought. But right now she had a good mind to tell this one that it was okay to be forceful, but drop the cockiness and down-right heartlessness. There on the streets the big policeman, while his partner held the gun on them, snapped, "I need to go on and see your registration and license, Doctor Desoto!"

Then he trailed her the few feet to the limo, her tipping on snow. Then right in front of the limo he pulled out his gun. The other policeman had remained behind holding Pops and Leon. Just outside the limo before the big policeman would allow Dassah to enter, he yelled, "You in there, come on out, right this second!"

Candy Man, in a knot on the floor only listened silently to the policeman's orders. Then, finally, like a baby, he got on his knees and hands and came crawling out.

"Up on your feet you!" definitely waving the gun.

Just as pale as the snow the coatless Candy Man stood dirty blond hair falling into his eyes before the policeman. The policeman harshly ordered his hands up. He frisked the now compliant homeless man. "Stand over there!" Then the big policeman stepped inside, subtle sniffing for drugs. He looked around at all the finery. Dassah had moved under the wheel and handed him a neat package of legal documents as he had now stepped outside and was at her window, snowflakes gathering on his cap. Flipping through the contents he found them all in order. "Beautiful picture," he handed the license back ". . . and nice ride too," he finally sounded human.

"Thanks!" she yet turned her perfectly shaped nose, her own, in the air. "These men are not maggots!" she hissed in a whisper between just them two.

Nevertheless, instead of an actual apology, he only softened his expression. She knew that was only to protect his macho image. As she had done earlier that morning, once again she found herself explaining her reason for being there.

"I know who you are," he simply said, knowing all the time. And as she sat slightly fuming, he said, "There's no evidence of drinking or drugs, so you're free to go. . . Do you still feel safe with these . . . *men?*" he reluctantly admitted.

It pleased her greatly that he finally got the message, so she shot him a soft smile. "Just a minute officer," she said. Then she turned abruptly to Candy Man. "Are you sure you're okay now!?" she asked Candy Man before the policeman would be gone. "If not, I can just leave you where I found you!" she now found the need to be a little sterner with him.

From the other side of the limo, the shivering man quickly nodded, "I'm fine, Ma'am! I- I- I promise!"

That was the second time she had heard him sound somewhat sane. Also, by Candy Man's real voice, she surmised he could even be 19 or 20. And from the driver seat she took on the role of a mother and glared as sternly as possible, "Okay, one more chance mister that's all you get!"

The policeman watched amazed at the way she scolded the grown man. Her light brown eyes in the day light sparkled as she glared at the policeman. "I know what I'm doing. . . Believed me!" she assured. "I didn't purchase my credentials from a catalog I earned them with 9 years of mind and butt busting at the mental mechanic of people . . . 4 years of college, 4 more of med school and 1 year in residency." The Christian in her usually was not one to boast. But she felt this one needed a crash course in humility. She felt that if she could hang out with these, so called less revered citizens, so could he at least show a bit of respect to them. The doctor had come to realize her love for them was not merely for the mega profit they brought. "I could very well survive off a psyche's income . . ." she thought. "I surely wasn't hurting for any good thing even before the makeover program happened."

As the policeman stood there he finally said, "I'm leaving now." Then he beckoned the other policeman to bring the other men who then marched them back at gun-point. Once by the limo the big policeman motioned his partner to put away the gun. From the driver's seat Dassah glanced down at her documents and a business card was now among the papers. It read, Steven Lake, Private Investigator and circled in red were both his home and office phone numbers. She had also noticed his bare wedding ring finger. "A Bare ring finger doesn't mean a thing these days," she whispered under her breath. "Married people cheat more openly than single ones!"

Then with a subtle smile he walked off with his partner, ordering the crowd to disperse.

Dassah was safe behind the wheel of her comfort once more. She peered out at the homeless men just gaping through the window at her. Again she wanted to cry about the layers of dirty clothing they had on. "But they have to keep warm somehow!"

The snow had let up in the shabby neighborhood.

She noticed Pops, who had no memory of who he was. He still appeared confused, a thin trickle of blood dried in his ear. Then her eyes moved to Leon for whom she really had high hopes. "Would you guys still like to come along?" her expression was fatigued but serious.

The men out in fine snow flurries exchanged glances, remembering the leftovers in the car. Leon began to move quickly toward the burnish vehicle. "Yeah we have to get our coats anyway!" was his excuse. Actually he preferred the leftovers.

She sighed of relief. Though Dassah had compassion for Candy Man's mental demise, she would not fret if he and Pops remained behind. She looked at Pops knowing he needed the emergency room. He had been hurt on her property so her insurance would pay. In her Christian walk the doctor wanted to save everyone both physically mentally and spiritually, but knew that was impossible, because not everyone would confess Christ, even if she fed them. "After all Dassah," she thought. "Jesus did not save everyone he encountered, though he's still trying, so how do you feel you can?"

Then the three homeless men climbed eagerly back into the finery, taking the same seats by their tattered coat. "Buckle up guys," her tired, but sexy eyes moved from the men to the clock. It was 1:25. She recalled getting up at five this morning, prior to staying up late, reading. Saturdays are usually her day to sleep late, but she desperately had to replenish the makeover program.

PART FOUR

CHAPTER 14

I n Neal, New York that Saturday morning Doctor Dassah Desoto had three homeless men in her limo. Her bodyguard Stephanas Carter had been arrested for inadvertently killing a Latino boy, whether accidental or deliberately would be for the court to decide. In the doctor's opinion, he had done that protecting her. She and the homeless men would make a decision about recruiting for the program. They would ride along with her to the little town jail to get Step. Afterwards they all would take a two hour drive to Manhattan and from there take a short jet ride to her farm in Georgia.

Meanwhile, back at the small brick police department Step was in a clean little holding cell with several tough looking men around his age of 25. The Latino hoodlum was 17 and taken to the juvenile. Step consciously tuned out all of the distractions in order to reflect on how just a couple of hours earlier he had killed a young boy. "Dassah only went into that alley to do well for those poor souls!" he thought, ignoring the simultaneous conversions. Some were swearing their innocence, others wishing for drugs or a cold beer. Step, a buffed Black man only sat silently with his hood partially covering his face, hiding some of the frustration. He was surprised the guards had allowed him to keep the coat—maybe because the jail was not as warm as state regulations required. They had to cover their wrongs. Nevertheless, he was cautious of how the men eyed his new black Timberland boots. They, as well took heed to how he eyed their every move with a blazing dare. "Go on!" he thought. "Finish making my day!" On the other hand he knew better than to dig his hole any deeper. "Come on Boss before I have to lose it up in here!" he said aloud as he tried to will the deputy to appear down the hall with good news. Though he had only been in the cell for a few minutes, he stood up with a sigh and began to pace again. And just like debris does for the wind, the men also mowed a path for the mammoth. Step's martial arts had taught him to move with confidence. He sat back down to meditate and practice self-discipline. "It's a little too late for that now!" he thought. "If only I'd used more self-control this morning!" The boy's screams echoed in Step's hooded head. He realized it was the boy's provocation that had injected him with a dose of momentary insanity. "I would never deliberately harm any child!" he thought with another big sigh, willing his mind on a cosmos journey to calmness. Thinking of outer space always was euphoria for him. As a boy he'd always dreamed of being an astronaut.

Meanwhile, back in the limo Dassah put on another pair of durable boots. "I'll be prepared this time for whatever comes next," she thought of the bad day. Then she invited Leon to come sit up front in the passenger seat with his leftover plate. She sniffed the air and the fumigator worked well now. She felt safe with Leon since he had protected her twice already. "He can be my temporary bodyguard," she thought.

Putting the empty plate in the bag, Leon beamed within but hid the glee. "I just hope the job she's offering is legit!" he thought. Pops had become lethargic acting and was not as responsive as before. Candy Man was in the very back now, snoring. She turned around to Pops, "I'd better drop you off at the hospital for sure!"

"No! I'm fine," he sat straight up.

"Well okay!" As she eased the limo from the snug space she crept along the snowy streets, "I still don't know where I'm going!" she said, faintly cutting an eye at Leon. At his silence, she shot a quick glance at Leon, and then at the car ahead as the wiper swiped snow. Apprehension yet glinted in her brown eyes. "Now Dassah, which way is that police department!" idiotically, she asked herself.

"Take a right at the next light," Leon finally offered "This is my hood you know."

"Yes, I know. Thanks," she sighed. Of all her cars, the limos were not her favorite to drive. Her soul-mate was the new SUV she kept all shiny. "I really miss Step!" she finally sighed aloud, carefully steering the long car into a sharp right turn, barely missing a parked car. She glanced into the rear-view mirror at the other two passengers. "How are you Pops . . . your ear . . . you keep rubbing it?"

No reply this time—just a blank stare. The stream of blood had dried into the thick grey hair in his ear.

"Hey Pops?" Leon turned partially around usually always getting some kind of reply from his friendly, mature homeless peer.

Finally, Pops simply lifted his green eyes to Leon, "I'm not Pops!" he frowned in an unfriendly tone. "I'm a brain surgeon, Doctor Blake Clancy. . . Clearly, I now remember who I am, and my family."

Her foot hit the brakes behind a car. Leon gaped at Pops. Even Candy Man from the back gawked at the older, now stranger. Then after the shock had absorbed into all of them, Dassah laughed, "Well that whack on the noggin was good for something' huh?!" She glanced in the rear-view mirror at the new solemn faced man. Leon snickered. She glanced over at Leon and was taken aback by his wide manly smile, "What an absolutely nice smile . . . dingy, but nice," she thought, brown eyes twinkling with joy. "I wonder what's really beneath that fuzz." She tried never to flirt with the men, "But I am a woman!" she thought. "What red-blooded woman wouldn't drool over the 'after' make-over of some of them?" even after today's horrendous ordeal she managed to snicker under her breath. Suddenly her mind went to some of the magnificent 'after' snapshots she always took of the men. Whenever the cautious doctor did date, she preferred men in the church of Christ, or in her professional league. Not that she overly inflated herself as a person. "Nevertheless, I have a rep to uphold both as a Christian and a psychiatrist!" she always says. In her third opinion, if an ex-homeless man were to prove he was rehabilitated by maintaining his small business, she might consider going out with him. Though, while driving, she became more curious about Leon Davis's background. "He seems shrewd, sensitive and strong-willed," she thought. "Those three S's are positive characteristics for a positive come-back in life . . . and if this one's not married with a boat load of kids, he'll soon be spoken for by some, hopefully, prosperous woman like Callie perhaps!" It was her goal to help the men find success. "Even if not happiness, I hope he will be successful!" In her opinion, as a psyche happiness was something that germinated deep within, with the Lord inside. "And happiness doesn't necessary materialize just because one come into a chunk of money . . . riches may offer pleasure, but true happiness sits in a class of its own," she thought.

From the passenger seat, "Now go about four lights and make a left," Leon pointed. "Can you get some music in here, Ma'am?" he suddenly became polite again. "I haven't heard a nice song in a month of Mondays!"

"Sure, help yourself," she handed him the remote, stopping for the light, the wipers swiping silently back and forth.

"I've never seen one this fancy," he gawked at the million buttons. "H-m-m, a DVD player too . . . that explains all the five-car pile-ups on the roads."

"For your info, the television is in the back . . ." she smiled over.

Reluctant to just start pushing buttons, he frowned, "How do you work this anyway? The last remote I worked had only ten buttons and an on and off button."

Then Blake strained on the seatbelt and reached up to Leon, "Hand it here," he finally demanded. Then skillfully he tuned to a classic music station. As the symphony blasted the surround-sound, Blake hummed along and daydreamed lovingly for a change, about his past. Candy Man, on the sofa-size back seat, was snoring again.

"Nice tune Blake!" Dassah said, waiting at the third light. "What kind of doctor did you say you are?" she had understood he was a brain surgeon but prompted more conversation from him.

Blake shook out of the joyous stupor, "I'm pleased to tell, I'm head of surgeons at North General Hospital in Manhattan," he almost gloated. "A-h-h-h, how good it feels to remember!" he closed his eyes and began to hum again.

She left him to his serenity. Then she said, "After we've gotten Step we'll take you guys to clean up a little bit."

The light changed and she slowly, on the developing slick, pulled off. Then Leon quickly said, "Whoa, not so fast Doc!"

Dassah glanced confused over at him, slammed on the brakes. "This is only the third light. We have one more to go, right?!"

"No, no! I'm sorry. Go on Doc."

And from behind they heard the screech of brakes in a desperate effort to stop. With the help of snow tires she also barely escaped plowing into a car ahead. Horns began blast her to scorn. Pops had sat straight up again. Candy Man was now peering up to see the commotion.

With the doctor nervously sitting in the middle of the streets, and cars moving on both sides, Leon finally breathed, "I'm so sorry to cause this confusion, but you're not taking' me nowhere to clean up until I know what's up with this job deal!"

"Why are you giving me such a hard time about this, Mister Davis?!" she said, with a quick glance his way but carefully pulling off. "I'm only trying to help you get off the streets . . . doesn't it appear by now that I'm honest?"

"Yes it does and for that I'm grateful, but I need to know what's in store for me. . . You could be one of those doctors that like to shoot medicine into a body. . . And I ain't down with that . . . that experimenting stuff!" he gestured firmly with now halfway-clean hands.

"Neither am I," Blake said. "I'm going home to my darling wife of twenty-five years, that's after I've gone to the bathroom."

Now slowly on her way to the fourth light, "Help yours elf to the toilet," she breathed now in frustration, "It's all the way in the back."

Suddenly, from the back, Candy Man made more than four sensible words, "Neither do I like being poked with needles, nor taking medicine!" the youthful voice declared.

"Guys, I'm not a medical doctor. . . I'm a psychiatrist only looking for homeless men to clean up and put to work in one of my stores . . . though I can prescribe medicine to those who need it." she glanced over at Leon, and then at the car ahead, and was forced to go on and reveal her purpose, "Through a makeover program I have you'll earn a new life . . . nothing about the program is free . . . like all of us, you also earn your living, getting paid a small salary."

"How much pay are you talkin'?"

"I'll get to that in time . . . but it'll be more than what you've got now," she went assuredly on "After you successfully finish, you would have saved so that you and your four business partners will combine monies, along with a small government grant, and start you own business."

Leon frowned, "What kind of business!?"

"Any small business you may choose within your financial and mental limits . . . In the meanwhile, you'll have learned the art of being a knowledgeable entrepreneur . . . And while you may not get rich in the small business, you will be self-reliant and an up-standing citizen."

Blake, now from the bathroom, sat beside Candy Man, who was now wide awake, and buckled up. "What's in all this for you Doc?" Blake asked with interest in his bloodshot eyes. Suddenly the Caucasian, ex-homeless man became the business-minded doctor he really was.

Dassah braking for the car ahead, "Well, It's obvious I didn't buy this baby by just dishing out money at will to everyone!" she pat the steering wheel. "This black-beauty is a up to date free gal." She tapped the plush wheel again as she cruised down the streets of Neal, New York that snowy afternoon. The three homeless men now stared with interest, Blake as a business man wishing to get in on the makeover business itself.

Leon from the passenger seat, "So we make you rich and you get us on our feet?" he glanced questioningly over.

"That's about it," she nodded. "My stores and farm can't very well work themselves!"

"Count me out!" Blake quickly announced from the back. "That is, unless you're selling shares!" Then he reflected back momentarily on his own hefty wealth. "But right now I want to go to my cozy mansion in Upper Manhattan."

Not surprised at Blake, she simply asked, "What about you Leon?" She turned in his direction and choked back nausea from the smelly sneakers. The fumigating system had not reached under the dash. She usually did not have homeless men in the front. "I never considered the smell when I invited him up here," she thought with deep regret. "I dare not insult him now." So, like she had done as a girl standing in front of the rancid air-conditioner that day, she took her senses back to her little room at Big Ma's.

Through the music, Leon said, "By the time we get Step maybe I'll have a decision Doc."

"That's fair enough." Nevertheless, she already knew he was game. "No sane person wants to be homeless for the rest of his life!" she thought. "I sense that Leon had a good home life at one time."

"What about me?" Candy Man asked timidly from the back seat.

"We'll figure out something," Dassah was careful not to set him off again. Without Step there to protect her, she was vulnerable. As a psychiatrist, she knew if Candy Man became too upset even the other men would not be able to control him. From the mirror she saw disappointment in his blue eyes and he began to rock. Dassah knew she had to get him to a hospital in order to fill out committal forms to a mental facility, if he would agree. "Without a doubt he needs medication whether he wants it or not," she thought glancing back and forth from the road to him. "If he won't take a tranquilizer by mouth, he must get a shot—which he already declared hatred for . . . if he refuses, there's nothing more I can do." She would have to return him to the streets where he would only pose a danger to himself and others. "Sad, it's only when he has hurt someone that he'll be put away without his approval," she sadly thought. She knew she could say he assaulted her and have him committed. "That's exactly what I'll do," she thought, staring at his retched rocking through the mirror. At just the thought of him getting care compassion overshadowed her. It was at that very moment that the doctor discovered what would make her cry. Tears formed in her beautiful eyes, but the tissues in her dash came in handy.

Then blowing her nose, "Cold weather always gives me the sniffles!" she excused. She knew that not being able to cry had everything to do with her abusive childhood. She would begin to cry, like now and then suppress the tears, leaving her chest with a load of weight. As a doctor she warned her clients time and again, denial of tears was bad news.

Driving slowly to the last traffic light on the way to get Step, snow began to really pelt the windshield. She glanced at the clock. It was 1:36 that Saturday. Leon in the passenger seat said, "When you get to the light, hang a left . . . the station is on the right."

Soon Dassah pulled into the snowy parking lot and found ample space as there were only about five police cars and a couple of other cars. "Candy Man," she turned and calmly said, "I'm only going to get Step, now don't you go worrying about the police." Then she looked at the other men. "If you'll wait until I get Step, we'll have lunch and then I'll explain the entire deal to you Leon." She planned to have lunch in the Bronx at her smaller restaurant. The other two bigger restaurants in Manhattan were another two-hour drive.

"Before you go, Doc, may I use your phone to call my wife," Blake took off his seatbelt and moved anxiously to the front.

Suddenly, as if it just sank in, Leon, eyeing Blake as a stranger, laughed, "You mean to tell me all this time I've been hanging out with a doctor who works in the most prestigious hospital in the North? Will wonders ever cease?!"

"I'm afraid so!" Blake, typical of a physician, matter-of-fact replied, his white but dirty hand reaching for the phone that was responsible for his memory returning.

"What's the number, I'll dial," she said, still smiling at what Leon had just said. Then Blake recited his number without missing a digit. She dialed it. When it began to ring, she handed it to the anticipating tattered doctor. As everyone also anticipated hearing, Blake nervously cleared his throat. Finally a woman answered, "This is the Clancy resident."

Blake hesitated clearing his throat again.

"Hello?!" the impatient woman now insisted.

Finally, "Hello Tessie it's me, Doctor Clancy."

Without another word, Tessie screamed for Mrs. Clancy to pick up the phone. "Ma-am, its Doctor Clancy!" she partially laughed and screamed.

"Oh Blake darling where are you!!" Mrs. Clancy sobbed.

"Hi Honey! I'm okay. . . I'm down in Neal . . . I really miss you!" he also began to cry and laugh.

Dassah passed back the box of tissue.

"Where in Neal are you Blake!?"

"Come to the police department. . . I'll be waiting. . . Oh, by the way, I'll be the one with the same suit I had on the last time you saw me," he teased through tears. For some reason Blake had not been able to tear away from that suit and get other clothes at the mission.

CHAPTER 15

In Neal, New York that snowy Saturday Doctor Hadassah Desoto a famed psychiatrist was about to exit her limo leaving three homeless men. One of those men had just newly discovered his name was really Doctor Blake Clancy. She asked them to wait in the limo for her. She was at the police department to bail Stephanas Carter her bodyguard out. Step was locked up for the suspected murder of a Latino teenager earlier that morning in an alley. Three homeless men had been picked up by Doctor Desoto and propositioned to become part of her lucrative makeover program to make them ex-homeless men.

Blake Clancy the late fifties, White homeless man had just snapped out of amnesia and discovered he was the Chief of Surgeons in a famous hospital in Manhattan. Leon Davis another one of the homeless men was unsure if he wanted to become part of Dassah' 'slaves' so he suspected. But she truly wanted the mid-thirties, brave Black man in the program and she had hoped to recruit as least five men that day. Candy Man, so he was named by the other men, was the third homeless man in the car. The younger White, early twenties man had deep mental issues that Dassah had not time to handle the un-intellectual challenges.

Being a psychiatrist she would persevere until she knew if his illness was self- inflicted or hereditary. "Is he trying to suppress something?" she wondered. She noticed how he often would retreat into his own created world. Her speculation was that his autism was purposely willed. "Which undoubtedly proves a recent onset of ill events in his past," she thought. Then she said, "I just hate going into that place!" glancing over at Leon still in the passenger seat. Just in that short time, snow had mounted on the windshield. As she was about to exit bundled up, Blake quickly moved along with her, "Hold it!" he said. "I'm coming along . . . my wife is picking me up here." He smiled, straightening his shirt and tie to impress his wife. He slipped on the badly stained overcoat, "How do I look!" he beamed, head high.

"Like the rest of us . . . dirty and funky," Leon snickered.

But Blake impatiently, snarled, "How did I ever put up with the likes of you anyway!?" overlooking how he had once adored Leon like a son.

Dassah was totally displeased with the sheer hurt in Leon's dingy eyes. To her one of her helpless children had been insulted. She knew that Leon suddenly felt that Blake now thought he was more superior to them. She noticed that even Candy Man took on a sour note to his ex-friend's new self. But she was glad to know that Candy Man even had that manner of comprehension. The doctor sought every possible opportunity to diagnose Candy Man.

Dassah glared meanly at Blake with a mind to intervene but knew Step was waiting. So there in the limo, she simply said, "Well guys I'll come back as soon as I can." She took out the keys, got her purse and the registration papers from the compartment. She looked at Leon in the passenger seat, "If you get cold, just push this button . . . you can adjust it with this knob," she pointed them out. Then she and Blake got out and walked across the snowy lot and into the police station.

Back in the limo Leon immediately went to the back for a drink of water and also got a cup for Candy Man. He grabbed a couple of packs of crackers from the cabinet he had rummaged into. Seated in the back, and after fumbling with the remote he finally turned on the TV. Then the tattered men stretched out to watch. "Did you think we'd ever be riding in a limo man?" Leon smiled across at Candy Man.

"I've been in plenty!"

"Is that right!?" Leon also eyed him anew. "He did come to us with a roll of green-backs," Leon thought. "Just who are you really Candy Man?" he then asked for the first time since knowing the evasive young man.

However Leon backed off when he saw that Candy Man had begun to snore.

Meanwhile, on the highway in a tan on brown, 2014 Mercedes SL, in that late Saturday afternoon traffic, Mrs. Clancy and her beautiful red-headed daughter were already on the way. They now filled the car with happy chatter instead of sad piano music. For once they were ecstatic to take the two-hour drive to Neal, a town they normally would never visit. "There are simply too many homeless bums pestering in that place!" Mrs. Clancy had once complained. "Can't those lazy folks get jobs or something and quit begging like dogs!" she had turned her keen, attractive nose in the air.

Then changing that depressing thought, the sophisticated woman, under the wheel, glanced over at her daughter, "Maybe we should've taken Blake's car just to blow it out a bit." Back in their three-car garage sat Blake's 2013 Mercedes. In another side of the garage sat their daughter's 2015, sports BMW. "I always thought we'd keep the Benz in the family!" he had teased her when she deviated.

"That's right Mother" her daughter said from the passenger seat. . . Daddy's car hasn't burned rubber in three months . . . since they retrieved it abandoned a few miles from the hospital. . . Oh, I can't wait to see my Dear Daddy!" the green-eyed, twenty-three-year-old beamed. She was only home for the holidays and was scheduled to return in a few days to finish her second year of med school at the university—she was anxious to become a doctor like her father. She bubbled to finally see her idol. "Daddy's been gone through the entire holidays!" she reminded her mother.

"Yes Dear, I know!" was the bubbly reply, eyes on the car ahead.

Back at the police station inside, Dassah noticed everyone so busy. So much that they barely noticed her and Blake come in. "We could have a bomb in our hands for all they care!" she leaned over and whispered to Blake, who in return didn't seem to care. His dignity was back and he was terribly ashamed of his shabbiness, and his mind was on his family.

Shaking her head disappointed at the government workers that had just displayed the utmost apathy she yet respected the law. "It's a known fact that bad people always set a negative example for the good ones on jobs!" she whispered again to Blake.

"Yeah, I guess," he finally whispered. . . Some shoddy security our tax dollars go for!"

Dassah glanced surprised at Blake because he suddenly sounded like a concerned citizen instead of an ex-homeless man. Though, she took a mental note that his comment was only about money and that quality customer service was the least of the new Blake's worries.

"Hello officer," Dassah, in jeans and coat that did not have wealthy written on them, said to the mature uniformed woman at the desk. "I'm Doctor Hadassah Desoto and this is Doctor Blake Clancy . . . I'm here to post bail for someone."

And without even a hello the tight-pores, smooth skinned Black woman glared at Blake's tattered clothes, and then at Dassah' somewhat nicer ones. Then her eyes locked oddly on the dried blood in his ear. Blake had tried to wash it out but declared it had been too painful. The woman finally, snootily replied, "Name of the person to be bonded out?"

Dassah gave the info. The woman began to speed-type into a computer. "He's under a one-hundred thousand-dollar bond," she eventually said. "Take these papers to the second floor and someone will take the ten-thousand it'll take to get him." Without as much as a glance up she jutted three sheets of paper at Dassah.

"May I wait here for my wife?" Blake asked the woman, who only glared at him in silent scorn. Then with the pen she impatiently pointed him to the waiting room.

Dassah hasted to one of the two little elevators, in-door-out-door carpet underfoot. As an eager psychiatrist Dassah muttered, "I surely would love to put that one on my red couch and see what's in her puny mind!" On the way she noticed a wall-to-wall shadow-box with missing persons, mainly children. A loud gasp escaped as there in living color was a picture of Doctor Blake Clancy whom she would never recognize had she not known his name. "That picture seems so . . . so fresh!" she snickered. Though, it was no surprise that his family attached a twenty-five-thousand-dollar reward.

Dassah had a mind to wheel around and inform Blake of the ad but instead went on up to get Step. She had already written the ten-thousand-dollar check. "My poor Step has been in this place about long enough!" she thought. Then she took the paperwork up. In approaching the desk Dassah braced for another rude encounter. "May I help you Ma'am?" the young woman sang with a bigger than life smile.

Taken aback, "Yes you may," she smiled back. "Now I can tell Blake his tax dollars aren't all lost," she thought. Dassah handed her the papers. "I need to get Mr. Stephanas Carter."

"Yes Ma'am," she looked over the papers and asked for Dassah' identification. "That'll be ten-thousand dollars, which you will have refunded when Mr. Carter appears in court. Of course, if the court charges a fine, that amount will be deducted from the ten-thousand," she patiently and articulately explained. . . If the defendant fails to appear in court, the money will not be refunded. . . Do you understand Doctor Desoto?"

"Very much so, and thanks for your kindness!" She handed her the check that had to be verified through a machine. "Now, who in his right mind would try to pass a bad check to the police department?!" she snickered to the woman.

"You'd be surprised at the kind of people that comes through here!" she also snickered. And while verifying the check, the woman said, "And you're quite welcome for the thanks, Doctor." Knowingly she smiled. "Negativity is all over this place, but respect is a rare commodity I'm determined to share. . . Some of our workers tend to treat the family like they're the suspects!"

Dassah eyed the young woman sensing her heart-felt sincerity. It impressed Dassah that the woman had been nice before she even knew she was a doctor. Then Dassah took out a business card that she was picky to whom she gave one, and handed it to her. "My brother can use someone like you on his inside security team. . . He pays very well with good benefits, double what you make with the city."

"Gee thanks!" the young woman gawked at the fancy card. "Doctor, you may have a seat and I'll call for Mr. Carter's release," she eagerly said. "You would normally have to go through a bonding company, but we are pleased that we can handle some cases."

"I'm grateful for that, too, because I'm flat worn out today!" the thirty-eight year old doctor breathed. "I'm not twenty anymore!" They laughed.

Dassah returned to Blake sitting impatiently staring at the door. But all he saw was strangers began to rush in brushing snow off their shoulder. Dassah sat down close beside him on the wooden bench. She glanced at her watch. It was 2:10. "It hasn't been thirty minutes since you called your wife Blake," she reminded him. "You know it'll take a couple of hours for her to make it here in this weather." She gently patted his dirty, damp shoulder. People stared at her being so affectionate to this obviously homeless man. Having been with them all morning Dassah felt a warm closeness to all three men. She thought about Candy Man and her heart ached with pity. Then a sudden brilliant idea sat her straight up. Sliding closer to her ex-homeless friend, "Blake!" she almost cooed. "Come with me" she stood up and tugged his sleeve, forcing him up.

"B-but, where are we going!? I have to wait. . ."

"It's just around the corner there." She grabbed his cold gloveless hand and led him to the missing person's board near the elevators. "Look!" she pointed to his picture.

"Well I'll be . . . that's my best picture up there!"

"Now look at this reward," pointing.

"So, what's your point Doc?" he didn't seem at all surprised to see the twenty-five-thousand reward.

"Blake!" she cried with seriousness. "You know how compassionate we doctors are when it comes to helping others . . . that's why most of us got into the healing business in the first place, right?"

Puzzled, staring through dingy eyes, "Yeah."

"What I'm trying to say is that Candy Man could really use that money for his stay at a nice mental institution." She pleaded into his weary eyes, "After all Candy Man was responsible for you getting your memory back . . . you know . . . when the phone hit you in the ear?" she touched the dried blood. He flinched and shied away in pain. There by the elevator with people boarding, Blake was silent as he pondered on that. Dassah hated his newly acquired remoteness. "He seems almost snobbish," she thought, dreadfully waiting for his reply.

Then finally, "Well it wasn't like he called in that he found me, or anything. Let me sleep on it, okay?" he assured.

"What can I say? It's your money. . ." Then Dassah reached into her tiny purse for the second time. "Here's my card, and as a humanitarian please consider that reward to Candy Man."

Suddenly, with a ding the elevator opened and out came Step. Dassah wheeled around and flew into his strong arms—something she had never done to her buffed bodyguard before. Their bodies had never been that close. "I told you I'd get you out today, didn't I!?" she smiled up into his grinning handsome face. He continued to hold her, surprised to finally have her in his grasp. "I could get used to this!" he only thought. Then he glanced again surprised at Blake, whom he knew as Pops. He could only wonder about Pops' but before he could ask, suddenly the young pretty police in the patty wagon, stepped around the corner. She gaped meanly at Step embracing his beautiful curvaceous boss. Then tossing her nose in the air, she walked abruptly away. "Hold up Paula!" He released Dassah so quickly she almost stumbled. "Again, this is Doctor Hadassah Desoto my boss as you know," he smiled softly at the lovely, uniformed officer. "Doc, this is Paula Clarke." Though not personally but the women had already met in the alley and at the wagon.

After formal introductions Paula disappeared onto the elevator but not before giving Step a seductive wave. Then Dassah teased, "Well, well, it wasn't such a bad stay in here after all! Maybe I should've given you a little bit longer for play-time!" humor.

"No, no! That's okay."

Then Dassah glanced at Blake impatiently waiting there by the elevator. "Step I want you to meet Doctor Blake Clancy!" she anticipated seeing Step's shock at the news.

"What?" Step did startle. "And what scientific breakthrough occurred since this morning!" he roared as people gaped boarding and un-boarding the elevator. "Is it suddenly possible for a homeless person to get a two-hour course in doctorin'!?" he laughed.

Dassah smiled to see Step in a good mood. She worried he would be feeling excessively guilty over burning the teenager to death. "But I know Step well enough to know he'll always carry some remorse about this, even if it was in the line of duty protecting me," she thought. Then she looked at her bodyguard, "I'll fill you in on Doctor Clancy once we're back in the car. The others are also there. . . I hope!" But she knew the men could not drive away. She had the keys. But they could very well have changed their mind and simply walked away.

"Are you alright!?" Step suddenly recalled suggesting she not recruit the men today.

"Yeah you know me." She dared not mention Candy Man's attack on her.

Then with an obvious display of apathy over the formalities, Blake wheeled impatiently around and headed eagerly to the waiting room where he sat down and began to rub his head with a deep frown. Dassah feeling intense mistrust toward the new Blake told an officer Blake had been brought in. And at her request, he took down the picture and the promissory reward and gave it to her. She slipped it into her pocket. The officer said that he would also take Blake's name out of the system. As she and Step headed out, she discretely showed the picture to another officer at the desk. Blake was still rubbing his head with his tired eyes sharply on the door. Dassah informed the friendlier officer that she had brought in Doctor Blake Clancy. "When his wife comes, and you take him off the list, would you please give her this card and have her contact me?" Dassah felt that the new Blake would never easily hand over twenty-five-thousand—even if it was justifiable. She was mentally preparing to force him to honor the reward in court if need be. "It's a known fact that some folks are just nicer when they're broke!" she angrily thought. Afterwards, she and Step finally headed for the door. They passed Blake sitting on the bench intently watching the door. The tattered impatient middle-aged man barely returned Dassah' farewell. She walked back to him. "Blake, as one doctor to another you really should have that lump looked at," she suggested.

He startled at her presence in his space. "Oh! I'll be okay." His perturbed eyes went back to the snow covered people coming in.

Walking back to Step at the door Dassah whispered, "I liked him a lot better as Pops!"

"Yeah he is a bit weird now!" However, Step had not spent as much time with the older homeless man.

Out on the snow once again she was happy to have Step at her side. As they walked to the limo she glanced at her watch, "Can you believe it's already one o'clock?! Where did the morning go?" she sighed. She dreaded wasting Saturdays because she normally use that day preparing her mind for Sunday worship. "To bring spiritual sacrifices to the altar of the Almighty is truly my oasis after an exhausting week," she had once said to a sister in Christ.

The doctor and her bodyguard walked across the parking lot toward the limo. Then, all of a sudden, a car pulled up to them, too fast on snow, and abruptly stopped. Step instinctively snatched Dassah behind him. He peered in at the driver and recognized him as the dead boy's uncle. The tight-lipped man began threateningly to exit the car. Step placed his hand on the gun under his coat that he had gotten back, because it had not been used in the death and it was registered. Dassah bent to get hers, "Oh no!" I forgot to get my gun!"

"That's okay. I didn't forget mine!"

Dassah noticed a Latino woman also seriously evil-eyeing Step. After a brief standoff in the fine snow flurries the man recoiled back into the car. He slowly pulled off and into a parking space. They had brought his son to the jail. When the couple headed towards the station Dassah and Step also proceeded in the direction of the limo. "What about your gun boss?"

"Oh never mind!" her gloved hands went up in frustration. "I've had enough excitement for one day. I'll just get it some other time. That's not the only one I have . . . my favorite one, but. . ."

They proceeded to the limo. Back in the alley earlier she thought the uncle understood why the boy had fallen victim to death. All evidence had pointed to him being at fault. "If he had not come into the alley with criminal intents, he'd still be alive!" she huffed to Step.

'I'll be the first to totally agree!" Step walked along beside her. "When we came out today I hadn't the foggiest idea I'd be returning as a child-killer."

"Yeah, and I feel we're in for it. . . But I'll stand firm that you only did your job, so don't you worry. . . Our defense is set for the arena. . . I've already alerted Mad-Callie," she sometimes called her because of her flatfooted way in the courtroom—not to disrespect the court, but only whenever she felt she had justifiable causes.

"That's good she's on our side!" a big sigh sent steam through the Black bodyguard's moist defined lips. Then he said, "I'm really grateful you bailed me out boss!"

"What? Did you think I'd leave my sidekick to rot in jail? You must be crazy!"

"Those few hours seemed like a whole lifetime," he huffed. Those jokers in there eyed the black off my Timberlands!" he glanced at his feet as if to assure his boots were still there.

"Then I know they would've had a brother all over 'em up in there!" wagging her beautiful head, laugher became her. They were still laughing when Step escorted her to the passenger door. He unlocked it.

"Who is that?" Leon jumped up. The nap and food had the men lethargic. Candy Man stirred aggravated on the far back seat.

It's just us!" Dassah frowned under her breath as the stench had strong-armed the fumigation system. She looked at Leon's tattered socks and knew it was time to turn on the air to aid the multi-standard system. "That's what you get for leaving homeless men in the parked car that long!" she thought. Now she felt rushed to have the car detailed, even though the fitted seat covers were always in place on a trip out.

Though once inside, her chilled bones welcomed the warmth. She had not yet gotten over the lengthy stay in the alley earlier. "Are you guys ready to go clean up a bit?" tact was in her more confident voice.

Step, her employed reason for being braver now, also slid under the wheel. Candy Man simply turned over, grunted and resumed snoring.

"A bath would be the order of the century . . ." Leon said, running his fingers over his dirty locks, "but we have to talk first . . . remember?" Then he looked at Step. "Oh, hi Step . . . glad you're out," covering his mouth from a wide yawn. "Forgive me, but I haven't slept that well in years . . . ya'll didn't stay in there long enough."

"That's easy for you to say!" Step flashed a mean glare back at him.

"Oh, right! I wasn't thinking straight, man." Leon excused.

Dassah quickly said, "That's exactly what I told him . . . he didn't stay long enough," laughter about Step and Paula.

Step and Dassah laughed. Leon hadn't a clue what the humor was all about.

Still parked, Step said, "That peaceful sleep you just had, you can get plenty more of that, man! All you need to do is say the word!"

From the passenger seat, Dassah said, "He wants us to explain his role in the program before he commits."

"Sounds a lot like myself before I would consider joining," Step sneaked a glance at the tattered Leon through the rear-view mirror hoping to stir his interest.

Leon's dirty eyes lit up, "No, man! I don't believe you ever were a bag-man."

"Oh yes he was . . . When I discovered him, he was not asleep in his box, but lived in one . . . just like I hope I've rescued you." Dassah turned around against the seatbelt and looked into Leon's eyes. "On the way to Manhattan to clean up I'll tell you all about the best rehab program in the United States for ex-cons and homeless men. The farm is only an hour in my small plane. . ." a smile crossed her fatigued beautiful, defined face, knowing she was financially able to have a plane. In the comfort of the limo there on the lot, she gave Leon a brief overview of the program, then asked, "Give us the word, Leon, and we'll ride away from Neal." I'll explain more as we go."

He pondered shortly on that. "Word!" he said. "What do I have to lose?"

Staring at the snowflakes on the windshield, she let out a deep breath. "What about you Candy Man?" She then peered all the way in the back at the stretched out young man without his seatbelt on. He now began to fill the car with teeth-grinding. As a psychiatrist Dassah recognized the teeth-grinding behavior as a highly stressed condition called, Bruxism. She knew that was brought on because he was asked to make a decision concerning his future. "Do you want to come along Candy Man?" she repeated. She knew Candy Man feared that if he committed to anything in the future, then he would be forced to reveal his past. "I wonder what was so horrid in his past," she thought. "The poor man's entire body is rigid with fear." She and the others patiently waited.

Finally, Candy Man sat up, dirty blond hair in his eyes, "Yeah I-I'll go." He barely muttered through the grinding.

She was not proud to admit she was not as excited over his answer. This was the part of her practice she dreaded to most. Though, she always loved a success story, she knew her work was cut out with Candy Man. So, she leaned over and whispered to Step, "First, I'll have to put him up until Blake can get the reward money to me. . . Which I feel I'll have to fight Blake to get. . . Then I'll have to do some convincing Candy Man to admit himself into a hospital."

"Doc, don't ask me to exchange places with you right now for any amount of money!" he whispered back pulling out of the snowy driveway. He glanced concerned over at Dassah, as she was pensively shaking her head and easing into thought. As usual, he knew when she did that to leave her to her meditation. Nevertheless, if she pondered too long and too deeply, he would gently nudge her out of it. She allowed that. "That's just the way psyches are I guess!" he thought, pulling into the sparse Saturday afternoon traffic.

While Candy Man snored and unsuspecting to Dassah and Step, Leon had heard her plans for Candy Man. "I think that's a good idea, Doc," Leon whispered. "Candy Man hasn't slept like this since the two years I've known him. . . "He usually gets up during the night and just paces 'til day light. . . The teeth grinding has become more intense lately."

"Why don't you move closer," she whispered. "Not that anything's wrong with your hearing, because I nearly non-verbalized that to Step." They laughed softly.

CHAPTER 16

Doctor Hadassah Desoto, Stephanas Carter, Leon Davis and Candy Man were in Dassah' limo, as Step drove carefully down the snowy interstate headed to her restaurant, but would first stop at her hotel and allow the men to clean up. The snow had slightly let up that Saturday afternoon. It was one-twenty. Dassah and Step had been scouting for homeless men since eight o'clock that morning. In the passenger seat, Dassah was disgusted that the scouting trip had not materialized as planned. They had run into an unfortunate stumbling block that suddenly turned fatal. It grieved the sensitive psychiatrist that her bodyguard was forced to kill on her behalf. "But, after all, I did hire him to protect me," she thought. So Dassah decided she would smile anyway in that she had gotten one good homeless man much needed, for the makeover program. "Maybe I've found two," she glanced in the back at Candy Man. "Maybe with a lot of therapy he'll turn out okay and work keeping the farm clean if nothing else."

As they exited the little city of Neal, New York, the traffic suddenly became stop and go. "What in the world are so many people doing out in the cold today?" Step huffed under the wheel. "If I weren't working,

I'd be in bed—with all this snow out here! Some people just love to sight-see and hinder working' folk!" he stepped on the brakes for what seemed to him the hundredth time in just five minutes.

Dassah snickered. "That's exactly why I hate driving in winter in New York!" she un-buckled the seatbelt and headed to the back to make coffee. She passed Leon, who was still was smiling over Step's frustration about the traffic. Delight shone in her light brown, very attractive eyes at the dread-locked, smelly man's sense of humor. Passing the snoring Candy Man, she shook him, "Please buckle up!" she warned. He grumbled, then fumbled and did so. Afterwards, he was snoring again, leaning into a strain against the seatbelt.

As she prepared coffee, she began to seriously explain to the men the pre-requisites for entrance into the program. She was not sure Candy Man even heard. "By makeover," she began, "That means you must have actually had a stable life at one time . . . that is the basic meaning of 'restoration,' isn't it?" she paused and glanced over her shoulder at Leon.

Leon yet confused, frowned, "Sounds to me like you're describing a piece of furniture."

Step kept his dark, youthful eyes on the white slick, but kept his ears peered as he broke frequently. He was anxious to learn how Leon wound up on the streets. "Looks like he's been homeless for years," Step thought, turning up the wipers and the fumigator. He sneaked a glance through the rear-view mirror at the hairy-faced dread-locked man. Step had a feeling they would be spending plenty of time together in the future. "The boss really likes this one!" he thought. He also admired Leon's spunk and tenacity back in the alley against the boys in their attempt to rape and rob his boss. Both Step and Dassah knew that if the incident had not occurred, the bond with Leon would never have developed. They normally found the men, fed them and took them to the farm for therapy and full body purging. Then, Step thought, "Leon would be un-afraid to knock heads on the farm, whenever things got out of hand!" The men on the farm sometimes tried newcomers. Driving along, he recalled being a freshman on the farm, and some of the men trying him only later, with lumps and knots, to express regretting they had. He envisioned the grueling wrestling competitions that took place for fun, and as usual, temples would flair up. Dassah also needed more men with spunk and leadership to be in charge of the farm and of her demanding stores for the three-year makeover period.

Then, from the coffee pot in back, she continued, "I run a strict program and expect the recruits to be honest with me, as I likewise will be with you!" She returned with three cups of coffee on a server with sugar and cream and bagels. As she passed Leon, the smell of hot bagels filled his nostrils and he immediately grabbed a raisin one. Once again in the passenger seat, as she prepared Step coffee, she said, "The minor details of a man's past are not that important . . . only he must not have any outstanding warrants. If he's on probation, he must uphold that commitment to the end." Exotically, she swiped a lock of auburn hair from her eye and took a slurp of coffee. "The man must not be a child-molester or woman abuser. . . The only way I'll hire an alcoholic is that he agrees to get help and completes an AA program on his own," she took another sip of coffee and then became even more professional. "A background check will be thoroughly carried out before final acceptance," she said. "Whoever is rejected because of warrants will be brought back to the exact place he was picked up. When he turns himself in and clears himself then he can look me up from the card I'll give him."

Leon listened as he gobbled down bagel and coffee. Candy Man's snoring occasionally broke in as he half listened.

"Are there any questions Leon . . . Candy Man? Although she knew Candy Man was in another world most of the time.

"Yeah," Leon swallowed the last bite, "What if a man had spent some time in prison?"

At that Dassah exchanged glances with Step, who broke frequently in the traffic. Then she looked in the near back seat at Leon hoping he had no major record that would disqualify him. "Just like I said . . . any *minor* offence can be overlooked. One of my goals is to help struggling ex-convicts too. Basic offences like petty robbery or substance-abuse can be pardoned. . . As long as he wasn't convicted of murder, child-abuse or long-term woman-abuse. . ." The experienced doctor knew that some men may hit a woman while merely protecting himself from her abuse and get unjustly charged for that. When in such a case the convicted man had simply been forced to protect himself from the woman in self-defense. And in most cases, in the end the man became the culprit with a jail record that would follow him for life. She recalled having enrolled more than a few homeless men where these men had served long spreads in prison and came out homeless and mentally stressed—all of that just for standing up for himself. Dassah was so fair that she advises young women that if they do not care to be beaten by a boyfriend, then they should also bestow the same honor on him. "What's good for the goose is also good for the gander," she would say to them. "Some of you women have some powerful slaps and kicks that can really harm a man, you know!" However she knew there were certain cases where the man consistently exercised power over the woman and the doctor viewed that as chronic spousal-abuse. She recalled a few cases where the woman was the aggressor and the man was too ashamed to admit to being that weak under her. The doctor also recalled a sad true case where a woman whose son at that time was being horrifically abused by his wife—a new lump on the head daily. Then a friend of the abuser warned the man's mother that if something was not done, the abuser, her friend, would eventually kill the man. There was really nothing the mother could do except what she had been doing all along—pleading with her son to leave the woman—which he never did, claiming he loved her and felt too helpless to leave. Then one night, to the mother and family's grief, her son was brutally bludgeoned with an object—which the woman always would use on him. The woman was given life in prison due to the long-term abuse that finally resulted in death. The judge refused to hear her lawyer's plea of temporary insanity.

Then, there in the limo on the snowy highway, headed to clean the up Dassah awaited the homeless men's answer. She had paused briefly, and then asked, "So, should we keep driving guys, or should we bring you back to your tenthouse in the alley?"

Leon pondered on that, "Yeah! I mean, no, keep going. . . I never killed anybody and I don't beat children or women!" Leon found himself sigh of relief this time. He was now beginning to feel it was he who must make a good impression to get in, "I spent almost three years in prison, wrongfully charged for armed robbery," he huffed.

"They all claim they're innocent, Man! Step said.

"I know but I'm really innocent!" he shook his head. "After I had spent two and a half years, this man was arrested for several other major crimes and robberies and had the heart to admit he also pulled that one. . . I can't understand how anyone can look at his face in the mirror while another person is suffering for his sins. . . But then, later I learned the only reason the man confessed was because he had a forty-year sentence without parole—he killed a bank guard and was already sixty years old. . . I heard he just didn't want to face God with that lie. . . Afterwards, I was apathetically apologized to by the judicial system, released and sent on my merry way," Leon sighed loudly. "They didn't even ask whether I had a place to go! I thought I had the home I'd left, but when I went back there my wife had moved and conveniently forgot to leave a forwarding address!" And in an 'under-statement-of-the-year' tone, "Now was that a hint she had left me, or what?" He struggled to fight back the tears clouding his dingy eyes, "After all the years of nothing but honesty from me it seemed she was convinced I robbed that bank too. . . some faith in the man you were married to for nine years, huh?" he had asked himself a thousand times in his tenthouse trying to fall asleep. "She got rid of all my clothes and everything! Now something like that really makes a brother want to commit murder and cut her up in a million little pieces!"

Dassah from the passenger seat suddenly observed that Candy Man, upon hearing the mention of murder screamed, "It-it wasn't me Mister . . . I didn't!" It appeared as if he was talking to someone other than those in the car. He sat straight up, perspiring, dirty face, hair wet. With all eyes fixed wide on him, he, straining against the seatbelt, gawked strangely around the limo. And with a deep breath he slowly eased back in the seat. Being used to that kind of behavior Dassah only shook her beautiful head with pity. She knew for sure there were demons haunting him. "But what and why!" she thought. Finally, everyone returned to the business at hand.

Step, careful of the snow broke for the car that had suddenly pulled in front of him. "How did you ever become homeless, Man?" he glanced in the rear-view mirror.

"Well, when I got out, I only had about nine-hundred dollars in an account my wife didn't know about. . . My daddy always told me to keep a little 'mad money' but when I began saving it I never dreamed I'd be this mad. . . Of course I had lost my job as a high school basketball coach. It wasn't that people didn't believe I was innocent, but who would want me around their kids after doing a stretch in prison? People tend to think the worst of a man that once mingled with hardened criminals. . . There was nothing I could've said to prove I hadn't turned gay or worse," he sighed, his fowl breath reaching out to Dassah who simply bore it. In back of her he went on, "And that really hurt!" hopelessly and throwing dirty hands up. "Those parents were the same ones whom I led their little angels to victory 3 straight years!" He tried to push down a stubborn lump in his throat. Dassah and Step, empathizing, waited for the lump o go down. Of all the stories they had heard from the men Leon's touched them most. As a psychiatrist that certainly was not the saddest she had heard, but rather it was that special bond they had developed over the past few hours. Leon finally gained some composure, "I couldn't get a job, I was totally stressed-out, and my savings had run out. . . I borrowed from people who would trust my unemployment checks until those benefits even maxed out. . . That was almost four years ago," he shook his head, his long locks giving his beard a spanking.

"So essentially you've been out of sorts since then?" Step asked the obvious.

"Yeah, I'm afraid so, man!" bitterness.

Dassah glanced over her shoulder at Leon. She was glad to hear he was a college graduate but was not surprised. It was not her expectation that all the men be college graduates but preferred the intelligence enough to earn a GED. "And I can always send them to school on line," she thought. Then she glanced around, "Where's your family?"

"My family helped as much as possible. . . I lived with some of them but guilt about taking food out of the children's mouth got me down. . . Now listen! I never run from hard work, but people just don't trust jail-birds, especially Black jail-birds! And there're just not enough Black business-owners to hire each other."

"That's one thing I know!" she sighed big, "And that's where the makeover entrepreneurship program comes into play. . . If we can just get Black businesses built up in every State, that'll solve a lot of the high unemployment among Blacks! And as it stands, many ex-homeless men have begun small businesses nationwide. Each business has been able to hire at least five or six employees." she happily nodded her pretty head. "Where are your parents Leon? You look like a fairly young man."

"I'm thirty-six, if you call that young. . ."

"I did say *fairly* young." she laughed. They laughed.

Leon went on. "My mother's in Kansas and my dad's deceased. Kansas is where I was born."

"How in the world did you end up in New York?" Step asked, braking again and turning down the wipers again.

"Well," he shifted, aggravated to think about that. "That woman . . . the one that lost faith in me, was also living in Kansas at the time and enticed me to move here to her hometown . . . before we finally got married we dated for two and a half years. I figured we were lifetime lovers."

"How many little Leon's are there?" she raised a professionally shaped brow, holding her breath. Since so much had gone sour today she automatically anticipated another setback. "But from the information he has given so far, I can put him directly into the program," she thought. "I can't wait to see what he looks like under all the dirt and rags!" she eyed him. The anxious doctor smiled at her roller coaster ride of seeing the men transform into proud citizens once more. And another thrill was her increasing bank account behind it all. Her plans were to later retire and then travel by the tender age of fifty. "That is, if the good Lord is willing that I should live that long!" she thought of the incident in the alley and one not knowing when their time was up. "What's the use of getting rich if you can't bask in the light of that?" She was mindful that some wealthy folks worked in some fashion, all their lives and never really enjoyed life. Her plan was not to leave her riches without tasting of some of it. She recalled an older rich co-worker having said, "Dassah, one day you'll look in the mirror and won't even recognize the person staring back at you! Then, mystified, you'll ask yourself, "Where did that smooth, tight woman go?" Then, after that rude awakening Dassah decided to start enjoying some of her money. "But, only along with the truly needy benefiting from it, too," she had said to the co-worker.

As a Christian she realizes that when she dies her money had to remain back here in this physical realm where it belongs. So with intense joy she constantly visualizes relaxing and also leaving a legacy of doing well before God calls her into the spiritual world. "And I mean *really* relax, not returning to work any time soon, to prescription pads or a therapy couch! And when I say put my money to good use, I mean making sure some of the truly needy gets food and shelter . . . preferably into their own businesses," she smiled.

As snow pelted the windshield, Leon, from the back said, "We had no children, thank God! When my wife told me she didn't like children that should've given me a clue where her heart was. . . So, during our marriage, I always played with someone else's kids, her nieces and nephews and at work."

"Is that why you became a teacher?"

"That probably had a lot to do with my remaining a teacher. I was one when I met her. Though, I never figured out what made me hang in there with the puny teacher salary until she had abandoned me—my love for children!" But, man she was so dog-gone beautiful I thought I was just blessed to have her look my way at all, ever having children or not, I was one happy camper just to have her!" he shook his head with sheer regret over losing her.

Silence in the limo as Step drove cautiously on the snowy highway as traffic had slightly thinned. Suddenly, along the way they discovered an accident that had caused the earlier traffic jam. "Some nut didn't have snow tires. . ." Step huffed, "Must be from Georgia." They laughed, knowing about the fender-benders and everything on lock-down for a mere inch of snow. Dassah thought about what Leon had just said about how much he had loved his wife. She found herself feeling a bit of envy towards his wife. No doubt his wife had a very good man and good-looking to boot. But she had simply allowed him to slip right through her grip. In Dassah' opinion, Leon would be a good father and a superb husband. In her line of mental therapy she had seen so many people come to realize what a gold mine they had abused. But they had not missed the water until the well ran dry. Afterward, they had tried to rekindle the burnt out relationship, but there were just not enough fuel left to jump-start it. The abused partner had simply moved on to sweeter waters. At that it is said, "Watch out what you discard because someone will salvage it and find underneath a priceless jewel. Dassah recalled a true story where a young girl had been dating this boy ever since tenth-grade. They graduated together and were very much in love and attached at the hip. They dated way up into their early twenties. Then she claimed she found God and wanted him to come along with her but was not ready. So she married a man in her church. Well, several years later with two children, she had not forgotten her first love. He had also married someone else. Needless to say, she left her husband and ran off in search of the love of her life. She found him and proceeded to try and break up his marriage. But

CHAPTER 17

Meanwhile back at Neal, New York Police Department, it was 2:57. Doctor Blake Clancy, after coming there with Doctor Hadassah Desoto, was now in the men's room frantically scrubbing his smutty face. The fifty-something, White man as a homeless man had been living with amnesia for almost four months. In front of the mirror with a wet paper towel he began to dab painfully, trying to clean dried blood from his ear. As Pops just a few hours earlier, he had accidentally received a blow to the ear—his memory was now restored. Abruptly, his months of homelessness were a nightmare of the past. With much pent up relief and fright his wife and daughter was on the way from Manhattan to get him.

As Blake tried desperately to tidy up, a man walked into the men's room and began using the urinal, all the time sneakily keeping an eye on the shabby Blake. It was not unusual to see a homeless person using those toilets, if they had not been intercepted by the cops before getting in. That was one reason for many street people smelling of urine. Not many businesses would dare allow them into their clean toilets. And just like everybody else, whatever goes into the gut, assuredly must come out! In too many instances if no one let them in, then in came out either in bushes, against walls, in stairways or in their pants.

There in the restroom the ex-homeless doctor, in pain, growled, "What, haven't you ever seen a man wash up before!?"

Hurriedly, the distinguished man speeded up the leak and almost ran out, glancing curiously over his shoulder. There before the spit-shine mirror, Blake stared long at his image. If he did not know it was himself, he would never recognize the face frowning back. Some of the newly grown in grey hair shone under the light. Once milky skin was now splashed with ruddy haggardness. He cringed at the blimps under his eyes. The same grayish three-piece suit the night he lost his memory was grossly stained. Only the outdated overcoat given by the mission was somewhat presentable. Blake stood in the spotless restroom thinking he must have lost his memory somewhere around his job, the hospital in Manhattan about 20 miles away. He recalled that aside from work he only went out with his family. He racked his brain trying intensely to recall something—anything else. Finally, he willed images to appear in the mirror as to how he'd lost his way. Suddenly he recalled leaving a tedious meeting one evening three months earlier. Just before the meeting he had performed a lengthy brain surgery while his own head throbbed miserably. Afterwards he had changed into a suit, the one he still had on, he had walked through the well-lit parking lot, hoping today's surgery would still be the success it had been during surgery that morning. He would know for sure the following morning during routine hospital rounds. Finally in the lot he got into the Mercedes in his private space, and pulled off. Then, suddenly, after a short drive down the street the headache intensified. It felt like a temple bell ringing in his ears. It sounded louder in the right ear more than the left.

There in front of the mirror, Blake recalled that before that night he had begun to experience milder headaches. He would take a Tylenol and within a few minutes it would be good to go. "It's only fatigue," the intricate brain surgeon would find excuse. Finally the CAT scan (Computerized Axial Tomography) that his doctor forced him to get had revealed no abnormalities at that time. "I told you I just needed to take it easy," Blake had smiled about the results.

Then he recalled that night when the ringing headache had ceased, and he stared out into the night, not having an inkling of an ideal where he was—neither were the surroundings remotely familiar. Behind the wheel he somehow had a feeling he had traveled that road before. But he could not figure out why he was there, who he was and where he was headed. He recalled getting out of the car and standing on the street beside the car for some time. He had stood tying to recall the slightest thing. He had left his brief-case locked in his office because he had to be back at work at 5 am the following morning. There beside his car he groped panicky for his wallet, frowning, searching—he just could not remember. Then he had glared at the ID that told him he was Doctor Blake Clancy and where he lived, but not even that was a clue. He had money and credit cards in the wallet. Then, he hopefully searched his pockets and found a cell phone. He recalled pulling it haphazardly out. The small phone fumbled out of his sweaty grasp. Then he gaped at the broken pieces of his only hope. The battery had popped out and it seemed the dark night simply gobbled it up. The slight portly doctor, who'd had little time to exercise, was there on his knees. He had felt all around for the pieces and finally gave up in a frantic huff. And climbing frustrated back into the car he drove for hours. In which direction, he could not recall. Ten o'clock at night in New York and he never saw a police. However, in that part of Manhattan the presence of the police was unusual and totally unnecessary. He got out of the car hoping to have more luck on foot. After asking several fast walking strangers to make a call to the police, or tell him where the nearest station was, they only glanced at him oddly, shrugged and kept on moving. After several blocks he eventually also lost his car. Now a ways from the urban area, riding one bus after another, he wound up running out of change, but had several five dollar bills, a couple of 10s and 20s. Suddenly the group of homeless people he ran upon was the friendliest of all his snooty encounters. Subsequently, when Blake began living on the streets of Neal, he knew he had a past with which to reckon. As a street person the amnesia victim often wondered if he had been happy or not so happy with his past. "Maybe I'm better off out here!" he often thought. "Maybe I wanted it this way and willed it!" Finally as far as he was concerned, he was one of the homeless. Then sleeping one night he get robbed of his wallet and the money he had. He often wondered if the robbers tried using his credit cards—he could not use them because his pin number had vanished along with his mind. And there on the streets his real name also slipped out of mind. The headaches began more impromptu, sometimes during a conversation, and more frequently. In no time the older, unusual homeless man became known as 'Pops' because he would spend his last dollar to pop off-brand aspirin—Tylenol had not fit his budget.

Now that Blake had his memory back through a freak accident he was proud of his past. "I probably should've done this sooner!" he thought. He recalled being a notable surgeon and the numerous brain surgeries he had performed in his twenty-year career. He was fifty-nine years old soon to be sixty in March. Now Doctor Blake Clancy, in the men's room at the police station, being suddenly ashamed of his appearance, hung his head and went back to the sparse waiting room that Saturday afternoon. After a while, as he had watched the door for almost an hour and a half hastily in rushed two familiar faces. His wife and daughter, brushing off snow were anxiously scanning the waiting room. He stood slowly up, caught his wife's eyes from across the room, looked down at himself, and a tear flickered in his dingy, tired eyes. The two well-dressed females stood momentarily stunned, unable to believe it had finally come true. Then his wife took wings into his outstretched arms almost bowling over a few people. His daughter screamed, "Daddy!" to her idol just like when she was little and he had just come in from a tedious day. She trailed her mother into his arms and he made room for both. The tattered doctor ignored people ogling at the unfolding of Beauties and the Beast there in Neal Police Department.

As Blake and his lovely ladies headed toward the door, the young desk police, yelled, "Please, wait!" She rushed around to the curious trio. "Doctor Desoto asked me to give you this," she handed the card to Blake's wife who frowned, reluctantly and disdainfully pinching it between her index finger and thumb. The desk police added, "She said to call her about the reward. . . May I take your name out of my system as missing, Sir?"

"Yeah, I guess that would be in order, Officer."

"First I'll need a family member to fill out some papers that you're no longer missing."

After they had finished the papers and fingerprinted Blake, he said to his baffled wife. "I'll tell you all about it honey!" He hurriedly ushered his family out and into the refreshing snow. He had assuredly grown used to being out in the winter weather of New York.

Meanwhile, back in the limo on the way to her hotel, Dassah was in the passenger seat. "Well, Leon we'd love to have you come aboard!' she smiled turning partially to only one of the two homeless men in the back. "I feel you have that special tenacity of standing back on your feet in no time!" she smiled. "And when you finish, the sky will be the limit. . . With your priceless experience in sports you can have your very own sporting-goods store, and contract as a sports counselor to boot!" she bubbled over.

"You can help me do that!" he strained against the seatbelt to see if sincerity was in her light brown eyes.

From the driver seat, shaking the image of the dead Latino boy out of his mind, a firm voice said, "If you make it through and do as you're asked; you can do that and much more!" Step broke for the car ahead.

"Now that's what I'm talkin' about!" Leon lit up with a dingy smile, briskly rubbing his dirty hands together. "Where do I sign?"

Step smiled through the rear-view mirror and then at the car ahead as the wipers swiped away snow. Again Step was grateful to God for snow tires as he broke hard for another car that suddenly swung in front of him. As he patiently held his peace from swearing at the driver, he glanced at the clock. It was 1:55. "About another thirty minutes to the hotel," he said, peering out at the thickening snow. . . The way things look we might be spending the night at the hotel and flying to the farm tomorrow! What do you think boss?" She preferred not to stay overnight in the hotel, even though he would be there with her. She liked sleeping in her own bed, not that the entire hotel was not hers. Candy Man was all snores in the far back seat, very slender, youthful body straining against the seatbelt.

"Maybe we will stay in town," she peered out through snow flurries. Then she said to the now very anxious Leon prodding her to sign him up, "Whoa! We need to talk salary!" It was she who did the scrutinizing halting him this time. She was very careful about the men understanding their salaries in particular. "Now for the first three and a half months you get no pay at all. . ." she went on. "You'll reside on the farm with three-hundred-fifteen other men waiting to either work full-time on the farm or to be placed in a store to work. If you prefer to work the stores, you'll live in my special boarding house in Manhattan. I have a temporary home for ex-homeless men who work the stores and one for ex-homeless females. You could be placed on the farm to work the cotton field."

Upon hearing of that, Leon sat straight up again, "Wait just a minute!" he quickly hollered. "Are you talking' cotton as in the kind our ancestors use to pick!?"

"Well yes, but not using quite the same method they picked cotton back then," she snickered as most of the African American men had the same astonishing question about cotton-picking here in the 21st century.

Step laughed heartily, but Leon remained wide-eyed, truly serious. "What's so funny!?" he cocked his head.

"Calm down Leon!" Dassah threw her hand in the air, "We have machinery that does all the picking, fertilizing, embedding, weeding and harvesting of cotton. . . All you do is man the machines and know what you're doing.

"I don't know the first thing about machinery. . . I teach . . . I meant taught basketball, remember?"

"You'll have a couple of weeks of in-service training on how to use them first. . . Don't worry, everyone had to learn. . . That is, if you wish to continue to work on the farm during the remainder of your rehab. You do have a choice to work in other phases of farming. . . I also own stores away from the farm, so the choices of placement are pretty vast, Okay?" She really needed him.

With a big exhale, "Oh, okay," he lay back.

Dassah knew that once Leon would, as all the men had, love running the two huge mechanical cotton picking machines. So she proceeded to explain the makeover program. "There will be ninety days of total body refreshing with nutrition, sufficient sleep, exercise and mental therapy," she said. "After you've satisfactory passed that segment, you'll begin working the farm . . . and I repeat, without pay for fourteen more days. . . At all times the farm is running even outside of harvest. . . Besides fruits and vegetables, there's raising and slaughtering meat for my restaurants and in a few select private grocery stores and restaurants. If after about three and half months, you've earned full-time work on the farm, you'll begin to receive a salary, which will be below minimum wage. . . However, most men prefer working in the mall or restaurants away from the farm. . . Those are a bit easier work!"

"Isn't it illegal to pay below minimum wage?" Leon raised an unkempt brow. "And I ain't afraid of hard work!"

"It's not illegal when room and board is free. . . The only out-of-pocket expense you'll have is toiletries. Some prefer their own brand of those personal items, and I'm glad to hear you do not shy away from hard work!? So many has. . . Do you understand?"

"I see." his dirty locks dangled around a light brown face in the seat behind her.

"You will never be forced to pay rent or buy food for the two years you're in the program. . . However, the only place you will be allowed to reside *is* on the farm or the boarding house."

As Step drove along on the snowy highway, Leon slid to the seat behind Step so that Dassah could easily see him from the passenger seat. Suddenly Leon leaned hard towards her, and in an un-restrained tone, "Are there any women on this farm?" he whispered. "I haven't had a serious date in a long time, Doc," his breath punched her hard like Laila Ali.

"And why haven't you any ladies knocking down your door?" Step smirked mischievously, trying to get the dead Latino boy off his mind. But also being once homeless he really knew the answer to Leon's demise. Bur Step never missed an opportunity to poke fun at people he liked. "If Step doesn't rib you," a friend had once teased. ". . . then chances are he doesn't like you very much!"

Leon also in good humor acted the proper gentleman, "And, pray tell, whom do you recommend I wine and dine in my tenthouse . . . I meant penthouse?" he bowed his bare tattered head.

They laughed, including Candy Man this time. He had now sat up.

Being a doctor of the mind Dassah noticed that every time something was mentioned in regards to a female, the young Candy Man reacted with sudden interest. . . "He's like any adolescent whose hormones are crushing the sense out of his brain," she thought, yet trying to analyze the young man. "Maybe he's a severe sex offender." She hated to even think of that as that would cause her to painfully recall her own brutal rape. Plus she would surly have to reject him from joining the program.

Then she turned to Leon, "Unfortunately, there are no women on the farm now . . . And for the first three months during your purging that means to abstain from women also. . . Then, afterwards as you work the farm or another job you'll be given one day per week to date. Those eight-hours will be for as long as you live on the farm. Additionally, you will never know the way to the farm, or its location," she seriously eyed him. . . The busses that will get you to town have black-out windows which the police are all familiar with on the road," she paused.

"Not knowing where you are at all times sort of plays with your mind, ya know?" Leon sighed, having second thoughts. Then he pondered long on whether he could take that kind of seclusion.

Suddenly came loud snoring again from the back. The dirty young, homeless, obviously mentally disturbed man began to stir restlessly, thrashing his head from side to side, he began to mumble something. Dassah and Leon peered back at his erratic movements. Step was curious about Candy Man's behavior, as he was the driver and controlling the car on the ice was crucial. The instinct to protect Dassah weighed heavy on his mind as his dark eyes darted to the mirror at the fretting man, and then back on the highway. The normally fearless bodyguard knew that if the slick was provoked, in spite of the snow tires it could be fatal. "Don't you dare try anything crazy back there!" he thought, panic closing in.

As Candy Man continued to stir frantically and aggravated, Step quickly said, "Should I pull over boss?"

Just the opposite of what her bodyguard was feeling, she quickly put up her hand, "No," she calmly hushed Step. As a true psychiatrist she was anxious to hear what the young man insanely muttered. Ears erect like a Cocker Spaniard, she fine-tuned the radar.

Then Leon whispered, "He does that a lot, but not as bad as this one!"

As the others became still Dassah heard him say, "No! No!" He screamed, tight fists vehemently beating the seat at his sides. "I told. . . . I told you it wasn't me who . . . who beat you . . . killed you . . . cut you, shot you. . ." Then Candy Man sat straight up, face white as the snow on the windshield, sweating, wide-eyed, and bucking dingy blue eyes all around. "Where am I!?" he stared strangely at everyone, staring at him strangely. Then, "Oh!" he finally said.

"Do you know who we are, Candy Man?" Dassah soothed.

"Yeah, that's Leon," he pointed naming only Leon.

Dassah noticed he was calmer but the doctor in her throbbed of curiosity transforming her into the capable shrink. "Candy Man, I demand that you come clean right now! What's your problem other than being homeless?" she glared firmly at him as she moved to the back and sat beside him, buckling her seatbelt.

Step quickly objected, "Do you think you should be back there boss?" eyes in the rear-view mirror.

"I promise I'll be fine." She knew she had two strong men this time at her disposal.

Step cruising the snowy road, marveled how psychiatrists too often took their lives into their own hands. "Why didn't I pursue a more civil profession than taking care of a psyche?" he thought, and then in the same thought, "What am I thinking . . . Which is the lesser of two evils, a bodyguard for any other person, or one for a shrink? I chose a career with her!" So he resolved to keep one eye on the road and the other on his boss, if that were even possible, both eyes in different directions at the same time.

By this time Candy Man was trembling like a child about to get a shot as he shied from the doctor beside him. "What's wrong Candy Man?" she pried gently touching his tattered knee. She also, almost cringed from his breath, mingled with today's digesting food.

He jumped nearly out of his skin at the mere touch of her hand on his knee. "I-I-I just can't talk about it now," he whispered. "I throw up every time I think about it!"

"Would you like something to calm you down? Then do you think you can talk?"

"M-M-Maybe I might"

At that the doctor diagnosed one of his illnesses as, Abreaction. His emotional outburst was due to an event too painful to bear remembering. She knew that even he had been surprised by his own out-cry, in that he had suppressed it for so long. Subconsciously he had his past licked by waking up in the middle of the night and pacing. Whenever he slept too deeply, the dreams came. Sitting there staring over at the young homeless man she gathered that his earlier attack on her was to relieve some of the caged frustrations. Suddenly another problem arose. She knew it was illegal to administer a tranquilizer without an examination. So she planned to take Candy Man along to the farm for a mental evaluation. Then she unbuckled the seatbelt and stood up. "Guys, may I take some blood from your arm?" she eyed Leon.

"Oh heck no," Leon held up a long finger-nailed hand. "I just knew there was a catch to all this niceness! Now you want to go all vampire on a brother!"

"No, no!" She sat beside the rebelling Leon. "This is really normal procedure, but I need to do it now as oppose to later for Candy Man's sake, okay? He needs medicine and I can't legally give it to him without a simple blood test."

"Go on get it from him. . . I'll wait," he flatly suggested.

"I just figured we'd go on and get yours too, and get it over with. . . It's got to be done sooner or later!"

"Naw! I have to be psyched up for a needle, Doc. I haven't have a shot in years, ya' know!"

"Well, okay." She only agreed because of the hopeful plans for Leon in the program. She went back to Candy Man, "You'll have to have blood work before I can administer something to calm you down." Then she moved on to the little refrigerator, bending slightly to avoid the roof. "You do want something?"

She was pleased that Candy Man began immediately to roll up his raggedy sleeve. Leon sat rigid, watching as Dassah took two tubes of blood from the fearless, white arm of his homeless peer. She was relieved to see no signs of him having shot any drugs into his veins. Finishing, she placed the red top tube in the refrigerator to take to the lab for a bio-chemistry, HIV, and Venereal Disease tests. The lavender top tube she took to the back and ran an H&H to test for low iron to be sure he was not anemic. And a microscopic differential test would check his red and white blood cell count for any infections.

As Step drove cautiously along the snowy highway in the limo Dassah went to the counter where the microscope was and uncovered it. In about 20 minutes she had the results of Candy Man's hematology profile. Looking at the results, "Just as I thought you're borderline anemic," she said, "However, your white cell count looks normal. . . I can go on and issue a mild sedative." She went to the back again and returned with a paper cup of water and two small blue pills. "Here, take these," she handed them to the curious, tattered, homeless man.

"W-what are these?" his dingy, youthful eyes glared up at her but avoided direct eye contact with her.

"Those are Valium and will temporarily make you feel as if you haven't a care in the world. You're too tense and need to relax! Valium is the mildest sedative I can give you until I know your chemistry results." She would administer Stela zine, but was unsure whether he was schizophrenic or not.

Then Leon said, "He could really use something to loosen him up a bit, Doc. I'd love to see him happy for once. He's been like that ever since I've known him!" Leon seemed very fond of his young homeless peer.

The nervous young man finally downed the 2 small tablets and slid back in his seat.

From the rear-view mirror Step tried as much as possible to keep an eye on Dassah, all the while braking for cars on the icy road. Then after holding his breath, a big sigh escaped when she finally was again seated beside him. "Good to have you home Boss."

"Now, all we have to do is wait to see if he responds to the sedative." She glanced around at Candy Man, "I know you don't want to, but please buckle that seatbelt!" she said. He had expressed how restricted he felt with it on.

"Are you still up with going on, Leon?" Step asked. "If not, then take it from me, you'll be sorry! And how would you be able to help other homeless people?"

With a hint of envy in his dingy, nomadic eyes, Leon zoomed in on Step's expensive true-fleece sweater and then at the fine jacket draped over the seat. Then his eyes moved to Step's grand haircut, which himself, for years had worn a cropped cut. He also envied that Step sat proudly behind the wheel of the most coveted car in the world. Finally, Leon said, "Yeah, man, I'm game."

"Okay!" she said. "Now that you're willing to join, you must trust me on this one tiny matter."

"What now, Doc?"

"You guys must ride the rest of the way in blindfolds." She would only allow them to know directions to any of her places of business until they had signed up.

He hesitated with a sigh. Then finally, "Okay!"

She handed him a durable blindfold mask. He put it on. Dassah and Step exchanged secret smiles over Leon Davis' decision to be a part of the program. Dassah felt no need to blindfold Candy Man just yet. He was snoring, and she was glad, much softer now. "Listen!" she said. "Yes!" silently clapping. "No more teeth-grinding."

Masked in the near back seat, Leon began to stir uncomfortably. "Well," he said. "Let's back up a bit . . . like I said earlier, I spent time in jail for something I didn't do, right?" Again he stirred nervously.

Dassah and Step were also on pins at his sudden uneasiness. "What is it?" she glanced over her shoulder.

Meanwhile, on the same road far behind the limo on the way to their home in upper Manhattan, Blake Clancy, his wife and their daughter were deeply catching up on lost time. "I just can't wait to get one of your home cooked meals!" Blake put his hand on his wife's knee as they sat in the back staring at the back of the most beautiful chauffeur they ever had. He then tried to pull his wife closer.

"Oh, no you don't Doctor Blake Clancy!" pinching her sharp nostrils together she scooted as far to her side as the seatbelt would allow. "Have you had a deep sniff of yourself lately?" They all laughed.

"Mother, its sure good to hear your lovely laughter again!" her youthful, green eyes glanced in the rear-view mirror.

"I'm afraid you ladies have about . . ." he peered down at the diamond watch on his wife. "An hour and some to smell this Blake's special aroma!" he said. "Do you think I ought to patent it!?" he laughed, grabbing his paining ear. It was 2:00 leaving the little town of Neal, New York

"Don't you even think about bottling, that fragrance! We'd all be homeless the same day it hit the market," his wife laughed fanning her nose.

"We can always stop at a hotel, Daddy," she broke for the car on the icy road.

"Are we also buying new clothing, or should I just slip back on Blake's special aroma?" They laughed.

"What's another measly hour or so!" his wife shrugged. "You know, Darling, I did marry you for smelling better or worse, so I can certainly endure your worse aroma," but all the while waving her nose. "Nonetheless, you stay over there!" she roared of laughter. Then suddenly turning serious, "Anyway, who is this Doctor Dassah Desoto?" she pulled out the card and jutted it at him. "Why does she want to talk to me about the reward? Did she, by any chance, find you?"

"Oh, that," he sighed and slid his weary body down in the seat, head on the head rest. He began to massage his throbbing temples again.

"How is it that she wants to talk about the reward, Blake?" she insisted. "So, did she find you or what?"

"No she didn't . . . I mean . . ." Blake whispered groggily and then was snoring extra loud.

Mrs. Clancy stared curiously at the card, and then at her tattered husband crouched back. She noticed the dried blood in his ear, and then concern wrinkled her already aging forehead. She stared empathetically at her husband not looking much like the notable brain surgeon he really was. He was covered with months of facial hair, and a breath that reached all the way up to his daughter. His wife cringed, fearing what might have happened to him if left on the streets any longer than three months. It finally dawned on her he was no longer the young man she had married. She became painfully petrified at the thought of ever letting him out of her sight again. However, she knew it would be virtually impossible to get him to retire after this. She wished there was some way to convince the hospital not to take him back as head of surgeons. The hospital had given him another chance after his first episode of amnesia a couple of years earlier. Only he was not far from home when that episode had hit. Having been discovered in a nearby park by a neighbor, he had been escorted home the very next day. That warm day Blake had been found curled up in the recreation hall where he had spent the night. He was always so well dressed and couth that no one had pestered him that time. When he was fully recovered from that episode, he gave a vivid description of what amnesia was like. He described it as total confusion of mind. "Having amnesia is almost like you know you're you, but what to say or do evades your memory . . . and then someone ask you something you can't answer . . . or you proceed to go somewhere you don't know," he had shuttered to his family that time.

CHAPTER 18

Meanwhile on the other end on the snowy highway of New York, in Doctor Dassah Desoto's limousine she was in the passenger seat, Stephanas Carter, the driver, Leon Davis in the seat directly behind Step, Candy Man in the far back seat snoring, Valium at work. They were in route to get the men cleaned up or maybe fly to the makeover farm down in Georgia. Leon she hoped to have a new future in life. In her plans, Candy Man's future was dim for the present.

The beautiful psychiatrist had blindfolded Leon to assure he never found his way to any of her places of business until he had become a full member—but never to find his way to the farm even then. Only her staff knew the directions to that undisclosed farm. Leon behind Dassah and Step, "I think I should let you in on a little scarlet secret," he said, and then grabbed the collar of his tattered shirt and began angrily to unbutton it. And turning his head sideways, "This!" he said. "I figured you'd see this sooner or later . . . better sooner, I suppose."

Dassah gasped at the gruesome scar around his throat that reached almost from ear to ear. The doctor knew that African Americans were extremely prone to permanent scarring if not properly stitched in time.

She gawked as the un-kempt locks repeatedly reclaimed their rightful place. He managed to keep the scar exposed to his audience of two. Step tried to see while driving in traffic that had drastically slowed down.

"How in the world did that happen and where were you when you got arrested?" she asked. Also the calmer young Candy Man was now craning his neck to see from the back seat.

As Leon, blindfold, pulled back his locks, he began to explain, "I got this in prison," he said, letting go of his hair and buttoning his shirt back. "Five gang members took pride in braking in newcomers— beating them up and forcing them to do drugs just to get them hooked . . . so the first week I was the chosen one." Leon slid his tattered coat on to hide the scar as usual,

Dassah, from the passenger seat, "And why did they hope to get you hooked on drugs!?" she truly was not that naive to prison life but wanted to hear the whole story.

"You know more drugs are sold in prison than on the streets!— turn one into a junkie and he'll lie to his family to keep money on his book just as if he was on the streets buying. . . I had told those suckers many times that I never touched the stuff!" he huffed. "But what those punks got from me was the farthest thing from their puny minds. I was prepared to die rather than take what they had done to other freshmen!" a smirk of satisfaction about having stood up to them, he went on, "That day they'd decided to force cocaine into my veins. They had sneaked up on me in the workshop when it appeared no guards were around . . . but later I learned that some sick prison guards, the ones who really had smuggled in those drugs, got a thrill out of standing back watching any kind of sordid violence unfold. . . Then with a home-made knife to my neck they managed to twist my arms and me to my knees. . . Now that was the first mistake they made, having me kneel to them when the only I kneel to is God. . . I was already pissed over being on lock-down for something I had begged the judge to believe I didn't do!" As the blindfold homeless man unraveled the sad story Dassah could almost smell smoke from his flaming eyes. She was also impressed that he admitted to kneeling only to God. And pensively he went on, "As one man had his filthy hand clamped over my mouth and the knife to my throat, another one told me to just relax my arm and let them shoot me up to the moon . . . I knew that would only be the beginning of the few weeks it would take to get that free addiction. I had seen so many other men succumb to that demon!" With anger there in the limo, seated behind Dassah and Step, the homeless man continued, "It was when I heard them talk of doing other things to me too, that made me ballistic . . . Even with the knife around my throat I suddenly reached out and grabbed the one who already had the tip of the needle into my arm. Not even caring if my throat got cut, I grabbed the wrist of the one with the needle and slung him into a couple of the others. As I felt a little relaxing of the knife, I kicked furiously out at another one, landing point-blank under his chin. He fell backward into a working machine and screamed when a stamper came down on the tail of his shirt and pinned him under it. And from that point on, all I recall was one of them glaring into my face and then the blood in my mouth. Then there was hot stinging around my neck. . . I awakened in a hospital bed, throat throbbing like pepper sauce was in it, and bandaged from chest to skull. . . They said I had been semi-comatose for three days. The doctors never expected me to ever talk again. . . Thank God the home-made knife had not been sharp enough to even cut up a chicken let alone my Adam's Apple . . . I can thank my dad for giving me a thick neck just like his!"

"What else happened man?" Step peered in the mirror then back at the snowy road, wipers mid-speed.

"Well they told me I had bitten off one inmate's nose, the one that had been in my face, thus the one with the knife kept his promise to split my throat. . . I heard they now call him, Nosy-Rosy. Doctors tried to re-attach the tip of his nose but it had been trampled to severely in the scuffle. . . I could've told him that, not only did I have a neck of leather at that time, but Dad also gave me jaws like a crock," the once buffed man said. Then Leon comically bared his dirty teeth and growled like a mad dog, whether he tried to be funny, his audience was unsure. So, for the moment they simply gawked in uncertainty as he continued, "I wish I would've just gone on and chewed 'em all up like an alligator!" Behind the blindfold he hesitated while Dassah and Step busted their gut to go on and laugh out loud. But they were not sure if this was the appropriate time for humor. Then the homeless story-teller finally broke out with laughter at himself, reliving everyone, even Candy Man, to hoot with laughter. Still laughing, the doctor in Dassah said, "You know, the more you try to hold in the emotion to laugh, the more you'll burst to belch it out!"

Dassah stopped long enough to marvel at the young man in the back now seemingly back in this present world, "Candy Man, you need to put this on," she tossed the blindfold back. "Sorry about throwing it!" And, again to her amazement, he readily slipped it on. As a doctor of the mind she discovered that a mask acted as a tool of confidence for some of her clients who lacked self-expression in front of others. "Some just don't like to have people gawking at them!" she had said to a fellow doctor.

"Yeah, for sure, that kind should never quit their day job for Broadway!"

Then when the limo riders had gained some composure, Dassah asked, "What happened to . . . Nosy-Rosy?" she snickered, and then became serious. "Surely, after that the gang sought revenge . . . you might have been killed in prison."

"Well, apparently that had been the big idea!" he said. "But as soon as I was released from the hospital, I was transferred to a facility in another county. But word of the fight had beaten me to that prison, so I finally got the respect that I deserved in the first place," he sighed of relief that his fear was no longer a secret. "It feels so good to ventilate!" he said. "And to answer your question about where I got arrested. . . Well, I was rudely arrested one evening getting into my car with a full cart of groceries. . . One of the three officers immediately snapped cuffs on and informed me I was under arrest for an armed bank robbery where a guard got shot. . . They didn't say I was a suspect, but that I was *already guilty*," he huffed. "To mine and my wife's shock, later in a line-up a bank teller pointed me out as the one who walked out with a sack of un-recovered money. The irony is that the man on the surveillance camera looked a lot like me . . . only he was a very tan-skin, Caucasian. I even told the judge those were not my clothes and that I did not own any outdated clothing like he had on, but I was roughly accused of being a liar, and it was rationalized that I probably got the clothes for just that purpose! I even pleaded for them to give me a lie-detector test! Even my lawyer believed I was guilty and obviously my wife did too." From behind the blindfold he turned his head in Dassah' direction, "Will any of this matter, Doc? I'm not a brawler or a hard man!"

"Why would it matter?" a sigh of sympathy. "I still would like to see you back on your feet and already I know you're no cold-bloodied shooter. I'll simply get the court records and your release records." She assured. "I'll even go as far as to have my lawyer administer a trusty lie-detector test just to make the judicial system look as careless as they sometimes are. I'll make sure that their carelessness hits all the news media. They use lie-detector tests on these stupid reality shows as nothing but the truth but will they use them on all the innocent Black prisoners?!" Knowing she would take care of that issue she reclined with a smile and turned up the music. She looked out at the snow and then a glance over, "Are you okay Step?"

"Yeah, I'm as cool as a snowflake Boss."

Leon lay back also feeling a load lighter. The music, along with Candy Man's calmer snoring, the Valium to be commended, sent Dassah into a sleepy drift. But she never slept with any homeless man aboard even with Step having her back. As a doctor and employee she felt adamant about closely monitoring each men's every reaction. Step had now come to a complete stop on the highway, and she said, "At this pace I'm now convinced we'll never make it to the farm as I hoped. . . Plus I need toothpicks just to hold my eyes open!" Suddenly in an attempt to keep alert she propped her tiny olive colored feet on the dashboard, her pedicure the perfection of a top model. Step discreetly glanced over, "My sincere compliments to your pedicurist!" he only thought. He was indeed a feet man. She also was aware that he liked pretty feet, so she did a little innocent flirting, wiggling her toes. "Maybe Paula has nice feet, too" sweetly, she referred to the pretty policewoman.

"I sure hope so, because if not, goodbye!" They laughed as guilt also prompted her to take her feet down. She knew it was not Christian to entice anyone to lust.

Dassah peered in the back to see if the men still had on blindfolds. They did. "If we decide to go on to the farm, we should arrive at the airport soon," she said.

"Good,' Leon said. "I have to really go!"

"There's a restroom in the back," she gestured.

"Naw! I'll just hold it. I can't go in a car, on a plane maybe, but not in a car where folk are in such close proximity. . . I might feel the urge to do number two, which I haven't done for days. You just might not be able to stay in this car after that!"

Suddenly, Step slammed the brakes. The limo went into a sideways slide and then suddenly stopped. Again he thanked God for the snow tires. The sudden hazardous stop was just short of the commotion ahead on the highway. "What is it now!?" he huffed, watching state patrols swiftly setting a road-block. As he also rubber-necked, "Great!" he gripped. "This is just what we need . . . appears to be a three-car-pile-up" squinting ahead.

Leon and Candy Man began removing their blindfold but Dassah quickly forbade them. Candy Man had sat straight up. She said, "Just another bad accident, guys we're fine!"

"How much longer do we have to go?" Candy Man asked, scratching his dirty blond head.

Leon, locks hanging unkempt around a very light-skinned face sighed, perturbed.

"What's the word Boss?" Step glanced over as they sat there awaiting the next move. They were the first in line at the road-block with several cars behind. "Looks like it'll be a while before that mess is cleared up!" he sighed.

The frustrated doctor thought about that, pulling on her boots again "Let's just go clean up and go to my restaurant . . . the smaller one," she added that for her passenger's information. "That restaurant is closer and my hotel is only minutes away from here, on the perimeter of Manhattan."

"Okay," was the happy reply from Step as he cautiously backed up the long car and took a detour off the highway. And since she no longer feared her security was in jeopardy, she allowed the men to remove the blindfolds. Concerning blindfolds, Dassah recalled how, except for God, she never trusted anyone else a hundred percent. She picked up the phone, "I'll call the hotel," she announced. "Hey Trisha," And as usual natural authority sounded. "Step and I are about twenty minutes away and I have a couple of men who needs to clean up?"

Besides the smaller and two very large restaurants and the mall, she owned the hotel in Lower Manhattan. "Yes Ma'am," quickly replied Trisha, the hotel manager, an ex-homeless woman.

Leon let out a big sigh, and added to what Dassah had just said, "And to go to the little boy's room. I've got-ta piss like a race horse!" Everyone, except Candy Man this time, laughed. He had begun to fidget again and the panic glare in his blue eyes warned Dassah the Valium had almost waned. Over her shoulder, "Candy Man, there's truly nothing to worry about. . . Haven't you guessed by now you're among friends?" However, the doctor of the mind knew it was not that he was afraid of her, but rather it was that skeleton lurking in his closet just waiting to boo him into a crazed fit.

From the back, the tattered young man simply reluctantly nodded his head, rubbing his thigh in helpless anxiety.

After about 25 minutes the burnished black limousine pulled slowly under the awning of an immaculate, 6-story, polished-stone hotel. A neon sign flashed a big smiling pillow that simply read, Happy Haven Hotel. This was not a franchise but she'd had it built. Step glanced at the clock. It was 3:25 pm that light snow flurried Saturday, in New York. As he parked, "Well, here we are my fellow passengers!" he exhaled, mentally exhausted. The bodyguard had all the way, relived having killed a Latino boy protecting his boss earlier. As a result, he had shamefully ridden in a patty wagon and then spent several hours in jail. He had never even been to jail when he was homeless. And to top it off he had just driven in sluggish, snowy traffic forever, "Now this mind just must relax!" the 25-year-old thought. Then realizing a bodyguard had to do whatever it took to keep his employer safe, he exhaled that he had done just that, glancing over at the pretty woman pulling on her coat. But, feeling worn out he yet dreaded the date last night that had lasted until early morning, "My boss also pays well enough for me not to be complaining," he thought. Then he recalled being a homeless, 19-year-old almost bank robber, "Had it not been for Dassah I would be in prison or shot dead by the bank guard possibly" he sighed under his breath. Dassah had rescued him in the nick of time which had botched up his plans to rob the bank. The handsome, buffed bodyguard glanced over at her with the deepest respect. "I can always catch up on some shut-eye tonight!" he thought. "But a wonderful boss is irreplaceable!" he smiled.

"Let's go guys!" she finally announced to the homeless passengers in back. Leon moved quickly to the door and Candy Man, a bit more cautious, attempted to follow Leon. Dassah waved them back. Then she and Step got out first, as Step gentlemanly held the door for them. Teasingly, she bowed her beautiful head, "Curb service for our special guests!?" naturally full lips smiling, looking so very youthful.

Leon humored her and beamed, "Why thanks Madam!" He stepped out under the sturdy awning, tattered, stained overcoat on. Typical of a very warm-blooded, young person, Candy Man simply had his coat draped over his arm and was close on Leon's heels. But then a North wind prompted Candy Man to hurriedly slip the smelly coat on.

"Just follow us," she led the way. Soon they all stood in the plush reservation office. "Hello Trisha," Dassah and Step greeted the early-thirties, fair looking woman.

"Hello Doctor Dassah. . . Mr. Step," the uniformed woman came hastily to the counter with two card-keys.

"We have that many vacancies!?" Dassah startled. "We're usually full this time of day, and on a weekend!" Then looking at the woman, Dassah recalled how Trisha had not long since gone from tenthouse to penthouse. She had been an abused girlfriend and fled to the streets which she felt was the only way she could ditch her stalker of a boyfriend. Trisha, handing over the keys, "Two, besides your special suite is all that's vacant," precisely she pointed out. "Let's just hope no other seekers come in the meantime!"

"The men only need one room," Dassah said. "Step and I will share the suite just in case another guest arrives. If so you can offer them at least one room... We'll probably be staying overnight too. We can't drive to the airport on the expressway nor get home. Her mansion and Step's penthouse were also located in Upper Manhattan."

The tattered Leon and Candy Man were close behind, eyes lowered, already feeling misplaced in the plushness. Leon had trouble recalling the last time he felt like holding his head high. Then the doctor pulled the blushing men in front of her, "Oh Trisha, this is Leon, and this is Candy Man." It was for confidentiality that Dassah withheld last names before the men were officially in. Trisha, from behind the very shiny, sturdy counter, eyed Candy Man just as oddly as his name sounded. Yet Leon sneaked a once over at Trisha's well-formed figure. "Any nice clean woman looks good at this point!" he thought. "And she doesn't even have to be beautiful, just smell good and fresh!"

Step went back out and parked the limo. Afterwards, while following Dassah and Step down the movie-scene hall and up to their room, Leon recalled how he desperately yearned to be on his feet again. "If this one is another farce, I'd be one disappointed brother!" he thought. Sadly in the past 4 years of homelessness, he'd entered one program after another that only made idle promises. Even now at the lowest ebb he had ever been, he yet tried to avoid falling into any unlawful ploys. "No drug-peddling or prostitution for me, so I'll just keep my ears cocked and eyes wide open." He had not made up his mind or promised the doctor anything—the accident on the highway had served to bide him more time. He was glad for the delay in that spending more time with Dassah and Step would give more enlightenment to this offer of hers.

"Here you are gentlemen!" Step announced, running the card-key through room number 416. Dassah stepped inside the posh then

Leon, and then Candy Man. Leon totally sucked in a breath and held it. Besides the other finery, the huge room had a 60-inch plasma television mounted on the wall and a big built-in refrigerator. "A fridge usually means food!" Leon thought, stomach growling again. On his honeymoon in Florida, they'd had some luxury but nothing like this. The cushioned furniture lured the tattered men with their dirty coats now draped over their arms—Candy Man not seeming too excited, almost like he had been use to this. Leon's eyes moved the length of the exquisite draperies that matched the décor to a total tee. Finally exhaling, he had trouble taking it in all at once because his heart was racing faster than his eyes could roam. "Am I legitimately on my feet!" he thought, noticing the printed partition dividing the huge room and was especially taken aback by that. "How magnifico!" he could not hold back using that slang.

"Thanks!" from the middle of the room, the beautiful doctor said. She marveled that Candy Man did not seem impressed with the finery as most of the homeless men usually were. "Your compliment goes to the ex-homeless for making things so very tasteful. . . They're also in the program and works here. You'll clean up here for our dinner-date."

Leon frowned down at his clothes that reeked to the ceiling. Dassah curvy in blue-jean quickly stood at attention with a playful salute, "Say no more, Generals! March yourselves to that closet," she pointed like a drill-sergeant.

Leon grinning at her clowning around, and Candy Man on Leon's heels, moved to the double doors. He swung the doors open and sucked in another breath as he beheld all the appealing suits and casual outfits, even down to new neatly folded underwear. Finally, Candy Man's dingy, blue eyes did light up. Dassah smiled about that with a victory wink at Step. "So, he's a typical teenager into fashion!" she whispered to Step, him grinning big. As the men stood baffled as to what to choose, she assisted in making up their mind, "Only casual attire for now," she said. "Later in the program I'll treat you at my Fine Cru sine restaurant, and then you may really dress to kill but today it's slum-out!" she added, "I must testify that the Good Lord has smiled on every single one of my businesses!" she testified.

Then she and Step went to the door and back over her shoulder, "It's now two-forty-five, so we'll return around three-forty-five. . . You have an hour to primp and pretty-up."

"Can you make that four-thirty?" Leon respectfully asked. "My hair has to be washed. . . It'll take this bush forever to dry . . . Candy Man has undoubtedly has to wash his too."

"Four-thirty it is. . . We can't have anybody catching pneumonia?!" Though the doctor of the mind realized that if they had not caught their death sleeping in the snow, chances were they were safe to wash and go now. She knew it was the excessive exposure to the weather that caused street people to catch fewer colds than non-homeless people. "That's the nature of adaptation!" she had once said to a fellow doctor. "If, and when a homeless person contacted the flu that's usually the end of the line for 'em," she had sighed.

There in the exceptional splendor Leon and Candy Man took turns in the sunken-tub bathroom. And then wrapped in huge beach towels they went and picked casual outfits from the closet. As the carpet cupped his bare feet Leon wished to just melt into the finery. Finally, it took only fifteen minutes for his hair to dry with the super dryer, even straightening some parts of his locks. Candy Man's fine hair dried shiny clean in about five minutes. Having lived together on the streets Leon and Candy Man had no problem working in unison. And merely a yes or no to any of Leon's questions was Candy Man's usual manner.

Finally, after an hour and a half the two homeless men were decked and standing before the full length mirror. Leon in brown corduroys and a beige knit, pullover sweater. The brown turtle-neck underneath served well to hide the scar. The tan boots proved the streets had not taken away his style. Staring in the mirror, flashbacks of how he used to look transpired. Street life had rudely snatched away memories of how good-looking he really was. He smiled knowing later he could taper his locks, "I've been growing these for four full years," the thirty-six year-old said to Candy Man now at his side. Leon was outright stunned when Candy Man verbalized, "I've always wanted to touch Black hair. It looks so hard," staring curiously at Leon's head.

Leon had to search for words, "Well," he finally found some, "Just like Whites, some Black folk have course hair and some have softer hair . . . go ahead, feel it!"

Very slowly he moved his cleaner, white hand to one of Leon's locks. "It's soft like cotton."

"Okay that's enough, man. . . Let's finish getting ready."

Candy Man gawked at his image in starched, baggy jeans. The dark-blue sweater that hung over the jeans complimented his straight blond hair. His choice of clothes was age-appropriate. He took a rubber band and pulled his hair into a long ponytail. "How do I look, Le?" he offered more conversation, beaming like a little boy.

Again, Leon, shocked, gawked at his young homeless peer. Then he grinned, "Okay, who are you, and what did you do with Candy Man!?" Suddenly, with a start, Leon looked at the clock. It was 4:27. "They should be coming any minute," he nervously said, "Why am I so jittery anyway?" He moved from the mirror. "Let's just ball up these old clothes, they've seen their better days, or should I say better years?" They cramped the smelly clothes and all into a plastic trash bag.

CHAPTER 19

A t four-thirty pm sharp, the soft knock on the hotel door yet startled Leon Davis and Candy Man. The two homeless men had just transformed from tattered to new and hole-free clothing. They had on new clothing which Doctor Dassah Desoto, a psychiatrist, kept in the hotel room for her frequent homeless guests. She and Stephanas Carter her bodyguard had also gone to her personal suite and freshened up after a long day of one mishap after another during a scouting trip in search of homeless men. In the snowy city on the outskirts of Neal, New York, close to Lower Manhattan, they would all go to dinner at her smaller restaurant. If the doctor and her bodyguard would not have run into such tragedy that morning, she had planned to fly the men early, to the makeover farm to be evaluated and to take a tour. And if the men passed a mental, written, family and major criminal background check, they would be recruited. She had devised the written test based on their ability to simply convey their future goals legibly on paper. Though, the capable doctor had grim doubts about Candy Man having any goals, "But if he were to commit to go into a hospital he can always use the twenty-five thousand reward money for that," she had said to Step.

At the soft knock Leon asked who it was in spite of already knowing. With Candy Man at his back, Leon opened the door. It impressed him that Dassah had knocked rather than rudely entering unannounced— she had the key. At that he found himself feeling better about her and her purpose. "That Doc seems like a lady!" he gladly thought. Finally standing before Dassah and Step on the inside of the threshold was Leon grinning, "Well, come on in!" he flashed cleaner teeth after the vigorous brushing. He recalled on the streets like most of the homeless, neither did he own a toothbrush.

On the other side of the door Dassah wore a blue wool sweater and a long denim skirt. The denim fur-lined, wedge-heel boots richly set off the matching skirt. The caramel-color fur sports jacket and matching hat popped the outfit right out of a casual-styles magazine. Step now had on a manly green, fleece pullover and more pressed jeans. His camel, hooded jacket screamed expensive. From across the threshold Dassah teased, staring at who she saw as strangers, "We're here for two men named, Leon and Candy Man!" she laughed, stepping inside, "Wow, take a camera to you two!" Nevertheless, she knew they had a ways to go to be the made-over men she could finally check off, "But this'll do for now," she thought. "And it seems they've done the best they possibly could in only two hours, so calm down gal!" she thought.

The two men turned around beaming and modeling. Dassah discreetly sniffed the air, "They smell better, not good, but better." She noticed for the first time Candy Man actually was blushing. "I don't think I've met a homeless person yet who didn't feel better after a good cleaning up!" she thought, looking at Candy Man's youthful, shiny face, pimples, but clean. "And I won't stop until I've offered as many as possible another stab at life," she obstinately thought. "Now go on!" she gestured hastily. "Get your coats and let's hit the road again!"

They gawked oddly at her. "What coats?" Leon asked, "We already pitched 'em Doc!"

"Well, silly, it's obvious you guys haven't even looked in the coat closet!" she pointed. "Any way, you should always search closets and under beds whenever you go into a hotel!" as usual wisdom became the beautiful woman.

Leon swung open another closet and discovered several coats there. Proudly, he slipped on one and delighted in the durability, "They'd really try and snatch this one from a brother!" he thought of his peers on the streets. Candy Man slipped on a youthful, quilted fur-lined jacket and proudly pulled on the hood even in the warm room. Dassah felt honored having the men dress in something they liked, "No outdated clothing for my men!" she would firmly declare. Though, she sometimes used nearly new clothing given by the staff after only a few wearing.

Finally, after putting everything back in place, they were following her and Step out. Step locked the door. Silently, on the elevator with other guests, they rode down to the lobby. Leon and Candy Man now blended in—heads no longer hung down because of offensive stench. Once in the cushioned lobby again, Step moved to take the key-card to Trisha, the manager as bellboys rushed to take baggage in and out. But Leon jutted out his somewhat cleaner palm, "May I have the pleasure of returning that, Step?" he politely asked. The two African American men stood almost eye-to-eye, guests milling around. The twenty-five-year-old Step was only four inches taller than the thirty-six-year-old Leon's six feet. Once again Doctor Dassah Desoto noticed like in the alley, that the two now looked comparatively like princes rather than a prince and a pauper, "Leon really looks nice," she smiled. "I can barely wait to see him at his very best!"

Step looked at Dassah to get her approval for Leon to take the key. She nodded. Step said, "Here you go man," dangling it out to him. As Leon began the thirty-foot trek to the desk, Candy Man also moved to follow. "I'll be right back, man," Leon quickly halted him. Candy Man was calmer since the clean-up, and obediently stopped in his tracks. Leon arrived at the desk along with a couple of other guests. Quickly, his turn came. There before the professional young woman Leon leaned flirting over the desk, holding the key-card peculiar, between his fingers. Then looking into his dingy, smiling eyes, Trisha took it with a sultry smile, "Did you enjoy your stay, Sir?" she cordially asked.

And with immense approval, he ran his eyes the length of the two-piece uniform that loved her curvy figure, "I don't allow anyone to address me as Sir, unless I can have their digits," smoothness also had not evaded the homeless man.

Trisha smiled even wider, "I think you're cute and all, but I have a fiancée!" She wiggled the moderate size diamond in his face.

Leon snapped his finger, "I should have guessed an angel wouldn't be flying around free!" he sighed. "But what's your man got to do with it!?" he wagged his locks in fun. They both laughed, recalling that as the title of a famous oldie song. With a sigh of defeat he walked back to his awaiting group.

"Sorry!" she yelled after him, "But if I wasn't. . ."

Upon hearing that he grinned big because he was left with a ray of hope that he still had it going on with the ladies. "And I just may have a chance before she makes it final!" he thought. He knew that street living had posed many mental challenges to the self-esteem, especially for men. Women expected men to be the provider in the relationship—someone she could depend on and look up to—not a homeless bum as he now thought of himself.

As they headed toward the door, "You're doing a fine job Trisha!" Dassah said. "Keep up the good work!"

"I sure will Doctor Dassah," she replied. "And thanks for everything!"

Then Step led the way through the full, snowy parking lot, and back to the limo. The homeless men now strutted relishing in the warmth and clean coats, for a change, not able to feel the fierce whipping of the wind.

Inside the limo Dassah looked at the clock. It was 4:45 pm. She sucked in a deep breath. As fresh as the air had been first thing this morning put a big smile on her naturally full lips. "The fumigating system is showing its butt!" she whispered to Step.

"Good, he whispered from under the wheel, and then said, "Sorry about Trisha, Leon!" glancing back.

"That's okay, there're always another filly in the field!"

Candy Man snickered from his favorite seat in the back, again having heard something about girls. The doctor of the mind noticed Candy Man's sudden alertness, "How do you feel Candy," she peered back. "Would you like to come closer?"

"No . . . and I'm fine," he almost gave her eye contact instead of the usual aloofness.

Then the psychiatrist knew that, aside from having slight autistic tendencies, the young man showed mild signs of schizophrenic. "One of his dual personalities would simply retreat into hiding whenever the other became too aggressive," she took a mental note. Whether he was born that way was still debatable in her mind, "Some dreadful event could be the culprit!" she thought. "The mind, for sure, is a complicated mechanism."

CHAPTER 20

Meanwhile, back in Doctor Blake Clancy's car now in upper Manhattan, he, his wife, and his daughter driving, pulled into the long un-driven-snowy driveway, a stretch between the street and the gigantic house.

It was now January, and for the past three and a half months the middle aged doctor had been on the streets of Neal, New York known only as Pops. Now he was truly revealed as Blake Clancy a very notable brain surgeon. Before just this morning amnesia had robbed him of his past, casting him into a homeless furrow out of which he saw no light at the end. Providing a decent future for he and his family had been why he had worked so tirelessly through med school. Only, having the amnesia, he had not known what his past had been like. Now that Candy Man, one of his street comrades had, through a fit, accidentally hit him in the ear with a durable cell phone . Blake's memory was back and now he was required to pay Candy Man the reward of 25 thousand dollars, which Dassah suspects the new Blake may turn into a legal issue.

His daughter driving the Benz, they crept up to the house and she opened the garage with the remote. Inside the tool-shelved, 3-car garage next to the other two lavish cars, they climbed out. Blake stood appreciating that it all belonged to him—sadly he remembered everything about his tenthouse in the alley. Most amnesia victims recalled their lives of having the illness but nothing prior to. If he had not gotten that whack on the head he would still be with them on the way to being made over. And just as he had suddenly been flung into poverty, a few hours earlier he merged back into wealth. As far back as Blake could recall that waking up looking for a late night snack from an empty cupboard in med school, was the closest he had ever been to hunger. He had been brought up in a well to do family of which his father had been a famous cardiologist and now was an invalid.

Once inside his breathtaking showcase of a house his daughter flew upstairs. Blake paused and rubbed the throbbing lump over his ear, and then with a slight slump his wife had to assist him to the stairs. Deep down Blake knew his condition had worsened. Holding onto her husband, "I knew you were more ill than you let on Dear!!" she clung to him. "Maybe we should have stopped by the hospital . . . but you said you were okay. . . I should know you by now! " she scolded herself.

"I'm alright, just a little worn out," he lied again, hoping that was truly the case.

"We're going right up and run a bubble bath," she insisted. Then she yelled for her daughter to call the hospital, "Have them send David Dupree right over!" Blake did not argue as he normally would, "Us doctors make the worse patients!" he always teased. Then making his way up the spiral Victorian staircase, he took in the lavish sight as if he was an admiring visitor that frequented their home. "I certainly am a fortunate man," he was brought up not believing in 'blessings' but 'luck and chance' and his family still held firm to that. One would say they were Atheists. "Two beautiful women and a home like this," he breathed.

"It was your own blood, sweat and tears that got us everything we have Dear," she paused with him on the staircase, giving his tattered back a victory pat.

Once Blake and his wife were in the master bathroom, sluggishly he began to strip. The clothing he had worn on and off for over ninety days seemed glued on. He recalled only taking them off to shower every now and then and change into more at the mission, "Fetch me a big trash bag at once," he managed to order. "I never hope to lay eyes on these again!"

The wide, deep, sunken tub was finally full of bubbles, high and aromatic. He cooed like a dove as he sunk deep into the foam. His wife had put on a bathing suit and sat on a step in the tub behind him. Her still very attractive figure could easily be compared to her daughter's. As he lay back between her velvety thighs she gently massaged his shoulders and finally asked, "What about this Doctor Desoto Dear?"

"M-m-m, oh that," he melted, exhaling deeply at her familiar touch, "She wants us to pay the reward to the man responsible for getting my memory back. I don't know if we need to. . ." Then he was snoring extra loud. His wife was determined not to leave his side until the doctor would arrive. She knew something other than being tired and ex-amnesia was wrong with her husband as she gently rubbed shampoo into his matted hair. Then with a frown, she zoomed in close to the lump above his ear and the dried blood inside his ear. When she noticed that the lump was fiercely pulsating terror came cross her lovely keen face. She had been a doctor's wife long enough to know that was blood in a swollen vein under his flesh, "Just keep on breathing my darling!" she whispered in his ear as he still snored unusually loud.

"Mother, I called the hospital!" a yell came over the bathroom intercom. "How are you Daddy?" a youthful, voice fill of concern.

"He's going to be fine!" a shadow of doubt in her voice. She refused to think of what she would do if anything happened to her strong tower. She had just gotten him back and simply refused to lose him again, "Blake!" she shook him while rinsing suds from his hair with the shower-head. No response, only heavy snoring and deep gurgles. "Blake!" she shook—still, no response. Then she yelled for her daughter, "Dianna, call 911, right now!! Tell them to send the hospital helicopter!"

When the helicopter landed in the field of a yard in about ten minutes, Doctor David Dupree from the hospital arrived with it. Hysteria had now set in on Mrs. Clancy. Dianna remained a bit calmer to console her mother, even though her own insides were about to explode with fear. As paramedics were in the huge bathroom, Blake's nude body had to be exhaustively hauled from the tub by the strong paramedics. His wife had drained the tub and put a blanket over him. He was rushed to the hospital and placed ahead of the other patients where a battery of emergency tests was immediately performed. Those patients had gladly waved him ahead of them in that Blake probably would one day have to save their lives. His wife at his side, anxiously hoping a CAT scan and blood tests would assure he would at least live. Then to everyone's astonishment, Blake Clancy was now in a coma—for how long he would be that way, had the capable doctors mystified. And they were also his close colleagues.

There in his room the ventilation machine was loud and annoying, but she remained on the cot beside his bed.

Meanwhile, back in the limo, headed to her smaller restaurant, were Dassah, Step and the remaining two homeless men, Leon and Candy Man. Dassah glanced at the clock. It was 5:20 pm. After the fifteen-minute drive in the snow, Step sighed having completed the safe task of getting his boss to the restaurant, "This morning had not been as successful!" he sadly thought about the boy he had killed for attacking his boss. It always made him as a body feel good that he had done his job well but it did not make him feel grand to have killed a mere boy in the process.

"Well, here we are," Step said, pulling the long car under another awning, but this time in front of the restaurant. The snow-covered sign on the durable red canvas read, "Dassah' Tasty Eats." As a uniformed, overcoat man ran dutifully to the car, Step left the keys inside. Even though this was her smaller restaurant, Dassah still provided valet parking. "Hello, Doctor Dassah," the twenty-something-year-old Asian man grinned. "Would you also like it vacuumed?" he offered.

"Yes, Ton, that would be great! By the way, these men will possibly be coming into the program . . . the same way you did," she purposely seized every opportunity for Leon to see what good things were in store for him. And especially she needed men with a college education to tutor the GED students. Also some men were presently struggling through home-schooling there on the farm to earn high school diplomas.

Standing under the awning, coats on, Candy Man watched the limo being driven away. Then he displayed slight apprehension. As a psychiatrist Dassah eyed him, knowing that most emotionally unbalanced people dreadfully feared crowds, and an abrupt deviation from the norm. The limo had grown on him and his security blanket would soon be out of sight. From here on she would need to monitor him for sudden panic attacks. The doctor noted that, at first Candy Man's attitude was that he really wanted to come along. Now, as they walked towards the door he jumped on an uneasy roller coaster and literally crushed Leon's heels. So, immediately she stepped in and grabbed Candy Man's arm leisurely interlocking it with hers, hoping the closeness would calm him, "Come on Candy, we're going to have some good food! What mostly do you like to eat anyway?" humorously, dragging him along. And with no resistance from the young homeless man, a big sigh escaped her full, painted refreshed lips. Leon also sighed no longer having him nearly pull his boots right off by stepping on his heels.

Step authoritatively led the way in, and held the door. Since it was a Saturday evening in the inner-perimeter of Manhattan, quite a few guests followed them inside. Some of the middle-classed guests were casually dressed, and some dressed to head straight to the night club afterwards. Entering and seeing so many customers, Dassah whispered to Step, "Maybe even we should've called ahead . . . but I ain't complaining though! The mo' peoples the mo' money!" She teased in slang. "God has really blessed my finances!" she only thought the latter. She never boasted about her wealth before the less endowed, especially while they were in such a depressed frame of mind. But she believed that being saved and assisting others pleased God so that He had in turn blessed her with material things, "Godly peace along with earthly riches is the pinnacle of joy!" she thought. Then she recalled a scripture in John 15: 11. As she had read it she felt that Jesus was personally assuring her that as an obedient Christian her joy could be full.

Once inside the busy, wonderfully situated restaurant, "Hi, Doctor Dassah!" came from all directions, both male and female waiters rendering professional service. The aroma reached beckoning fingers underneath their noses, alluringly. On Dassah' arm, Candy Man was calmer, skillfully holding her like in escort fashion. It appeared he was no green horn at how to lead a female. She sneaked a peek at his red youthful nose sniffing the air. The doctor in her knew that he would become uneasy if she were to stare too long. So she only smiled warmly over at him, her just as tall as he, and then quickly looked away, "Still, I won't be satisfied until I've gotten inside that blond head," she thought. She recalled the fun she and her peers had had in med school picking each other's mind. Only she had put up an impenetrable barrier when they tried to delve into her past.

From the reception area, Step also led the way, following a Mexican male waiter to a table. He recalled how he had befriended that ex-homeless, ex-con man when he himself was in the program. Now at the lavishly set table, the smiling waiter pulled out a chair for Dassah. "Here you go, Doctor," perkily, in perfect English.

Thank you Mack."

As Mack helped with her jacket, she found convenient opportunity to impress Leon and Candy Man again, "This is the only one of the three restaurants without coat-check service."

Mack draped the jacket carefully over the back of her chair. She sat down. After she was seated the others followed suit and rested their coats in like manner. During introductions, Leon was even more impressed at the staff of ex-homeless people, especially the men working so fervently and picking up tips—big ones. The women, he bravely and openly gawked at from head to toe. His locks looking much neater, he glanced around at chatting guests waiting patiently to be served and some giving orders to the red, black and white, tasteful uniformed waiters and waitresses. Their pants and or skirts were all black over black polished shoes. He was also impressed that the table cloths, napkins and chair covers matched the uniforms. Then looking down at the gleaming, tile floors, "You can eat the crumbs you've dropped and not get staphylococcus!" he laughed, drawing laughter around the table.

Leon sat back, sipping lemon water like a pro. The soft music and mellow lighting cast him into a euphoric mood he had not experienced in a long time. He recalled the last time he had dined at a posh, but not as large restaurant was with his wife some years earlier, "Doc," he leaned over. "And this is the smaller restaurant!?"

"Yes it is!" she looked across at Leon and Candy Man, "And you'll fall in love with my mall that has a health club, a movie theater and anything else one might need in a mall. . . The only difference between mine and other malls is that I own ninety per cent of the stores . . . the rest is leased to vendors."

"May I take your order, Doctor?" a tall, tapered-waist, tight buns waiter inquired. Then the Afro-centric twisted short-hair man, engaged respectfully in small-talk with Dassah. Leon remarkably took in the scenario. He could not believe the doctor had rehabilitated all these people.

"We're ready now, Thomas," Dassah finally said to the man. They then, undecidedly, placed orders from the elegant menu. Thomas had sat a pitcher of water and a large bowl of salad on the table. After much deliberation from the table, Thomas was finally able to go place the orders. Candy Man, more relaxed, youthfully began to sway to the overhead golden-oldies.

Leon gaped after the well-mannered Thomas who walked away, "Was he also in the program . . . was he an ex-homeless man I mean?"

"Thomas is still in the program. . . Remember all of these men are yet being mainstreamed," Step cut in from across the table, shoveling salad onto his plate. "Only a few of these women were needy and low income at one time. . . Now they work for Doctor Dassah full time," he was pleased to report.

Then Dassah said, "Thomas has only about seven months to go before starting his own business . . . him and four other co-partners, that is." She took the salad bowl from Step who passed it around. "The five men will soon be the proud owners of a small printing company," she smiled.

"I did some printing in prison," Leon said, dipping salad onto his plate, "The jail system got too much free labor out of me . . . and me being innocent all the time," he sighed. "I also crafted and designed cabinets."

"But, now that's water under the bridge Leon," Dassah consoled. "Now you can begin life anew, maybe as a carpenter contractor since you can do cabinets and all!"

"But I can never get back three and a half wasted years, nor my wife back!" his voice escalated as if Dassah had been the convicting judge and jury. Odd gapes from surrounding tables made Dassah uneasy. At Leon's outburst Candy Man squeezed his eyes shut and began to rock. Dassah glanced over at Candy Man next to her. She would not have him retreat into a shell again. With a hearty 'hush' wave to Leon she hoped to alert him of the effect he had on Candy Man. As a psychiatrist she realized that both men had suffered a great deal in the past years. She knew that giving one issue precedence over the other would compromise her oath as a doctor, "But, thus far, I assume that Leon's problem doesn't go as deep as Candy Man's." she thought there at the table looking at the frowning Leon. Suddenly the doctor found herself in dire straits. Step there beside Leon, gobbling down salad, knew Dassah was out of harm's way, so he simply would keep his eyes peeled.

Finally Leon calmed down, his locks attacking his light-brown face, "But, you do feel me don't you, Doc?" an anguish whisper, "The way Blacks in America are treated and all? I was not even read my Miranda Rights before they arrested me, nor were any of the other Black men I talked to, read their rights!" He began haphazardly piling on salad dressing—way too much, "And if you don't demand an attorney, they just stash you away and lose the keys, sometimes even when some ask for a court appointed lawyer they never see one. . . I paid for one but was found guilty anyway . . . maybe my wife kicked me to the curb to be with my attorney. I noticed the way he was supposed to be talking to me but kept his eyes on my wife!" Leon painfully remembered, "The two of them was tighter than he and I should've been!"

"Is that right?" Dassah calmly said to keep the peace. She glanced over, "Candy Man, won't you try this wonderful dressing?" He opened his eyes and then slowly dribbled dressing. She let out a sigh.

There in her restaurant awaiting the main course and gorging on salad, Dassah looked across at Leon, "Oh yes," she muttered between bites, "I know what you're saying . . . I'm interracial and a woman, so I'm no stranger to racial, nor gender discrimination. Rejection of African Americans in a biased society is far from over. . . Women are yet fighting for job-equality and not to be sexually harassed in the work place."

Step said, "But life is what you make it, man . . . you either allow racism to better you by dealing positively with it, or let it reduce you to malignancy by hating back. . . and you do know what cancer can do!?"

Then Dassah said, pointing the fork, "And surely you don't intend to get eaten alive, having your mind consumed with the hopeless tumor of hatred. . . And you're justified in your feelings. . . But this temporal life is just too short and will soon be all over . . . get saved with the hope of eternal life in heaven . . . there's no kind of discrimination there," she soothed, "Plus the sweetest thing about the eternal place is, on the way up there, you'll meet the same people that wronged you, being sent to their home down in hell! And you can also have financial security right here on earth, you know!"

"That's easy for the two of you to say!" Leon became serious again but now with more self-control, "But what about the homeless who've been mistreated, and is so stressed out about being cast down, mainly Black homeless folk. . . And society passes us by, which dejectedly brainwashes us into thinking we're doomed to continual drudgery?" He tuned to Step, "Picture this, man," he almost pleaded. "A homeless person applies for employment, and the first thing the employer sees is dirt on top of black skin color. . ."

"Been there, done that!" Step's dark mouth breathed between bites of salad and sips of lemon water.

"Oh I forgot you were once in my stinking shoes," Comically he jutted out a leg, exposing a new not stinking boot. They laughed again.

Then Leon went on to ventilate, "And to add injury to insult, the news media assists in projecting how Blacks are the lowest-rated in this society. . . In the everyday media, whenever a positive situation is broadcasted, that positivism is usually focused on other races," he sighed, pausing with the fork of salad halfway to his mouth. Frustrated, he harshly dropped the food back on the plate, "And as the result of that negative media exposure, it seems the world is resigned to feeling that all Blacks are slime-balls, especially if they've been to prison before! And why is it that when Blacks commit minor offenses, we deserve longer incarcerations, but when another race commits the same type of crime, rehabilitation to get better jobs, is their punishment," Leon huffed. "And why are they building bigger prisons instead of more rehab institutions? And you know who those prisons are going to be full of, don't you?!"

"No doubt about that!" Step assured, crunching salad, "Like I said man, been there, done that! Only I've never spent any time in prison. . ." he recalled the Latino boy that he had just a few hours earlier, killed, "Not in prison yet!" he sighed, unsure how the court-pendulum might swing.

Dassah had stopped eating. Whenever one of her men had a deep issue with society, that usually sent her into a 'how can I fix it' mode, "And if I have anything to do with it, you won't spend any time in jail either!" she assured Step. Then her freshly made up eyes moved to Leon, "And Leon," she said. "I'm really glad you brought up the issue of how *some* news media reports!" She lowered her voice so as not to offend her paying guests. She noticed with surprise how attentively the cleaner, blond Candy Man seated at her side listened so she went on, "It seemed that some news channels doesn't afford the public the opportunity to view the inside truths about successful Blacks who've contributed just as much to America's technology and growth . . . I've always felt that if the news were to distance themselves from hanging around poverty stricken neighborhoods, Blacks would not be so scrutinized, because any exceptionally poor group are prone to be in and out of trouble. . . If they had jobs making a decent salary, it's unlikely they would have time to disrupt society," she pointed out. "We know that reporters' livelihood depend on how well they make the headlines . . . and society, by nature, loves a story that makes the ears tingle! Thus, in light of all that, the poor seems to be the only citizens not likely to sue for slander, which the rich would sue without blinking an eye and win!"

Finally Leon there at the lavish table had gotten an opportunity to take several bites, and then said, "That's a good point, Doc. . . In my opinion, Blacks should start suing for the filming of so many under-aged kids, unless they're seeking to help them! And it really bakes my cake when I hear in the media, other races claiming that a Black person committed the crime just to through the police off them. Later only to discover that Black person had absolutely no involvement with that crime," Leon huffed, "You know, there's only so much a race can bear! We have the right to sue for defamation of character too!" then glancing around at the paying guests, he continued more calmly, "And, were it not for the couple of Black television channels on cable, not even on regular television, Black achievements would hardly receive any attention at all . . . and poor people surely can't afford cable, thus getting no positive Black feed-back at all from regular television."

Then Dassah said, "It sort of makes me shiver to think Blacks are so severely cast out merely for being a color God made us, though she was part Puerto Rican." Suddenly she pulled a pen from her tiny bag and began writing on a paper napkin, "Leon, when you get settled, here's a scripture for daily mediation." She wrote Matthew 5: 44, "God commands us to love our enemies." she said, "In that passage Jesus stated, '*But I say unto you, Love your enemies, bless them that hate you and pray for them which despitefully use you, and persecute you.*'

Then, suddenly, to everyone's total amazement, from beside her, Candy Man softly interjected, "Additionally, in verse forty-five Jesus went on to say, ". . . *That you may be the children of your Father which is in heaven: for he makes the sun to rise on the evil and on the good and sends rain on the just and on the unjust*". Then he said, "I ... I used to think all Blacks were," he paused, cleaner white face and blond hair shining under the dim light.

Dassah slid surprised back in her chair. And as all had stopped eating, she glanced over at him, "I didn't know you knew the Bible. . . What were you about to say about Blacks?" For the world she would not miss the opportunity to find out what had flung him into a seemingly bottomless mental abyss and homeless degradation. "er pretty He certainly doesn't fit the profile of a regular street person," she thought, "But it's apparent he has a past to be reckoned with. . . And it does my heart good to see such a young, homeless man knowing the bible!"

Candy Man had simply ignored her question regarding what he was about to say, cleared his throat and eagerly lit back into the salad. Dassah' pretty eyes lit up under the dim lights for the first time since she befriended the young homeless man. She was exhausted from the scuffle in the wet alley, but to evaluate Candy Man was a challenge she would not forfeit for all the diamonds in Africa. . . "I'd have to think about that one!" she snickered under her breath. "I could rehabilitate plenty of homeless people with just some of those diamonds!"

Meanwhile, back at the hospital in Upper Manhattan, Doctor David Dupree came softly into Doctor Blake Clancy's private room. Though Blake was unconscious and on a ventilator, he looked much better than he had as a homeless man with amnesia. Now Blake, the chief of brain surgeons at that same hospital, had his memory back and was reunited with his wife and young adult daughter. He laid comfortably in an uncertain coma—in a bed, a clean bed for the first time in almost four months. Mrs. Clancy sat reading on a cot by his bed and vowed not to leave until he would walk out beside her.

Mrs. Clancy stood hastily up when Doctor Dupree came in, "Hello again, David! Any good news?" she searched his aging face.

"Hello Marie. . . Well, we have a bit of bad news."

A gasp escaped her thin, now unpainted lips. The many applications of lipstick had been her meals.

"Wait, don't panic so quickly!" he hushed her, "There are a couple of methods to remove the hematoma. The (MRI) Magnetic Resonance Imaging revealed the tumor is expanding an artery in his brain . . . at some time in the past he must've received a serious blow which caused bruising, which led to the collection of blood in the vessel in question . . . we'll try Coumadin, a blood-thinner," he held her hand. "However, the blood tests revealed he has been popping aspirin, which in essence, should have dissolved the occlusion, but didn't because it was obviously there for too long." He moved over to examine Blake, "He's blessed to have been found just in time," he said, checking Blake's feet for swelling, "Even though he was hit in the ear, it was just a matter of time before the artery would've ruptured and been fatal. . . But don't worry he's here with us now and the good Lord!" His faith that there was a God was stronger than the Clancy's faith.

"Thank God!" surprisingly, she breathed, which proved that most so called Atheists will openly call on God when all else has failed.

CHAPTER 21

T here in Doctor Dassah Desoto's restaurant that Saturday evening it was 5:35. She, Stephanas Carter her bodyguard, Leon Davis and Candy Man, two homeless men were dining in Lower Manhattan. It had been snowing all day and they had spent most of the morning in Neal, New York, where Step had burned to death a Latino boy. Against the beliefs of the boy's uncle, Step had dutifully protected his boss from being raped, and then car-jacked by the boy and the bay's two friends. Dassah had gone into the alley to recruit homeless men for the psychiatrist's makeover program that was in dire need of replenishing since so many men were leaving to begin their own business, a few remaining to work on the food farm. Now, she and Step were at a point of taking the men, who are not totally convinced. Then a serious wreck on the highway had prevented them, and they wound up going to the hotel, and then to the restaurant. Dassah still wondered about Candy Man's true name and why he displayed such schizophrenic and autistic behavior. It had appeared that just a few minutes earlier, at the table that the young homeless man was on the verge of revealing his past. However all the doctor got was a bunch of disappointments when Candy Man clammed up and then Leon had a sudden outburst of race-anger. So, all she could do was sigh over today's catch of homeless men.

The main course finally arrived causing everyone to rub their hands together in anticipation. As usual, without missing a beat, Mack placed everyone's order with the correct person. The aroma of the savory, steaming dishes slapped them in the face. The cleaner, smiling Leon made up his mind right then and there, "Doc, you can count me in for this rehab program!" he had since calmed down. Joyfully, there followed a quiet, relaxing dinner around the table. Dassah was grateful for the serenity in that now no one would get indigestion from the stress of too much excitement, "All I need is for one of them to start throwing up!" she thought.

When dinner and small talk was finally finished, it was 7:30, dark outside and they were good for nothing but turning in. The doctor of the mind always flew the men to the farm in early day so that she could get back to Manhattan, "We'll just stay at the hotel tonight," she almost demanded. Then she said, "That is, if it's okay with you guys!"

"Fine by me," Leon also stood up. "Okay with you, Candy?"

He only nodded, standing up.

After a relaxed ride back to the hotel where the lonesome, homeless Leon Davis noticed another female a couple of years older than Trisha now minded the front desk, "Now this one is closer to my speed," he thought with a sheepish grin. But, with more precautions this time, Leon interrogated Step about her hooked-up status. Step, headed directly to the elevator, yawning in that he had not slept at all the night before, "As of yesterday she was as free as the wind!" he yawned. At that Leon immediately lingered to make her acquaintance. The calmer Candy Man tagged along with him. Dassah decided to trust Leon with the card-key. Handing it over to him, "Leon, you must not leave the hotel or have anyone other than Candy Man in the room," she clearly instructed.

"I can respect that, Doc," he smiled, dingy teeth failing to sparkle. He went and introduced himself to the woman who was impressed to have him interested, "M-m, at least he's tall!" the 5 foot 5 inch woman breathed inwardly, "This is the phone number to my own home," she smiled proudly, having once been homeless herself, resulting from a nervous-breakdown over a sudden broken engagement, which had also caused her to lose her job and nearly lose her only child. And refusing to seek professional mental help, she had simply run to the street crowds for company—the wrong choice many Blacks make. Too many Blacks refuse to succumb to psychiatric assistance. Then, one day, near the end of her rope of hope and crowded, in a shelter she heard about Doctor Desoto.

There in the plush lobby, before the doctor of the mind would allow Candy Man to leave, she asked, "Do you need another dose of Valium? You can have two more doses before the blood test results on Monday." They had to wait and get Leon's blood before dropping both off at the hospital lab. "Y-yes, I probably could use something," Candy Man said.

She had put them in her purse for that very reason. She knew he could possibly freak out in the new surroundings. She was glad Leon was there as a familiar face.

Then back in their room with two double beds, the homeless men were especially jovial over taking another long shower and watching cable. They could use as much hot water as they needed unlike in a shelter. Then wearing brand new pajamas the stink was finally all washed away. Watching an adult show, the youthful Candy Man was all eyes. Leon, in amazement at the liberality on the big screen in just four years, said, "Man, they do everything on television nowadays!" Nevertheless, the yet young 36-year-old man was compelled to gape, along with Candy Man. Leon took out the paper with the woman's phone number. "Sharon, huh?!" he smiled big at the paper.

Even behind full meals at the restaurant they took advantage of the bedtime snack left in the room. Afterwards, the television left on, the large room was filled with the sound of it, and peaceful snoring. For once in years Candy Man did not pace in the night.

The following morning, Sunday, the men hoped to sleep late. But at 6 o'clock sharp the phone rang. They were asked to meet Dassah downstairs in an hour for church. Groggily Leon answered, "But it's only six am, Doc," a mild complaint.

No other words but, "We'll be leaving at seven and service begins promptly at eight!" perky and bright eyed.

"Okay, be down by seven . . . Wake up Candy Man!"

"No! I'm sleepy."

"I think we have to! Let's go . . . You do want in, don't you?"

Barely stirring, "Yeah, I guess!"

After a sink-wash, Leon looked in the closet, "I knew these suits were here for a good reason." He chose a dark blue, perfect fit. Candy Man crept but was ready by 7. His brown suit was stylish for a youngster in his early 20s. Once in the lobby they received woof whistles from the dressed up Dassah and another desk woman. Step, looking like a magazine model, only stood there with an alert smile. Dassah loved to see the men blush, and for them to know that they could always look good while working for theirs and their children's future.

It was s7: 55 when the foursome entered the building of the church of Christ. Dassah was always proud to strut around with the new perspective recruits. The members were aware of the success of the program and sometimes even referred homeless people. At 10:30 when church service and Bible school was over, they had breakfast in the limo, and then were off to the airport in the fine falling snow. After taking the hour flight down to South Georgia they were at the farm. The men, like all the homeless recruits felt like royalty coming off the ten passenger plane. Then they fell in love with the farm. Leon and Candy Man met the many, many ex-homeless men who had also been to church and made it back to relax for the remainder of the day. The weather in Georgia was not snowy but was cold. The homeless men were also introduced to the overseers whom they would later get to know. The comfortable but rugged living quarters had separate rooms with cold hardwood floors, each with a private bathroom. There were recreational halls where the men met to interact and play when not working. "As you can see, I like things kept very, very clean, no maid service ever needed here!"

Then up drove Step, sitting high atop a Land Rover and picked them up to tour the 200-acre, un-harvested grounds—the usual frosted over vegetables and the fruit trees. The two homeless men got in the back, Leon was truly impressed with the raw cotton pods and mammoth machinery, "I know our fore-fathers wished they'd had machines like these!" he sighed, "That would've prevented the heat-stroke crippler among some of them. . . But, now that there's such modern stuff, most farmers won't even allow Blacks to man them. . . We can't even get a field job these days. . . When you aren't needed anymore, you get a bed with the fleas, and slandered by the news media for sleeping with the dogs!" He was aware that the news media was most Black folks' worst enemy.

Candy Man's blue eyes darted back and forth over the huge fields and all the fenced animals. Dassah asked, "Well, what do you think Candy?"

Hands crammed into pockets, "W-what do you mean?"

"Do you think you can handle the animals, the cotton and harvesting of fruit and veggies? Of course, I have to know who you are first!"

"I-I don't know. I've never. . ."

Once the soft young man was cleaned up, she could tell he was inexperienced at hard labor and with a short attention span to boot. "I'll find out about him and get him into a hospital," she thought with Step at the wheel of the Rover she by his side.

After about 45 minutes, "Well, we've seen enough for today," she announced. She really wanted to get back to Manhattan to her own house. She did not like to stay on the farm overnight. Even though she was sure the men had no weapons there. Even with her gun, Step's and the overseers', she still trusted only God. Being the only female and a beautiful one, she was yet uneasy about staying overnight, "I do feel I've gained all of my men's trust, but only with all my clothes on!" she always says. Plus Callie, her personal lawyer had said, "And don't go letting your guard down, Dassah! Some men can be dogs when he hasn't been with a woman in a while. . . Well you know what I mean!" she waved. She about Dassah' brutal rape at the age of 15.

"Sure you're right!" But the nurturing doctor would rather think of the men as her adopted children, even the ones older than herself, "I'm just the Old Woman Who Lives in a Shoe," the girlish looking doctor had sighed that day.

After having a leisurely lunch of tuna fish, spring salad and fruit it was three pm that Sunday on Dassah' makeover farm. She had convinced Leon to remain on the farm with a couple of the male therapists. She would take Candy Man to her office in Upper Manhattan. Though it was an ordeal just to get Candy Man to part with his right hand man, Leon, finally he agreed but very nervously. She could never leave such a mentally unstable man in the hands of even her finest therapists without being sure of his diagnosis. However, with his last dose of Valium and on the flight back, he did loosen up and became a little more verbal. The young, homeless man's name was Jacob O'Toole.

Then they left the airport and as Step drove the limo down the highway with Jacob blindfolded, Jacob displayed more confidence behind the mask and one-on-on with the soft spoken doctor. Dassah climbed from the front into her therapy chair and pulled out a note pad. Up until then she had mostly taken mental notes of the homeless men with the exception of a couple of small written notes. With fine snow occasionally swiped off the windshield, Step's dark eyes darter back and forth from the road to rear-view mirror. Jacob sat with his seatbelt on, stretched on the roomy seat across from her who was also strapped into her chair. She looked long and wondering at the young Caucasian man whom it had taken a day and a half for him to finally trust her, "I'm pleased to know your name, Jacob. . . Who named you?"

Hesitation, and then, "My dad." the yet youthful voice said, then silent again.

"Did you know Jacob was one of the Patriarchs of the Bible?"

"Yeah, he was the son of Isaac, who was the son of Abraham," he perked up a bit and Dassah stopped writing to glare at the masked man. Step startled from under the wheel of the limo. Then Jacob went on with the genealogy of the biblical forefathers, "Did you know Jacob had a twin brother named Esau . . . And Abraham had a son before he had Isaac?"

"What was that son's name?" she knew the answer.

Right away, "Oh, his name was Ishmael, who was the son of Hagar the Egyptian bondwoman, Sarah's handmaid!"

"You must have gone to church quite a bit, Jacob? Do you understand God's eternal purpose for the freewoman verses the bondwoman?"

"Not really," hesitation and then, "My dad's the minister of the largest church in town."

"And where's that?" quickly.

"That's not important."

Dassah let out an aggravated breath. She bent forward as much as the seatbelt would give, "Look, Jacob, you finally revealed your name, so you might as well come clean all the way!" She sat back, "You do want to come into the program with Leon don't you?"

"Or go home to my inheritance. . . My family is well off."

As Step broke for the car ahead he glanced back, exchanging stunned glances with Dassah. Then she asked, "And where is home, Jacob?"

A long hesitation, and then a whisper as if not wanting her to really hear, "The Bronx."

"Does your mother miss you? How many siblings do you have?" Then she caught herself, "Slow your roll, Doc!" she thought, anxious to get to the core of this mystery-man.

Behind the mask he finally said, "My mom is the director of the Christian University. . . I have an older brother about to graduate from there," he sighed. "I was in college, b-but then it happened!" his hands began to shake as he began to wring them trying to control the tremors.

"Why did you quit school?" softness in her well trained voice. Then she only motioned for Step to turn on the special music she used to sooth clients. Step also pushed a button to release a burst of the most calming, special-blend of aromatic spray. Those psyche-tools worked on Jacob. His hands began to sturdy, "A-a as a freshman, when I was eighteen, innocently I joined a fraternity. Then come to find out the Ivey Leaguers had a rep of practicing severe hazing." Shamefully, he threw his hands to his already covered face, "And if I refused to do the things they wanted me to do, they would brand me a bi-sexual and claim I tried to attack one of them!"

"That was a mean thing to do. . . Are you bi?"

"No, I had a girlfriend, a female!"

"What thing was it that they forced you to do, Jacob?" she was writing.

Step's handsome eyes darted back and forth from the rearview mirror to the snowy highway. "This is better than cable!" he thought. "White folks do some weird, crazy stuff!"

Jacob hesitantly went on, "A-a-at least every four months some older boys from the fraternity would go downtown and seek out homeless people. . . I mean really, really homeless!" T-t-then the boys would lure a homeless man with promises of food and money." He harshly shook his masked head, "I don't think I can talk about this!"

"It's okay not to talk, but the problem is obviously eating you and keeping you awake nights . . . and the next thing you know you'll be an old man, crying over a wasted youth," she paused for that to sink in, "However, at this stage in your life you've been blessed with an opportunity to retrieve your sanity!" The doctor of the mind had now discovered he could be helped—his illness was not innate. With therapy eventually he could be cured.

Only silence from the blond head-hung-down man, and then his head shot up, "Well, I was being forced and was afraid to tell my parents or girlfriend. . . And when it was my turn to be initiated, we found an old homeless Black man. That poor man was so hungry and malnourished . . . In order to gain his trust the two other boys and I carried packaged food to him for weeks," Jacob finally rocked with sincere sobs, tears wetting red cheeks under the mask. Step startled, broke behind a car, and fixed his protecting gaze momentarily on Dassah. With an assured wave that she was fine Step exhaled, eyes on the road. "Take your time Jacob," she soothed. "Would you like a cup of coffee or tea?

"Y-yes, ma'am, I would like some tea," swiping tears from his now paler cheeks.

She returned with a box of tissue and a cup of decaf tea. She handed Step a cup of real coffee. The doctor of the mind knew that caffeine along with Valium was bad news. He would be on a roller coaster ride for sure. She took her seat, "Now, Mr. O' Toole . . . Are you Irish?"

"Partially, on my dad's side," more relaxed now.

"Releasing that pinned up frustration through tears is just what the doctor ordered," she thought. Jacob was a rare client so she wanted him to cry it out. "May we resume?"

He took a slurp of tea, "Doctor Desoto, why do you need to know all this?" Suddenly and surprisingly no more stuttering, "You probably won't allow me into the program anyway and I might not want to come in!"

"Well, to tell you the truth I feel you should go home, get medical help and go back to school."

"But you don't understand," he paused frustrated again, and then, "I don't think I *can* go back. . . I haven't told my parents why I left or where I am. . . I've only called twice in the past two years I've been on the streets, begging them not to look for me. . . I'm twenty-one and haven't seen them since I was nineteen," Silence again.

Dassah said, "You can take off the mask since we've gone so far."

"No! I want it on. . . It has helped me to talk. . . I need to finish talking!"

Dassah was glad to hear that, however she worried he felt the need to hide behind a mask, "Its times like this I would like to change professions right in midstream!" she thought with the feeling she had taken a step backwards with this one, "Okay, you may keep it on." She glanced at her arm where her watch usually was. She had forgotten it, "What time is it Step?"

"Five o'clock," he said stopped at a light.

"Thanks. . . Now Jacob, where were we?"

Taking a slurp, "Well, after we had gained this particular homeless man's trust, all smiles we convinced him to take a ride with us . . . the two students I was with told the hungry man we were going to buy him some fried chicken. . . We did get the food, but as he was busy eating we wound up near a solitary wooded area. . . I know I should've backed out then and there!" a broken sob, "But I went along. . . The poor man was so naïve . . . but when I, the driver, was ordered to stop at a densely wooded area the man also stopped smacking on chicken and looked confused. . . The leader of the frat suddenly, furiously barked in the man's face to get out of his car, and stop stinking it up . . . and that if he didn't, he would shoot him, showing the wide eyed man the gun. I'll never forget the way his smutty face suddenly glared at me with total disappointment, mouth all greasy. . . I had been the nicest to him," Jacob wiped his mouth as if wiping the homeless man's greasy mouth, "After that day, every time I close my eyes I see those dark, dingy pleading eyes . . . whenever I close my eyes!" he repeated, and then choked, "The man got out of the car that evening around dusk and I stayed in by the clear road and watched the three disappear down into the woods . . . Ever since those shots rang out from the woods, whenever I hear shooting or any sound like shots, I retreat into my shell of safety," he admitted.

Then the doctor of the mind was suddenly enlightened why Jacob had become so terribly shaken back in the alley among all the gun-fire, "That was probably the first time he had heard real gun-shots since the homeless cold-blooded murder," she thought, looking sadly at Jacob's rocking sniffles.

Then his mind urged him to continue to unload years of burden, "Even now at night that poor man's dreadful face shakes me awake, him begging me to tell him why I did that. . . Why I helped kill an innocent man in cold-blood!" he sobbed, head hung behind the blindfold of shame, "I'd give anything to reverse that . . . I just can't take it anymore!!"

Dassah felt even worse for Jacob because he had been brought up with religious convictions all around him. Even Step's eyes became misty. He related on how it felt to snuff out a human life. He had just yesterday done the same. Only he did it in the line of duty, protecting Dassah, whom she depended on to keep her safe. Then from her chair, the doctor just watched the remorseful young man cry. He lifted the blindfold and wiped, but carefully replaced it.

"You know you can't hide behind a mask forever," she softly advised, holding her feelings in, as a psyche, "Are those boys still in school? It seems they're the ones who ought to be suffering! They pulled the trigger." However, she knew Jacob was also guilty, and must share the blame.

"I don't know . . . they were still in school when I left a month later and wound up in the alley where I soon maxed out my credit card . . . Well, I guess you have to turn me in now?" he finally asked, seemingly wanting to get punished.

"That's not for me to do. I'm a doctor not the police. . . Do you plan to take the total blame?"

Then Jacob sat quiet during the ride down the snowy highway. His thoughts were much clearer now. He no longer felt a dependency on Leon as a security blanket. Dassah knew that in Jacob's psyche he had attached to Leon in a desperate attempt to replace that homeless man. When he found Leon, he also lavished Leon with money to repay what he had done. Leon, all the time without a clue as to why this White youth had, magnetized to him had gained much love.

As she jotted down notes, Dassah noted that Jacob was pricked in his heart realizing that murder was a sin. And that he feared that just punishment from God would follow if he refused to repent. "Though, it's up to him to make his own decisions," she wrote. As he was in deep meditation over that, she had a feeling he was also seriously contemplating letting the cat out of the bag to the proper authorities. When he would go to court, she would certainly attest that she had evaluated him and found him to have been unduly under coercion at the time of the murder—and even had suffered a near nervous meltdown after that. She knew she had to bring him back to the alley or to a hospital, either one would be his choice. "Too bad I can't enroll him in the program now." She sadly thought. Still Dassah knew that he would gradually withdraw from his self-willed safety of autism. And he may have to depend on medication leading up to the anticipation of the trial. He also had to struggle with his feelings that God had not forgiven him. One of the makeover policies was not to take in a murderer, "And what he did was deliberately planned," she thought, "It's too bad that even though we're forgiven there remains post-traumatic consequences after we've sin!"

Back in Neal, New York around six o'clock pm that Sunday evening Dassah back in the passenger seat, Step pulled up to the familiar alley but did not park this time. Staring pensively at the alley, the ex-homeless bodyguard began to have flashbacks of the Latino boy's head aflame amidst snowflakes. Immediately, he shook that thought loose, refusing to retreat into guilt like Jacob. The few folk out, gaped after the limo. "Here we are Boss!" he said. Jacob, still with the fine suit, was fidgeting again in the back seat. He finally eased the blindfold over his head. His blue eyes blinked at the light. Dassah noticed Jacob's expression seemed more peaceful and alert. "Jacob," she said, "As a psychiatrist I must say you look as if your worries are a bit fewer!"

"Yeah, I feel a little better," more confident.

"Will you return to the alley now?" she peered back.

Looking out at the light snowflakes, he sighed, "Yes Ma'am, for a while anyway." The stuttering had completely vanished.

Dassah turned to Step, "Do you have any money?"

"I have about a hundred bucks," he pulled the bills out, "Take what you need."

She took it all and went back to Jacob "Take this. . . You can pay me back when you collect the twenty-five-thousand-dollar reward from Doctor Blake Clancy."

"What reward," he frowned.

Then, parked on the streets she found herself explaining about the phone accident that he caused Pops vs. Blake's memory to return, while Jacob was jaw-dropped all the time. All he knew was that an accident had occurred.

"You can go down to the police station to claim that you should get the reward," handing him her card, "Contact me if any problems arises. . . Blake's a changed man in more ways than just no longer being homeless!" With almost a smile, Jacob took the card and the hundred dollars and stepped from the limo onto soft snow. He stared sadly at his few homeless comrades, very tattered gathered around the alley. He looked down at his new clothes and really began to long for his family at home. It came to him how he had only been on the streets because of the guilt of harboring and supporting a murderer. He felt that by helping the homeless that would erase the pain of having taken one of their friends. As the young Jacob stood on the sidewalk contemplating, Step was about to turn the corner in to limo. Then suddenly, "Wait!!" Jacob took off after the limo, waving and slipping to catch up, his hungry peers gaping after him. And Step was unable to hear Jacob's shouting. But Dassah noticed him in the side mirror, "Hold up a minute, Step!" she quickly put a hand on the wheel.

Jacob slid into her window, puffing, "I want to go on to the hospital!" he puffed. "I'll tell the police everything!"

"Well, hop on in!" she smiled with an exhale.

Step grinned, "There might be hope for you yet Can . . . I mean Jacob!"

"Wait just a minute Mr. Step!!" Jacob said. "Let me go back there for a minute!" he pointed to his ex-peers, gaping after him. Then he slid running back to them, "Here you go, Guys!" he handed the four a twenty-dollar bill each. "I'll keep this twenty to contact my family!" He ran back to the limo "Bye forever, Guys!" he waved. "Bye Candy Man!" they called back. "You look and smell good!!"

Dassah and Step regularly recalls how it has been a year since they dropped Jacob at the hospital. The 21-year-old was admitted to a rehab facility and the whole truth about the homeless murders—other killings had occurred even before Jacob got involved. He led the police to the woods where the one he was involved had taken place. The body remains were discovered and identified by dental records. The 52 year old, homeless man had been in the service and had been honorably discharged. The family, whom he had run away from, was found in another city and he received an honorable burial from the army—a 21-gun salute of whose firing no longer un-nerved Jacob. The family forgave Jacob, but insisted that the other boys get what they deserved.

Jacob's family embraced him and he went back to school after rehab. He served a year in a halfway house for troubled youths, along with paying a stiff fine. Jacob's partners in crime are now 23 and graduated. They were found in California, expedited back to New York, and convicted. They were both given a 10-year sentence without parole.

Dassah recalls how Doctor Blake Clancy was still in the coma when Jacob tried to collect the reward from his wife, and had to wait until he recovered. Blake had an old blood clot in a vessel, which caused his memory loss. Since blood thinners had not been effective in flushing out the clot, doctors suggested intricate surgery. If Blake had been even a week later getting it removed, he would not be around to issue any reward. The apathetic Doctor Blake, after recovering said how *blessed* and not how *lucky* he was, yet grumbled about paying up. His family now goes to church occasionally. Instead of going back to work he decided to retire and really see the world. His wife immediately began contacting travel agencies. Their daughter went relieved back to med school with two years to go. Jacob used some of the reward money to pay his psychiatric stay in rehab. Now the handsome blond, blue-eyed man smiles a lot and sleeps drug-free. In the halfway house for a year he's allowed to travel to college in town and then back to the house. During support group meetings Jacob teaches his peers to respect the poor—and find out how they may assist, "Maybe give them a box of pencils to sell," he had suggested. As a self-inflicted ex-homeless person himself, he knows how important it is for a homeless person to work for his keeps. He also discovered that he needed to be more thankful to God for his lavish middle-classed home and loving family, "Just because you have a television in every room of your house, never take that for granted!" he would say to teenagers among other warnings. However, he knows that the well-to-do teens have no control over what gifts their parents lade them with but the teen can learn unselfishness. Jacob plans to counsel more when he becomes a doctor of theology like his father.

Step constantly recalls the short court procedure about the Latino boy's death. The jury had deemed it necessary for him to protect his employer in a lawful fashion. The judge had said that when those boys entered that alley with loaded guns, or not loaded, they should expect the victims to retaliate by any means necessary. And because Dassah did not press charges, the Latino boy was given 4 years' probation and a stiff fine for possession and assault with a gun which injured Leon. The Latino boy was pressed that if he refused to reveal the identity of his African-American friend that got a way, she would press charges. Then the Black boy was picked up without any resistance on his part. The same 4 year probation was dropped on him. There in the courtroom, afterwards, both set of parents hotly tongue-lashed the 16 and 17 ear-old boys all the way to the parking lot—and probably a long time after that. The Latino uncle had come to his senses that the boys were indeed guilty. He passed by Dassah and Step, and shot them an apologetic glance and then hung his head.

Doctor Dassah Desoto was out the very next day after dropping off Jacob, diligently searching for much needed homeless men and anyone she may be able to help. "Step, we need to go to Atlanta. . . I hear there're plenty homeless pickings down there . . . so many young kids in prison . . . seventeen and eighteen year olds, too young for this kind of program . . . they must qualify by being a homeless adult, but we still can do something for even them. . . At eighteen, some are still high school age."

"Yeah!" he shook his head, "Nineteen and up they can legally work within the program, like you did me at that age. And the south is the ideal climate for agriculture . . . ya' know, another farm down there."

"Maybe I should try something else that would be geared towards teens only!" she lit up. "The juvenile system is jam packed with minor offenders . . . all the judicial system needs is someone to offer a workable rehab solution," she smiled as they cruised the snowy highway, eyes peered for homeless people.

Two years have passed. The steadfast doctor of the mind still thinks a lot about her past, especially the rape that left her barren. But she found that bitterness lessens with time. In her present plans, whether or not she will ever get married, remains to be seen. The big red-faced police call on her quite frequently and she goes out with him. It surprises her how immensely enjoyable his company is, even though she does not practice dating outside of the church of Christ, "He ain't anything like he was that day in the alley!" she had teased herself inwardly, smiling on the first date, "Maybe I can get him to be added to the church." She recalls on their first date he had talked a lot about his son in Iraq and how he couldn't wait for the President Obama to bring the troops home. She mainly listened attentively and took it he had no one else to really listen. He has been a widower since his twenty year old son was thirteen.

Dassah recalls how her father surprised her with a visit to her office one day. And with many questions, she finally accepted him into her life, "Why, I don't know, because I surely don't need his puny inheritance!" she had told Jarvis her brother, who had a different father.

"He has never been there for me!" she had cried, "Now he only wants a comfortable place to die!" Though she knew he had his booming liquor store in Victory, Georgia, and was not so old. She finds herself trying to get him saved from turning so many people, especially the poor into alcoholics. His wife, who worked most of her life away, has meekly hung in there with him all these years.

Dassah always compliments Leon Davis that she wishes she could find many more men like him, "You've really worked this program like a pro, Leon!" Step always says to his sidekick, "I can't believe you're just about to finish and start your own business, man!"

In less than a year Leon and his partners will own a printing company there in Manhattan. He and Step has become close friends just as Step hoped. Leon also found true love in the woman at the desk, who had, herself been a long time waiting for Mr. Alright. He now proudly refers to her twelve-year-old son as his own. Leon would never go back into the school system, but daily coaches his new son in basketball. They are trying to get pregnant before her biological clock ticks down. "I want to give you a child of your own, too!" she would snuggle up to him during her fertile times.

The government proudly nominated Doctor Dassah Desoto for a Nobel Peace Prize for the many successful rehabilitation achievements. But she knows that award will be offered some time in the future.

During the ex-homeless graduations she always leaves these last words with the class, "Remember what God told the Israelites in Leviticus 23: 22 in commanding them that in reaping the blessings of their harvest, to leave some corn and fruit for the poor," she says, "And when you find yourself getting stingy, just you bear in mind where you once were. . . And giving food is just one means of assistance. . . Another effective tool is to seek out specific needy families that are in need of housing. . . And everyone in the hood knows a family who's sincerely in need of monetary help. You can go into indigent neighborhoods where the older child is struggling to be a substitute parent who works two jobs. . . Most apartment complexes have a Resident Services program, so to keep it legal, ask the leasing office if they know of a family about to be evicted. . . Help with a month or two of rent. Go to the unemployment office and offer some poor person a job in your store. . . And, just being a personal mentor to some boy never having a father to play ball with, will leave an everlasting impression on the child. . . You are the one he'll perpetuate in his thoughts, and who knows? Your paths just may cross again where you'll need him. God has ways of working things out that way. . . And God forbids that you forget others when you've reached your own financial peak! Don't be a bridge-burner!" Then Doctor Dassah Desoto had looked sternly out over the graduating class of well nourished, ex-homeless, made-over men that day, "Men, remember you can't out give God because He never runs out of blessings, and is able to fix it so that you'll never run out of receiving them! The more you give of your money and time, the more He gives of His blessings. But, first of all, never forget how He gave His only begotten son! Also remember the parable of the talents in Luke 19:12-27, how the nobleman trusted his money to his servants to be used wisely until his return . . . Then, when the nobleman returned to collect his money with interest, he found that one servant hadn't been faithful and that pound which he had was even taken away . . . Thus, the servant who had been faithful to gain more was given more . . . So when we work righteousness in money or in saving souls, and remain faithful until death, God will reward us likewise. . . And bear in mind that our money and lives are simply a loan from God, He will return to find out how we've utilized both," the sincere doctor had concluded her speech to the graduating men all of them looking very polished, some with families.

Just the other day on a scouting trip she said to Step, "I wonder if Leon will help me to follow up on that pursuit to have lie detectors reinstated into the justice system?"

From behind the wheel, "Why did they do away with that anyway? In my opinion, if the judicial system had honest law-enforcers who wouldn't tamper with evidence, then lie detector results could be truthfully the solution to the prison overflowing with innocent, Black inmates!"

"That's so right! And they surely seem to have no problem using lie detectors on those reality shows as the truth and nothing but the truth!"

"Poor Leon wasted almost five years of life and lost his wife when a simple hook-up to a machine could have freed him. . . And also in my opinion, if the law were to release too many of the innocent and minor-offenders, then where would the jobs for law enforcers and law workers be?" the buffed bodyguard sighed, driving the limo down the freeway of New York, listening to the depressing news on the radio.

"Well, those law workers would just have to join the long lines at the unemployment department with all the other citizens who've gotten laid off. They shouldn't be allowed to make a living off of injustice towards the innocent!" Doctor Dassah as usual, only sighing, shaking her head with pity at the broken system, trying her best to think of more ways to bring about positive change in the lives of the poor, "And another thing!!" she huffed,

"And what is that!"

"Since the government claims I'm doing such a fine job reinstating the homeless back into society, I'll just conjure up a justifiable petition to open all the cases where any non-Black race who may have blamed a Black man did it and then later discovered he was falsely, purposely accused. . . That person who had falsely accused the Black person should be made to spend just as much time in prison as that innocent person spent!" angrily, she wagged her pretty head, "Or better yet the false accuser should be made to pay monetary restitution to that innocent Black person!"

"Sounds, fair to me! That should send a loud message to stop blaming innocent Blacks!" Come to think of it, I've even seen movies where Whites have made fun that all they have to say is that a Black man did it in order to deter the law from the true offender!" also working up anger.

With determination, "Well, if I have to sit on the steps of Washington with that petition, that slave-tactic is just about to change, I promise that!"

THE END
© 2008-2016

REFERENCES

a. All scripture-KJV

b. This reference is from reliable historical, biblical resources and statistics about homelessness. Also there is a myriad of assistive information on how to help the needy at the National Coalition for the Homeless website. This site reveals all categories of homelessness in America and all that one needs to know to get involved.

c. For Slave Reparation see, 20/20:American Debate Reparation for Slavery, ABC News.http://abcnews. go.com/2020/story?id=124115

d. http://www.gettyimages.com/photos/roms-camp-for-homeless?family=editorial&phrase=roms%20camp%20 for%20homeless&sort=best&excludenudity=true

    Use image of Roms-Camp inside the book

ABOUT THE AUTHOR

Sara M. Harris-Bowditch is a member of the church of Christ. She is a published children's book and novel writer. Sara Harris was married to David Bowditch on May of 2012. She has one daughter and one grandson and is a native of Georgia. She attended college in Georgia, later to attend Saint Joseph School of Histology. She became a registered histology tech, ASCP-HT, with the American Society for Clinical Pathologists. She earned a certification in business plan development from Kennesaw State University Business Enterprise. She is presently retired due to an inherited eye disease that rendered her permanently legally blind though not totally blind. After retirement, she began writing where she discovered her real love of trying to solve the world's many pitfalls. Her books are of a fictional self-improvement genre. She enjoys floral design and interior decorating. Her long-term goal is to continue to lean on God's Word so that God will welcome her into a forever habitation with Hum.

Printed in the United States
By Bookmasters